REACHING OUT TO TROUBLED YOUTH

REACHING OUT TO TROUBLED YOUTH

DWIGHT SPOTTS & DAVID VEERMAN

VICTOR BOOKS

A DIVISION OF SCRIPTURE PRESS PUBLICATIONS INC.
USA CANADA ENGLAND

Bible quotations, unless otherwise indicated, are from the Holy Bible, New International Version, © 1973, 1978, 1984, International Bible Society. Used by permission of Zondervan Bible Publishers. Other quotations are from The Living Bible, © 1971, Tyndale House Publishers, Wheaton, Illinois 60189. Used by permission.

Cover design: Joe DeLeon
ISBN: 1-56476-279-3
1 2 3 4 5 6 7 8 9 10 Printing/Year 98 97 96 95 94
Printed in the United States of America

Produced for Victor Books by The Livingstone Corporation. David Veerman, Michael Kendrick, and Brenda James Todd, project staff.

#3031143

CONTENTS

This book is dedicated to the thousands of men and women who have given their lives to reach troubled youth—men and women who have understood what it means to "go the second mile." They're still going in order that young people will learn of the Lord who changes life forever.

With special thanks to Greg Monaco, Gordon McLean, Ken Goldsmith, and others in Youth Guidance, a division of Youth for Christ working directly with troubled young people.

1. Should You Be Working with Troubled Youth?

"**S**crew you!" shouted Jimmy as he shoved Mr. Hutchins against the blackboard. "If you tell the principal me and Bruce was fighting, I'll get suspended again. You keep your f_____ mouth shut!" Jimmy loosened his hold on the shaken teacher's shirt, glared at him, and then spun around and returned to his seat.

In the church bus, Brenda sat alone eating her lunch quickly and quietly so she could leave. She approached no one, spoke to no one, and looked at no one. She tried to be small and invisible. She was convinced that everyone was watching her and thinking how ugly she looked. Mostly she just wanted to cry.

John acts like the typical six-year-old. He often asks for help in Sunday School, pays attention only for short stretches, complains a lot, whines, and daydreams much of the time. But John isn't six years old; he is twelve.

You probably know young people like Jimmy, Brenda, and John. The first meets life with aggression, the second withdraws, and the third responds with immature and inadequate behaviors. All three are troubled youth, lacking the skills needed to lead effective and satisfying lives.

These youth come in all shapes, ages, sizes, and colors, and they are more common than one might suspect. They may live in your neighborhood or go to your church. They may be your children's friends and, quite possibly, the children of your friends. You don't have to look hard to find them. Sooner or later, they will find you.

Most people think a "troubled youth" is a juvenile who has had a run-in with the law or who has a mental/emotional disorder. In some cases this is true, but the most basic definition of a troubled youth is a young person who has problems which are more intense than those of a "normal youngster" and which prevent him or her from developing necessary life skills. These struggles and problems are more serious than the average person's but not necessarily criminal.

If you are concerned at all about young people and their struggles, then you will be concerned about the problem of juvenile delinquency. Juvenile crime has been sensationalized for years. Many people have become so alarmed that they fear any contact with troubled youth, not realizing that a troubled young person may be living in their home.

The most sensational cases scream at us in daily headlines. Usually they are serious, violent crimes which have been publicized enough to attract attention. Most criminal acts, however, are virtually silent—whispered about only by the people involved. In fact, research indicates that over 80 percent of America's young people

---

How Likely Is a Juvenile to Use a Weapon?

National Crime Survey data indicates that the older an offender is, the more likely he is to use a weapon. Juvenile offenders used a weapon in 27 percent of their crimes; 18–20-year-olds, 36 percent; and adults (21 or older), 41 percent.

From *Facts about Youth and Delinquency, a Citizens Guide to Juvenile Delinquency*, published by the National Institute for Juvenile Justice and Delinquency Prevention.

---

under the age of 18 commit at least one offense for which they could be arrested.[1] But only 3 percent of them are. It's not too far from the truth to say, "The difference between a juvenile delinquent and a 'good' kid is that one was unlucky enough to get caught." About 14 percent of the U.S. population is between 10 and 18 years of age; and according to records, juveniles make up 21 percent of all arrests.

Troubled youth seem to have a stigma about them, keeping most of us from becoming personally involved with them. We can discuss, analyze, and wring our hands with "someone ought to do something" comments, but we keep them at arm's length, safely tucked away in statistics and newspapers. The sensational cases, of course, are truly frightening. They make people thankful that they have chosen to steer clear of personal involvement with troubled youth. The average, less publicized situations, however, will have you wishing you could help.

● The 16-year-old girl in a Detroit ghetto who quits school to support her family and her baby. Her occupation? Prostitution . . . for her the simplest and most logical solution.

● The neighbor boy who attends the junior high program at church and even "accepted Christ" at camp last summer. He wanted to make money and now has a "job" stealing bikes and selling the parts.

● The kid who spends so much time at your house that he might as well live there. His dad is gone, and so his mom has to work. There is no one at home for him, so he has adopted you.

Coming into contact with young people who have been alienated from the church and, in many cases, victimized by society is a sobering experience. Reaching out with a helping hand forces us to count our own blessings while offering a new perspective on life. More importantly, it provides opportunities to confront firsthand two of the church's most stubborn challenges—troubled youth and social problems.

If you choose to become involved in the life of a troubled young person, you will embark on an emotional roller coaster ride: frustration, satisfaction, dismay, anger, humor, joy, sorrow. At times you will say, "I don't need this kind of frustration!" On other occasions, however, you will feel the warm satisfaction of helping a young person find meaning in life and in his world, helping him change his life for the better.

WHAT KEEPS US FROM HELPING TROUBLED YOUTH?

There are three main reasons why people tend to avoid troubled youth: (1) We are afraid of them (and what they might do to us); (2) we don't think we have the skills or abilities to help them; and (3) we don't see it as our responsibility. Let's look at each of these.

Fear

Why are we afraid of troubled youth? Perhaps we see them all as "criminals," young people with violence in their blood. So we try to avoid them whenever possible as "self-preservation" takes over. Being threatened or injured by a juvenile is far more frightening than most anything we can imagine. Fear, then, would be a natural response if, as mentioned above, we have formed our opinions from sensational headlines and TV news accounts. But remember, we are talking about a much broader group of young people than those who grab headlines for acts of violence.

Fear of Crime

The fear of crime is, in general, the fear of a random, unprovoked attack or robbery by a stranger. As far back as 1967, a presidential commission on crime concluded that ". . . fear of crimes of violence is not a simple fear of injury or death or even of all crimes of violence, but at the bottom, a fear of strangers" (*The Challenge of Crime in a Free Society*, a report by the Presidents Commission on Law Enforcement and the Administration of Justice, U.S. Government Printing Office, Washington, D.C., 1967, p. 52).

Over the last twenty-five to thirty years, Americans have become increasingly crime conscious. Our increasing awareness of drive-by shootings, gang violence, and random car-jackings has only served to heighten our fear of becoming a victim. Fueled by the L.A. riots, the bombing of the World Trade Center in New York, and murders in Florida, the national media and public officials are again focusing much attention on the volume of crime, its costs, and its effects on people.

Public opinion polls show that most people have mixed feelings about their fear of crime. Most say they feel safe when alone in the neighborhood and think that their neighbors are less dangerous than others. Yet they believe that people in general have limited their activities because of crime.

It is interesting to note that the groups who are at greatest risk of becoming victims are not the ones who express the greatest fear. Females and the elderly, not in the population groups most

Continued

victimized, generally express the greatest fear of crime. The risk of victimization depends on a combination of factors—among them male, 12–25 years of age, black vs. caucasian or members of other racial groups, and lower income.

Report to the Nation on Crime and Justice, U.S. Department of Justice, Bureau of Justice Statistics.

And just how dangerous are these young people? Statistically, juvenile crime is much less threatening than daily activities we take for granted. Our chances of being killed in an automobile accident are ten times greater than being murdered by a stranger, and our risk of death from a fall, slipping in the shower, or tumbling from a ladder is three times greater than being victimized by juvenile crime.

We may also fear troubled youth because we equate "strange" with "dangerous." How do you feel when you see a stranger, someone unknown who doesn't fit the setting, wearing old or "radical" clothing, exhibiting poor social habits, and carrying bored or hateful facial expressions? This kind of person is threatening. Troubled youth just don't "fit" in today's society, much less in most churches. Viewed as "strangers," socially and emotionally, they are feared and avoided.

The cause of this fear, then, is not the person but our lack of understanding of the person. We don't know him (or her), and we can only guess about his background and culture. This lack of knowledge and understanding translates into fear. But this fear can be transformed into care as we understand the person's values, family background, friends, religious influences, and cunning ability to survive. And when they are no longer strange *to* us, they become familiar *with* us. These new relationships will mean that:

● These young people will be less likely to hurt us (and others).

● They will finally have a friend who looks beyond the surface of their appearance, past, and behavior, and accepts them for who they are.

● We will have the opportunity to change lives.

A Lesson from the Good Samaritan

The Bible uses many illustrations to teach us valuable lessons. One is about a Samaritan man who stops to help a man on the Jericho road (Luke 10:25-37). Someone has surmised that when the Samaritan saw the man lying on the roadside, beaten, robbed, bleeding, and dying, he looked down and thought, "If I do not help that man, what will happen to him?" There were all kinds of answers to that question. But even more important questions penetrated his thoughts: If I do not help him, what will happen to me? What will happen to how I feel about myself, to my dignity, pride, and self-respect? And then, how will I be able to love God and others if I do not love myself? These questions suddenly became much more difficult and sensitive to answer because the focus shifted from the one in trouble to the one who could help. Thus, the Samaritan ministered to the man on the road and became the good Samaritan.

Abilities

Why don't we think we have the skills or abilities to help troubled young people? Perhaps the main reason is that their problems seem so difficult and complex that we wonder how we could even begin to help. "After all," we surmise, "you would have to be a psychologist or social worker to help those kids."

It is true that certain problems need *professional* attention, but most troubled youth need *personal* attention—loving relationships with people who take time to care about them. Just about everyone has that ability. Which of these five basic skills could you use to minister to troubled young people?

1. *Relationship building skills*—beginning and building a friendship with someone

2. *Helping skills*—helping young people solve their problems

3. *Sharing your faith skills*—introducing a person to Jesus Christ

4. *Teaching skills*—teaching youth to learn to do what the Bible says

5. *Basic life skills*—assisting any adolescent in a wide range of areas: e.g., decision-making, getting a job, caring for his body, talking to an adult

These skills will be discussed more fully in succeeding chapters. Needless to say, each person has a unique mix of talents, gifts, and abilities, and no one will have all of these skills perfected beyond the need for improvement. We must remember that *who* we are is much more important to young people than *what we know* or what we think we know.

Young People in Trouble

Our society tends to ignore children in trouble—usually preferring to remove them from sight. Some citizens even demand severe punishment for these children. An adult who would punish children stricken with measles or leukemia would be considered insane. Yet youngsters battered or neglected by alcoholic parents, children who run away because their homes are without love or because they are being hurt at school, or children who are being beaten and raped are often ignored or punished.

School leaders, church officials, and other professionals and volunteers who work with children in trouble tend to concentrate instead on good children. Many of those who care about problem children, including several thousand sincere, dedicated persons employed by various public and private agencies and institutions, continue to face much criticism and little support when the public cries out for reform. But the public is scoffed at as kid-coddlers and as permissive do-gooders by those who cling to tired myths and those who refuse to examine facts. Some become so frustrated that they now demand that the present system of dealing with children in trouble be scrapped.

Even if money, rather than children, is of paramount importance to the people of this nation, they would be well advised to reconsider the way they deal with young people because the staggering rise in the number of troubled youth will soon cost the nation dearly.

Neglect of children in trouble and in need produces misfits, drifters, welfare cases, delinquents, and criminals. The result is a tremendous financial drain on our nation and a tragic squandering of human potential.

From the White House Conference on Children—Report to the President, Washington, D.C.

Another reason we think we lack the necessary expertise to help troubled youth is we have been conditioned to think that all of society's problems should be solved by "professionals," people paid to do the job. Society now hires police officers, fire fighters, probation officers, teachers, and others to do what individuals used to do for themselves. Of course, professionals are needed in our modern and complex society, but with their proliferation grows the subtle idea that "someone else" *always* can be hired to do the work for us. We can make the same mistake in church, where we hire the pastor, youth pastor, and other staff members to carry out our spiritual responsibilities. Obviously this is a grave mistake; each person has a God-given mandate to reach out *personally* to others. We cannot hire someone else to do what God has asked us to do.

In addition, the *non*professional volunteer has certain advantages in ministering to troubled youth:

● A professional is expected to behave in specific ways. He or she must balance vastly different, often opposite roles within his profession. For example, the typical school guidance counselor must be the "good guy," providing counseling and help. At the same time, he must be the "heavy," holding the responsibilities of surveillance, truancy enforcement, and class scheduling. A probation officer is supposed to provide counsel and assistance to the youthful offender while being responsible for investigation and possible resentencing. Despite their best efforts, often these professionals are rejected by adolescents who cannot differentiate between their roles. Seeing the contradiction, they stay aloof and uninvolved. The nonprofessional has a great advantage because his/her chief role is to be the guiding, rewarding helper.

● The professional is sometimes perceived by troubled youth as someone who does the job only because it pays. Money—not personal interest—may be seen as the major motive for the professional's involvement. Many young people resent being the "problem" on which the worker's livelihood is based. They may vent their feelings by hurling the accusation, "If it wasn't for me, you wouldn't have a job!" The nonprofessional volunteer, then, has a distinct advantage because his/her motives are clear, unmuddied by financial considerations.

● The professional has a "behavioral sciences" frame of reference. Of course, this in itself is not a problem. His or her education has provided special expertise and insight into behavioral problems and societal structures. The problem occurs when they focus on certain "symptoms" related to something they have read or observed in others and consequently spend more time dissecting the parts rather than reassembling the whole person. The professional may concentrate on the bad actions or attitudes and forget about the *person* doing them. Most nonprofessionals, however, are not used to seeing people in parts. Instead, they see whole human beings with needs, desires, and longings for God's help. The nonprofessional is not restrained by the government to deal with symptoms only, but he can work with the whole person including the spiritual dimension.

● The professional has a heavy caseload. A typical caseload for a probation officer, counselor, or social worker ranges from 25 to 50 or more. With so many people to consider, he or she must be quite selective about who gets his time and how much. Many youths who need help will be neglected in favor of those who have more serious problems. The nonprofessional volunteer can work with relatively few young people (often with only one) and can devote quantity and quality time to building relationships and "prevention."

Far from being a person without the necessary abilities, you have unique skills which God can use to help troubled youth.

Responsibility

Any ministry to troubled young people will spend a great deal of time and energy just meeting their social, emotional, and physical needs. The result seems to be a "social gospel," sometimes exclusive of "evangelism." Christians have always struggled with this tension between social and evangelistic concerns, asking, "How much contact should I have with non-Christians?" and "What is my social responsibility?" Because of this, it is often assumed that working with troubled youth does not fit into our "theology," the biblical imperatives for our lives. But reaching out to people with "social" needs has always been an integral part of the ministry of the church.

In Acts, we read that seven men were appointed to make sure widows were properly cared for (Acts 6:1-7), and Paul tells us in 1 Corinthians that he worked with the people considered "social rejects" of his day: drunks, prostitutes, and thieves. Candidly, he describes himself as servant to all: "Though I am free and belong to no man, I make myself a slave to everyone to win as many as possible" (1 Corinthians 9:19).

In addition to the example of the apostles and early believers, the Bible teaches us, "Do not merely listen to the Word, and so deceive yourselves. Do what it says" (James 1:22).

Jesus Himself gave a dramatic motive for helping those in need when He said about those who are hungry, thirsty, alone, naked, sick, and in prison, "I tell you the truth, whatever you did for one of the least of these brothers of Mine, you did for Me" (Matthew 25:40).

If our faith is to have a real impact on the world, it must have an impact on real people, people in need. God's dealing in the Old Testament demonstrated His love for His people when

Social Responsibility of Christians

Every Christian and every Christian church is involved in society and its problems. There are no exceptions. Even the pastor, congregation, or denomination that claims to be ministering to purely spiritual needs is thereby declaring its position on the political, economic, and social issues of its community and nation.

This is true because the spiritual life of any person is profoundly social, no matter how individualistic or private it seems to be. Its origin is social, for faith comes by hearing, and human messengers are used by God to bring the Gospel message (Romans 10:14-17). Even when a person is alone with God, his emotions, sentiments, private prayers, conscience, language, religious concepts, beliefs, values, and attitudes toward himself, the world, and God are all modified by his past experiences in society.

"Social Responsibility of Christians" taken from *Christian Social Responsibility in 20th-Century America*, written by David O. Moberg. Grand Rapids, Michigan: William B. Eerdmans Publishing Company, 1965, p. 13.

He delivered them from oppression and gave them food and water in the desert. Jesus' actions in the New Testament demonstrated His concern for the whole man—mentally, socially, physically, and spiritually. When speaking of His mission, Jesus quoted Isaiah:

> "The Spirit of the Lord is on me, because He has anointed me to preach good news to the poor. He has sent me to proclaim freedom for the prisoners and recovery of sight for the blind, to release the oppressed, to proclaim the year of the Lord's favor" (Luke 4:18-19).

Church history is replete with examples of Christians who raised the moral tone of society, working for the elimination of gladiator shows, less oppressive Roman laws, rights for women, abolition of slavery, care for orphans, increased employment, improved education, care for the mentally ill, and on and on. Christian social responsibility is not a new concept.

If, therefore, we say that reaching out to troubled youth is not our responsibility because it is not scriptural or as worthy as other spiritual pursuits, we miss the clear teaching of the Bible and the example of great Christian leaders of the past. Ministering to troubled youth presents a God-given opportunity and a tremendous challenge. Invaluable lives can be rescued and changed through God's power as it is channeled through us.

If you want to become the vehicle through whom a troubled young person changes his life, you must associate with those kids who are neglected and left out. You must venture out of your secure surroundings and minister to the last, the least, and the lost. This involves the authentic telling of God's message in word and deed. How else will a troubled young person find out what life is all about un-less we proclaim the Gospel? Love for and commitment to others will propel us closer than arm's length. We will step boldly out of our safe environment and into "youth territory," accepting, loving, and caring for those who are different.

WHAT CAN WE LEARN FROM THE PRODIGAL SON?

The Parable of the Prodigal Son in Luke 15:11-32 may illuminate the special predicament of adolescents and point us to an effective approach to helping them and handling their problems. This illustration offers insights into the prevention and treatment of delinquency at the most critical stage. More importantly, it encourages us to replace our attitudes of isolation and fear with acceptance and concern.

The Prodigal Son is the third parable which Jesus gave to answer the Pharisees and scribes, proud religious leaders of His day. They believed that even touching a sinner made them "unclean" before God, and they criticized Jesus, who not only socialized with sinners, but even ate with them (Luke 15:2)! Jesus responded with the teaching stories—parables—to let them know that God loves every person and is willing to receive anyone who follows Him. Implicit in the Prodigal Son is the truth that God has not rejected the sinner and neither should we.

> Jesus continued: "There was a man who had two sons. The younger one said to his father, 'Father, give me my share of the estate.' So he divided his property between them. Not long after that, the younger son got together all he had, set off for a distant

country and there squandered his wealth in wild living" (Luke 15:11-13).

Evidently the time had come for the younger son to free himself from the family and leave home. He had no plan; he just left and wandered to a distant country, where he spent his money on himself, having a good time. Whether this trip was the natural and inevitable adolescent quest for freedom or simply an escape from home, the younger son was "running away" with no destination or goal. Even with personal resources and his father's consent, he was an up-and-coming troubled young person. Similarly, today many youth leave home to "make it on their own" or to escape the harsh realities of a dysfunctional family. The Prodigal's squandering his inheritance to satisfy his short-range desires and immediate pleasures may have been a simple act of immaturity, or it may have been an attempt to compensate for limitations placed on him earlier in life. Today many young people actively pursue substitutes for love (money, sex, possessions, etc.).

"After he had spent everything, there was a severe famine in that whole country, and he began to be in need" (Luke 15:14).

Famine devastates those without resources, exacerbating their most basic need—survival. Additionally, the famine forced the Prodigal to confront the emptiness of his life away from his father and his inability to provide for himself. As with many troubled youth, his self-image suffered, and he did not have the psychological base necessary to survive as a person.

"So he went and hired himself out to a citizen of that country, who sent him to his fields to feed pigs. He longed to fill his stomach with the pods that the pigs were eating,

but no one gave him anything" (Luke 15:15-16).

At this stage, the young man was near rock bottom, willing to eat food thrown to pigs. He felt almost like an animal himself, reduced to basic survival, living on the instinct level. "No one gave him anything" because no one knew him. And he didn't even know himself! It is this descent to the bottom, to the hopeless feeling of being a "nothing," that makes a relationship with a hurting young person so timely. This is when he or she will see the need for Jesus Christ who alone has the ability to truly change a life.

"When he came to his senses, he said, 'How many of my father's hired men have food to spare, and here I am starving to death! I will set out and go back to my father and say to him: Father, I have sinned against heaven and against you. I am no longer worthy to be called your son; make me like one of your hired men' " (Luke 15:17-19).

"When he came to his senses," the self-defeating behavior, the delinquent trend, was finally checked. This was his turning point, and he realized his personal need. Out of the depths of hunger and want he cries, "I have sinned against heaven and against you," betraying feelings of guilt and the desire to start all over again. And his words, "I am no longer worthy to be called your son," betray his fear of lost identity, his desperate need to find himself, and his realization that he was reduced to nothing, not even his father's son. Like so many delinquents, disillusionment and suffering shook him awake, forcing him to come to grips with his life. Now he was ready to acknowledge his need to trust and to depend on someone else.

"So he got up and went to his father" (Luke 15:20a).

Why did this independent youth in search of himself return to his father? It was not just the prospect of being forgiven; he was also motivated by his need to forgive others. In a delinquent young person's experience, there is often much that he or she must forgive. Many of those who run away will forgive just about anything—beatings, drunkenness, verbal abuse—if only their fathers will take them back and love them. No matter how weak, cruel, or indifferent the parent has been, the faintest possibility of love and acceptance, hidden though it may be by indifference and rejection, will evoke forgiveness. The need for love is critical in troubled youth.

"But while he was still a long way off, his father saw him and was filled with compassion for him; he ran to his son, threw his arms around him and kissed him. The son said to him, 'Father, I have sinned against heaven and against you. I am no longer worthy to be called your son' " (Luke 15:20-21).

Finally the son begins to pour out his feelings to his father—a carefully worded appeal prepared for this moment. His words acknowledge that he has done wrong, and they appeal for restoration, for help in reestablishing his identity. Contrary to popular belief, troubled youth do admit to doing wrong, and they don't naturally seek conflict and unhealthy relationships.

"But the father said to his servants, 'Quick! Bring the best robe and put it on him. Put a ring on his finger and sandals on his feet. Bring the fattened calf and kill it. Let's have a feast to celebrate. For this son of mine was dead and is alive again; he was lost and is found.' So they began to celebrate" (Luke 15:22-24).

The father took back his son. This is one of the main lessons that Jesus wanted to teach: God never rejects the sinner. He receives anyone who repents and asks to be restored. His love is always ready; it has never stopped and will never be withheld. But the Prodigal, the wanderer, may need to experience suffering in order to face his own emptiness and then to be open to the Father's love. In today's families, there are youth who have been rejected and need somehow to experience acceptance and love. But acceptance is meaningless if only expressed in words. This is where we provide a vital link when we build a relationship with a troubled young person. We model the truth of God's love and acceptance.

"Bring the best robe and put it on him," cries the father. Stripping off his son's rags, he clothes him with articles of beauty and dignity, clearly identifying his lost son as an individual, a person. "This son of mine was dead and is alive again; he was lost and is found." Thus begins the long, slow process of restoration.

So far, from the story of the Prodigal Son, we have learned that troubled youth do acknowledge their need for help and that they want to be loved and accepted. And the best way for them to experience God's love is through a loving relationship with another person.

But what about the "older brother"?

"Meanwhile, the older son was in the field. When he came near the house, he heard music and dancing. So he called one of the servants and asked him what was going on. 'Your brother has come,' he replied, 'and your father has killed the fattened calf because he has him back safe and sound.' The older brother became angry and refused to go in. So his father went out and pleaded with him" (Luke 15:25-28).

After receiving and restoring his lost son to the family, the father confronts a delicate problem. How could he fully accept this delinquent son without belittling the faithful older brother whose traditional family position made him highly sensitive and open to unintentional rejection by the parent?

"But he answered his father, 'Look! All these years I've been slaving for you and never disobeyed your orders. Yet you never gave me even a young goat so I could celebrate with my friends. But when this son of yours who has squandered your property with prostitutes comes home, you kill the fattened calf for him!'

'My son,' the father said, 'you are always with me, and everything I have is yours. But we had to celebrate and be glad, because this brother of yours was dead and is alive again; he was lost and is found' " (Luke 15:29-32).

Jesus does not tell us whether this diplomatic answer, tender and sincere as it was, really countered the elder son's anger and jealousy. Evidently at this critical moment, he needed to test and reaffirm his own acceptance and status in the family. The father responds as God would, with unquestioning love and acceptance.

The older brother's response is illustrative of our community at large which often reacts to delinquency and the juvenile delinquent with hostility, fear, anxiety, and, therefore, rejection. Often the church responds the same way. If anywhere, that is the place where total acceptance and love should be found! But full and quick acceptance, like the father's, must be encouraged, for the delinquent and the nondelinquent alike. This acceptance should not be seen merely as a therapeutic device to be administered in times of crisis or when a young person has committed a specific offense and needs forgiveness. It must be a quality characterizing all our relationships.

Parents, teachers, and even church leaders often present a world in which the individual adolescent has no place because adults tend to put themselves first and kids last. Troubled youth, therefore, are rejected by their parents, society, and the church. They are not seen as important. At times, churches have tried to be channels for acceptance, but they rarely succeed. Why? Because they fail to teach the truth that God will accept anyone who comes in repentance and faith to Him, no matter how far he or she has strayed. Even in their finest moments, programs cannot *teach* the love of God with words. Children must not merely be told about it; they must experience it.

Of course, churches are often thwarted by those most responsible for children—parents. This is why we must minister to the entire family, not just one member of it. In the parable, who was delinquent? Was it only the Prodigal? What about the older brother or other family members? They all share responsibility. Even the most exhaustive efforts of the church on behalf of delinquents will be in vain if the significance of the entire family is underestimated.

The story of the Prodigal Son teaches us that as individuals, as members of society, and as church men and women, we can make a difference in the lives of troubled young people.

WHAT WILL IT TAKE TO HELP TROUBLED YOUTH?

We have already outlined the five basic skills which can be used to help troubled young people. The following stories are examples of people who put those skills into action. See if you can find yourself in their lives.

● *Sam* is a Bible college student with a heavy course load requiring lots of studying. But every Saturday morning, Sam pulls on his jeans and sneakers and heads to the parking lot basketball hoop with a group of fellow students and five court-referred youngsters. His teachers understand and forgive Sam's absences on the first Wednesday of each month— court reporting day for probation volunteers.

● *Patty* is a supervisor in the claims department of an insurance company. She arrives before her crew and doesn't leave until they finish. She is a member of a national association of women in business and active in her church, serving on various committees. Patty is also a Big Sister to a girl in her apartment building. She and Beth, her "little sister," see each other daily. Patty even had to set limits on the number of times Beth could drop by each week. But for Patty, the loss of some privacy has been more than compensated for by Beth's openness to spiritual matters.

● *Walt*, in his 50s, owns his own janitorial business and lives with his wife and children in a comfortable suburban home. Regularly he receives calls from a prostitute, but Walt's wife doesn't mind. No, she is not a proponent of open marriage, but she does understand and support Walt's involvement with Angel's two teenage boys, Mark and Eric. Over

Breaking Out of the Box

In close-knit societies, people are willing to help one another. Think of a rural setting where a farmer becomes ill during the harvest. What happens? Usually a neighboring farmer steps in to help. He understands the other farmer's plight, and his sense of community spirit dictates his action.

In the urban setting, by contrast, we don't see our lives affecting others. We've alienated ourselves and tend to live in little boxes, scarcely knowing our neighbors. We're isolated. Inside the box called home, we watch another box called a television set. Seeing tragedy every day, we tend to become immune to suffering and need. We aren't even aware of our neighbors' hurts or needs; much less are we prepared to help him.

When we leave the box called home, we get into another box called an automobile and isolate ourselves once again as we speed through one neighborhood after another. Rushing through a neighborhood of a different ethnic group, we check to make sure that our box is secure by locking the doors. Arriving at work, we park our box next to a hundred others and walk briskly into yet another box, our office or workplace. At night, we simply reverse the process. All day we move quickly from one box to another, feeling insecure and unsure when we are outside our normal confines. Helping a troubled young person means that we have to venture outside of these boxes in which we feel so familiar and secure.

the past two years, Walt has taught them to shop for a week's groceries with ten dollars, to survive when Angel doesn't come home from the bar, and to properly present themselves for a job interview. Both boys have steady jobs and have accepted Christ as their Saviour as a result of Walt's involvement. (Walt always brings his wife to the restaurant when he meets with Angel to talk about her life and the boys.)

Sam, Patty, and Walt are too busy to go out of their way to spend time with the sometimes elusive and often difficult troubled young people in their worlds. But each has decided to reach out despite of the discomfort and impracticality of it all. They don't have all the skills or specialized training, but they are making a difference.

Of course, there are other factors to consider; and before you decide to work with a troubled young person, you should be able to answer the following questions with a firm "yes."

1. Am I willing to commit myself to more than a short-term relationship with this young person? Most troubled youth will require a minimum of one year, usually more, before significant progress is made.

2. Do I have a genuine interest in this youngster as a person, not just in his or her problem(s)? It is easy to forget that God is asking us to work with real flesh-and-blood people and let the young person's *problem* become the focal point of our attention. When this happens, the sin becomes paramount, and his or her need for love and understanding fades to a minor consideration. This is especially true if the sin is a "sensational" one such as assault, rape, pregnancy, or drugs. Instead, like Jesus when He confronted those who were ready to stone the woman caught in adultery (John 8), we should focus on the *per-*

son and be able to say, "Neither do I condemn you; go and leave your life of sin."

3. Am I willing to suffer personal setbacks and discouragement? These times will come when you will do everything you can imagine to help a young person, only to have him or her fail to respond, much less reach your expectations.

4. Am I willing to become involved in the total life of this person, not just on Sunday mornings and Wednesday nights? Am I interested in his or her home, school, hobbies, poverty, health? Every person is a mental, physical, social, and spiritual being. Real ministry treats the whole person, not just the "soul."

5. Am I willing to work cooperatively with others who also have an interest in this young person? As soon as you become concerned about a child's home, health, or school, you will meet other adults who have invaluable insight into his or her problems. Reaching troubled youth should be a team effort.

6. Am I prepared for defeat? Defeats can occur. Unfortunately, not everyone is willing to change or will even get to the point where they see the need to change. There are those who will not confess their sin and ask for God's forgiveness, and some will remain bitter. This can be discouraging, but often what appears to be defeat to us will be "seed planting" to God.

7. Do I recognize my limitations? No one is perfect, so if you have limitations and liabilities, you will fit right in. There are those, however, who act as though they have no weaknesses, believing they can be psychiatrist, social worker, teacher, probation officer, lawyer, counselor, and loving parent all at the same time. They may even believe that they have all the answers. To be effective in this ministry, you must identify your limitations and work in your areas of strength.

8. Will I make every effort to understand his or her point of view without becoming judgmental? If you pass judgment first and listen (and try to understand) second, you will lose. Hank serves as a good example. He volunteered to work with Roger, an eleven-year-old boy referred by the juvenile court. After getting to know

Should You Be Working with Troubled Youth?

	YES	MAYBE	NO
1. Am I willing to commit myself to more than a short-term relationship with this young person?			
2. Do I have a genuine interest in this youth as a person, not just in his or her problem(s)?			
3. Am I willing to suffer personal setbacks and discouragement?			
4. Am I willing to become involved in the total life of this person, not just on Sunday mornings and Wednesday nights?			
5. Am I willing to work cooperatively with others who also have an interest in this young person?			
6. Am I prepared for defeat?			
7. Do I recognize my limitations?			
8. Will I make every effort to understand his or her point of view without becoming judgmental?			
9. Am I willing to be inconvenienced?			

Roger for several months, Hank thought it was time to begin talking to him about God. Because Hank's father had always been loving and kind, he quite easily pictured God as a Heavenly Father who always loves and cares for us. So he talked to Roger about God as a Father who cared for him and who wanted him to be obedient. "I hate God!" Roger exclaimed, "I hate my dad, and I'd never obey him!" Hank's immediate response was judgmental, and he told Roger that he should always obey his dad. Several weeks later, Hank's perspective changed as he saw Roger thrown off the front porch by his drunken and abusive father.

9. Am I willing to be inconvenienced? Troubled young people are not "organized" and their problems cannot be neatly scheduled. Often you will have to adjust your schedule to meet their needs and crises. Again Hank is a good example. He is now a newlywed and has been working with Steve for three months. Steve is thirteen, lives with one parent, and has recently been expelled from school for cutting classes and for fighting. Steve really likes Hank, and they spend many hours together. Steve has heard about God's love for him. It is normal for Hank to get a phone call from Steve every evening, just to talk or to ask when they will be going minibike riding again. One call was at 1 A.M., from the police station. Steve was arrested, wouldn't go home, wanted to talk to his "counselor," and needed a ride. Hank decided to be inconvenienced (not an easy decision for a newlywed), and later he was able to introduce Steve to Jesus Christ.

Should you work with troubled youth? Are you ready to become a friend to a young person from a different background, with different values, and with critical needs? If we were to compare working with troubled youth with other types of ministries regarding the expenditure of time, money, emotion, and energy, this type of ministry would seem to be expensive. But if God lays the burden of troubled young people on your heart, the benefits will far outweigh any costs, fears, doubts, or setbacks. In fact, there may be a young person out there who can't afford to have you do anything else.

Notes

[1] "Juvenile Justice: Before and After the Onset of Delinquency," U.S. Discussion paper for the Sixth United Nations Congress on the prevention of crime and the treatment of offenders.

Although her last surviving parent died when she was sixteen, this little girl was an emotional orphan for years. At five, she was rejected by her mother because she was "homely." Her father, an alcoholic, was fond of her, but he was usually out of control. Eventually her parents divorced and soon after, Father died. After her mother's death, the girl was placed in the custody of her grandmother—a change from bad to worse. Also living in Grandma's house were four young uncles and aunts whom Grandma had been unable to manage, especially after her husband had died. One uncle was an alcoholic, and one aunt was an emotional wreck who sometimes tried to retreat from her problems by locking herself in her room. Grandmother decided that she would be strict with this child, so she prohibited her from having playmates, put her in braces to keep her back straight, and kept her out of school.

In his senior year of secondary school, a nervous breakdown forced this boy to leave school for six months. A poor student, he had few verbal skills and no friends. His teachers saw him as a problem, and his father was ashamed of him because of his lack of athletic ability. This boy had odd mannerisms, made up his own religion, and would chant and hum to himself. His parents and other adults regarded him as "different."

Three of this youngster's brothers and sisters had died before he was born. Because his head was so large as a baby, the doctors thought he had "brain fever," and most of the relatives and neighbors concluded that he would probably be abnormal. At age six, he went to school where his teacher diagnosed him as mentally ill. His mother disagreed, withdrew him from school, and taught him at home.

What became of these children? If you were their parents, teachers, or neighbors, what would you predict as their future? Will they outgrow their problems? Will they be mentally handicapped? Will they need special help? Will they be delinquents? Should they go to school?

Are these three children troubled youth? Possibly . . . but it is difficult to define exactly who is a "troubled" young person and what makes him or her that way. There are a multitude of theories. Psychologists think in terms of behavior, attitudes, and thoughts. Sociologists analyze the child's environment and his relation to it. Criminologists discuss broken laws, sentencing, and recidivism. Teachers describe content retention and learning disabilities. Social workers talk about the child's welfare. Meanwhile, parents are confused, but caring; hurting, but angry; wanting help, but refusing help. They are at their wits' end!

The truth is that many supposed "delinquent" children turn out fine. Our three case studies above, for example, were Eleanor Roosevelt, Thomas Edison, and Albert Einstein. Surprised? They weren't delinquent, but certainly they were "troubled." And who can predict which "troubled" young people have such potential?

Just about everything imaginable has been blamed for causing youth to be troubled: weak discipline at home and in school, a pervading disregard for authority, leniency in the juvenile justice system, violence on TV, divorce, drugs, alcohol, sexual and violent music lyrics, child abuse, poverty, pornography, mental disorders, and even physiology. All of these alleged culprits boil down to this: rejection, neglect, and parental unconcern. Admittedly this is a generalization, and there will be exceptions, but we believe it is the rule.

This chapter has been written out of concern for those children who do *not* turn out like Eleanor Roosevelt,

Thomas Edison, and Albert Einstein—young people who want to be understood but aren't, who want help from caring adults but are overlooked, and who have chosen to do wrong for one reason or another. This chapter's purpose is to help you understand these troubled young people, who they are, why they have developed this way, and what makes them different from "normal" children.

Recently a magazine cartoon pictured a group of bearded protestors carrying signs reading, "Ban the Bomb," "Cut the Budget," "Death to Star Wars," and "Get Out of Central America." In their midst was a well-dressed but depressed-looking young man with a poster which said simply, "Insufficient Data." Similar feelings arise as we try to define the "troubled adolescent." It is a complex issue, and there are no easy answers; but that is not to say that there are no answers. Research and information are mounting as troubled youth are becoming recognized as a significant problem in society.

To begin, we must realize that we cannot define a troubled youth simply by recognizing how he or she is different. A fourteen-year-old boy's earrings, long hair, leather clothes, and studded bracelets do not tell us if he has a serious problem. How a young person differs from our expectations, even a dramatic difference, is not indicative of whether or not he or she is troubled. For instance, the coauthor of this book, Dwight Spotts, was fortunate to be reared in a Christian home with loving parents. Dwight attended a Baptist church in the Midwest where his dad served as a deacon and his mom taught Sunday School. In the late 60s, it was normal for teenagers to identify with the "flower child" clothing styles; therefore Dwight owned several pairs of pants that any hippie would have been proud to wear—bright yellow, arrayed with green and orange flowers—and not exactly the attire of a normal Baptist young person. The Sunday he wore them to church, heads turned, eyes popped, and teeth chattered. Church pillars were certain that he was well on his way to becoming a delinquent—a deacon's son gone bad! Fortunately, "man looks on the outward appearance, but the Lord looks on the heart" (1 Samuel 16:7). Though Dwight had a lot of maturing to do, he wasn't a *troubled youth.*

Conduct norms vary from state to state, city to city, and neighborhood to neighborhood. Whether or not these norms are applied to a particular child may depend on the parents' social position and the community's law provisions. Schools, courts, families, and police all share in defining what is right and wrong for a child. The church also plays a significant role. And here is where many of the myths of "normal" can be exploded as biblical principles are stressed. For example, our worth as persons does not come from what we own (Luke 12:15) but from who we are . . . unique individuals, created in God's image.

What is "normal," then, for any young person, troubled or not, depends on what is taught and practiced at home, school, church, and neighborhood. From the child's perspective, of course, friends' ideas and standards will be most important. It matters little that we have been raised in a similar environment or can appreciate a child's friends. What is most important is to understand how he or she defines "normal." The alcoholic father, an ultrastrict teacher, a judgmental neighbor, and accepting friends will all contribute to his or her definition.

WHO ARE THESE TROUBLED YOUTH?

A troubled youth is a young person, male or female, who mistrusts others, lacks significant adults to provide emotional support and to model appropriate behavior, has primitive social values, turns to peers to find acceptance and approval (a troubled youth will do almost anything to find acceptance and love), and has virtually no relationship with God.

The following is a general profile of the typical troubled young person:

1. He lives for immediate gratification, and postponement of rewards is unacceptable.

2. He exhibits learned behaviors. Attitudes and behavior patterns are learned from others, a shocking and discouraging sign of the lack of mature, adult role models.

3. He is extremely self-centered. The universe revolves around him, and he expects the world to contribute to his pleasure.

It is safe to assume that delinquent behavior is an effort on the teen's part to say something to the world. It is a cry for help which should be interpreted as, "Love me, listen to me, accept me for myself, give me direction, teach me." Basically, the troubled teenager has the same drives and desires as the average teenager. His actions are less predictable, but his patterns of unpredictability are fairly consistent. Like the average teenager, he loves adventure and excitement, but unlike the norm, he is unhindered by convention or social restraint.

4. He finds comfort and a measure of fulfillment in delinquent behavior. Delinquent acts bring few feelings of guilt or remorse.

5. He has a peer group which usually reinforces his behavior. He is self-centered, but usually not independent.

6. He has a weak conscience and is less affected by guilt than the average person.

7. He is suspicious of anyone representing the "establishment." He is not anxious to develop relationships with those who uphold the standards against which he has rebelled.

8. He has learned to use people without becoming attached to them. People become "tools" in his quest for meaning.

9. He does not respect law, tradition, or people in authority positions.

10. He is capable of loyalties and selfish love. The bases for his friendships are difficult for the average citizen to understand, but these are realistic relationships for troubled youth.

11. He has achieved proficiency in "conning."

12. He usually has a stable personality.

13. He believes that his behavior is all right. From his perspective, his motives are justified and his behavior is reasonable.

14. He usually is not upset about his delinquent life . . . except when he is caught.

15. He is not interested in changing; little thought is given to how to straighten out.

16. He is not mentally "sick" and is in touch with reality.

17. He strives to achieve recognition as an adult by doing adult "things."

18. He is emotionally immature. Emotions run to extremes—elation to depression, submission to defiance.

19. He tends to be either loud and uninhibited or quiet and cunning.

20. He lives by his own set of rules and follows behavioral guidelines often set by a gang or peer group.

21. He accepts pleasure as his guiding life-principle. Self-centered, materialistic, and status-oriented values scream, "I want it, and I want it now!"

22. He enjoys shocking people with extreme speech and behavior; refinement is resisted.

23. He is lonely. The gang or peer group does not meet his needs for love and self-worth.

24. He may use delinquent behavior to get attention.

Often it is assumed that a troubled young person is a "juvenile delinquent." Delinquency is an act or course of conduct which could be handled by the court. Many times, however, the situation never comes to court and is handled by a social agency or the school or is forgotten altogether. Legally, "juvenile delinquents" are adolescents under 18 years of age who have been convicted of an offense. Until then, they are no different than many children who are not "delinquent."

The term "juvenile delinquent" was first used legally in 1897 with the establishment of the first juvenile court in Illinois. Before 1899, most disapproved behavior was treated as a family problem and handled at home. If a young person violated the criminal law, he or she was tried as an adult criminal and treated accordingly. The juvenile court was intended to substitute rehabilitation and treatment for punishment of children as adults.

Although the deferential treatment of youthful offenders has been relatively recent, troubled youth have been with us for ages. Young people did drink, steal, fight, and have "real" problems before the 19th century. Here is a sampling of a few:

● *Disrespect for parents*

"Our earth is degenerate—children no longer obey their parents." (Carved in stone 6,000 years ago by an Egyptian priest.)

● *Disrespect for those in authority*

"From there Elisha went up to Bethel. As he was walking along the road, some youths came out of the town and jeered at him. 'Go on up, you baldhead!' they said. 'Go on up, you baldhead!' " (2 Kings 2:23—9th century B.C.)

● *Sexual misconduct*

"Public schoolboys practice more vices by the age of 16 than anyone else would have by ____" (Written by Philippe Aries during the Middle Ages in *Centuries of Childhood*. He also highlighted their drinking problems and the attempts by the schools to control drinking.)

The fact is, troubled youth are not much different today than they have always been. They live in "broken homes" in increasing numbers and still have the unfortunate opportunity to be raised by inconsistent, unloving, or unhealthy parents. It is still possible to be born with mental or physical abnormalities. Sibling rivalries and troublesome relationships still exist. There will always be inadequate adult behavior models. On the other hand, these obstacles and influences do not guarantee delinquency.

Most behavioral scientists agree that there are three cultural influences affecting every young person: home, school, and peer group. Fifty years ago, the church would have been named as well. At home, in school, and in the peer group, the child moves to meet needs and develop potential. Unhealthy influences in any of these areas, therefore, can foster attitudes, values, and actions which lead to antisocial behavior. To understand a troubled young person, we must look at the strengths and weaknesses of his or her home, school, and friends.

We will not undertake an exhaustive discussion of the theories of youth problems. (A continual stream

---

Are Troubled Youth Like Troubled Adults?

A recent group of studies has revealed a striking resemblance between the serious juvenile offender and the adult felon. While the group of juveniles that repeatedly commit violent crimes is small, there seems to be a consistent progression from serious juvenile offender to serious adult criminal.

Serious juvenile offenders are like adult felons in many ways. Here are a few:

● Both are predominately male

● Both are disproportionately black and Hispanic compared to the general population

● Both are seen to be disadvantaged economically

● Both are likely to exhibit interpersonal difficulties and behavioral problems in school and on the job

● Both tend to come from one-parent families with a lot of conflict, instability, and poor supervision

of research and theories attempts to explain the psychological and sociological dynamics of troubled youth.)

Children come into this world without any frame of reference. They have no inherent scale upon which to judge their worth; they must ascertain their value from the messages they receive. Parents largely determine the ratings that children give themselves, at least until they enter school and begin to reevaluate themselves based upon the feedback they get from teachers and peers. It is no wonder that children whose parents have their own emotional problems have trouble assessing their own personal worth.

Just about any professional who is worth his salt acknowledges that there are a few basic essentials that human beings need in order to grow into competent adults. They need to feel powerful, that they can affect the world around them. They need identity, to know who they are and with whom they belong. They need acceptance from their parents and unconditional regard that allows them to experiment and make mistakes. They need consistency in order to believe that the world is predictable. They need to feel worthwhile. They need to be loved.

Parents who supply these essentials (with God's help) are more likely to have well-adjusted children. Parents who do not are likely to have children who suffer from low self-esteem, anxiety, lack of empathy, poor social relationships, drug or alcohol abuse, delinquency, suicide, or homicide. The simple truth is, more often than not, dysfunctional parents breed dysfunctional kids.

Hypothesizing about the possible causes of delinquent behavior is only helpful to a point. Then we must concentrate on the specific needs of the individual young person and develop a loving relationship with him or her.

WHAT ABOUT FAMILIES?

The family is still the basic unit of society. Here the child first experiences living with others, and this experience forms the foundation for values, attitudes, and behaviors. A distorted family is *usually* in the background of the delinquent. A bad home breeds antisocial attitudes. How can children emerge unscathed from "families" featuring alcoholic parents, promiscuous mothers and sisters, single parents, drug-abusing brothers, unemployed fathers, or a combination of the above? These conditions mark the homes of many delinquents and, in part, are the environment of nearly all troubled youth. Even the middle- or upper-class problem child is usually struggling at home.

Discipline in the distorted home is usually extremely permissive or extremely stern and harsh (the latter often physically enforced to the point of abuse). Extreme permissiveness communicates lack of concern and love. Extreme strictness is usually arbitrary and cruel and is inconsistent when administered by undisciplined parents and others. The ineffective parent often vacillates between freedom and law, leaving the child confused and without guidelines with which to evaluate his or her behavior. Parental affection or rejection is the watershed issue of home effectiveness. Few parents of troubled youth realize they communicate rejection to their children. Most are trying to love their children, but problems in their own character development make this difficult.

Today our cultural patterns of life put children and families last, behind priorities such as making money, achieving recognition, and fulfilling civic and social obligations. Parenting is to be done, of course, but it happens in the "spare time."

WHAT ABOUT FAMILY STRUCTURE?

The word "family" usually evokes a picture of Mom, Dad, and the kids, the "nuclear family," where Dad is the breadwinner and Mom is the homemaker. We assume that this is the only home environment in which a child can function effectively; any other family structure is a "broken home" where parents and children fail. But children *do* flourish in many families which are not nuclear.

Among the wide diversity of family structures exists a broad range of ethnic and racial variations. Here are some of the most prevalent:

● *Nuclear Family*—Husband, wife, and children living in a common household; Dad is the breadwinner and Mom is the homemaker.

● *Dual-Work Family*—Both parents are employed outside of the home.

● *Single-Parent Family*—As a result of death, divorce, separation, or abandonment, the family has only one parent and usually preschool and/or school-age children. If the other parent is living, he or she rarely supports the family financially.

● *Unmarried Parent and Child Family*—This is usually a mother and child where marriage is not possible or desired. A common-law marriage or a homosexual relationship could be other variations. The child could be an offspring of either partner or adopted, formally or informally.

In many ethnic and racial groups, a "kin" network develops, where many family members live close to each other and exchange goods and services. It is not uncommon for two or three generations to live in a single household with uncles, aunts, and offspring together.

Children may move from one family structure to another. The infant of a nuclear family may enter the single-parent family if the marriage breaks up. Then, if the single parent remarries, the child enters a new parent-child relationship, adopted by the new parent. New half brothers or sisters may also be involved. Now the mother may have to work, moving the child into a dual work family.

As mentioned previously, many of us expect young people from broken homes to be troubled and on their way to becoming delinquent. This is not always the case. But because broken homes are such a large factor in any understanding of troubled youth, it is interesting to see the perspective of science. Since the turn of the century, the "broken home variable" has had its ups and downs. On one side are those who argue that broken homes foster delinquency. This was the prevailing view for the first thirty to forty years of this century. Consider this statement by John L. Gilling in 1933:

> The broken home is decidedly dangerous for juveniles . . . the fundamental importance of a good home in the prevention of delinquency is well recognized everywhere.[1]

Thirty years later, Marshall B. Clinard proposed the following view:

> The effort to link juvenile delin-

quency with broken homes is probably a blind alley, since the concept of a broken home is by no means a constant factor, and the relationship of broken homes to delinquency has never been conclusively demonstrated.[2]

Though no research has proven conclusively that young people get into trouble because of broken homes, it is apparent that it is a potentially significant factor. Travis Hirschi summarizes the research well:

The closer the child's relationship with his parents, the more he is attached to and identifies with them, the lower his chances of delinquency.[3]

When the conditions required to develop healthy, competent young people are considered, one family form may be more supportive than another. Much more significant than the structure are the relationships developed within. Different forms present different issues and potential problems for family members. Developmental and relational patterns within the family are significantly affected by a variety of factors—size, money, environment, personalities, and others.

WHAT ABOUT PARENTAL LOVE?

Regardless of the situation, the key ingredient in every family is the relationship between parent and child. If the parent is loving, considerate, and understanding, the child will be able to grow and mature in almost any kind of family structure.

Though family forms play an important role, far more significant is the presence of a caring adult who loves God. Ideally, every child should have parents who model and teach

love for God. As we read in Scripture:

Watch yourselves closely so that you do not forget the things your eyes have seen or let them slip from your heart as long as you live. Teach them to your children and to their children after them. Remember the day you stood before the Lord your God at Horeb, when He said to me, "Assemble the people before Me to hear My words so that they may learn to revere Me as long as they live in the land and may teach them to their children" (Deuteronomy 4:9-10).

These commandments that I give you today are to be upon your hearts. Impress them on your children. Talk about them when you sit at home and when you walk along the road, when you lie down and when you get up (Deuteronomy 6:6-7).

If God-loving parents are not available, God can use other adults and other support structures to teach His truths.

The emotional bond between a child and a parent or parent figure is not as simple as it may first appear. When the adult leader is involved personally and emotionally, a relationship will develop and the child will begin to relate well to his or her world. When the adult doesn't care, the relationship will be incomplete, one-sided. To develop self-esteem, every child needs at least one person whom he or she can love and who loves and values him or her. But, unfortunately, unwanted young people are plentiful.

Infants born from unwanted pregnancies risk rejection from birth. Children pushed from families and into institutions begin with a disadvantage. And any child's welfare fades when an adult claims him or her with self-serving motives (e.g., using the child to gain a financial advantage, as revenge after a painful divorce, as a way to force a reluctant partner into marriage, to cement a shaky marriage, or to replace another child lost in death).

At the other extreme, being wanted loses its benefits when the parent's needs and valuation are excessive. There are parents, for example, who blindly believe that their children have never done, or could never do, anything wrong. Children from those homes may grow to become egotistical, spoiled, and self-righteous. And they can become almost unteachable regarding values and morality because they feel no obligation to win their parents' approval.

The quality of the interaction between parent and child is crucial. Troubled youth have needs like any other children. When they receive love and acceptance from parents, they learn to love and accept others. When they don't, they learn to be self-serving, hard, and "unlovable."

In *Delinquency and Parental Pathology* (Staples Press), Robert G. Andry reports these findings of research exploring the extent to which delinquent youth feel loved by their parents:

1. Delinquents feel loved most by their mothers; nondelinquents feel loved by both parents.

2. Delinquents believe that their fathers should love them more; nondelinquents believe that neither parent should love them more.

3. Delinquent boys think their parents are too embarrassed (especially fathers) to openly show love and affection.

4. Delinquents are too embarrassed to show love openly to their parents.

5. Delinquents feel hostility from their parents; nondelinquents do not.

6. Delinquents identify with their mothers more than their fathers and believe they are more like Mom than Dad; nondelinquents tend to identify with both parents.

In general, troubled young people receive less love and affection, and their fathers are less satisfactory to them than their mothers.

WHAT ABOUT DISCIPLINE?

Usually, consistent, loving discipline is lacking in the lives of troubled youth. Good discipline is based on a common understanding between parents and children and is carried out in love. Research has shown that the discipline in the homes of troubled young people is either extremely permissive or extremely rigid and harsh (physically enforced). As noted earlier, the discipline style in a home determines to a great extent the child's own discipline patterns and his or her feelings of love or rejection.

Discipline forms and methods can lead to even greater problems: child abuse and family violence. Abuse will be discussed later, but research has found that a large number of abusive parents (perhaps as high as 40–60 percent) were themselves abused as children.

Family violence is also a common ingredient in the background of troubled youth. Many of them are physically aggressive because violence is a way of life at home. They fight because Dad fights. In *The Family Secret*, William Stacey summarizes the problem well:

Family violence is widespread in

American society. It can be likened to a cancer, which is part of an organism but which at the same time fatally corrupts and destroys its host. From all indications, it is a growing threat to the future of our whole society. Moreover, it can even be passed on from parents to children, making some families literally training grounds for future generations of violent adults. Yet at the same time domestic violence often remains a "family secret." Many public officials ignore it as trivial. Legislators make it a low-priority item in their budgets. Even many of its victims try to conceal its effects from their relatives, friends, neighbors, and coworkers. Sadly, its youngest victims often have no one to turn to or cannot explain their dilemma. Victims of family violence from incest or beatings may remain silent out of fear, embarrassment, or the belief that there is nothing they can do about it. Commonly circulated myths that violent homes are somehow "sick" or abnormal, or alternatively "normal," do little to help bring the problem out into the open.[4]

Most troubled adolescents seem to experience inconsistent and unloving discipline. And there is usually no mutual understanding between parent and child on what is expected. Consequently, many hurting young people never learn the basic guidelines about how to act or relate to others.

WHAT ABOUT ECONOMICS AND ENVIRONMENT?

In the poverty-stricken family struggling for survival, hunger, cold, sickness, and despair cripple the capacity for human response. No person who spends each day searching for menial work and each night keeping rats from the crib can be expected to be the "ideal" parent, a stable example of love and discipline.

Though social "class" is not a reliable predictor of delinquency, research shows that a young person in trouble with the law typically lives in the poor part of town, where over-

---

In spite of the obstacles a victim faces in acknowledging family violence, a significant amount of domestic violence is reported to National Crime Survey interviewers. Considering that during a nine-year period 4.1 million victimizations committed by relatives have been reported to a government agency (either the police, the Bureau of Justice Statistics, or both), and that a substantial number of these occurred at least three times during a six-month period, it is apparent that family violence is a significant problem of large and currently ill-understood proportions.

Much work remains to be done before the problem of family violence is thoroughly understood. Historically, the problem is one that has been surrounded by secrecy and shame; many victims never talk about it to anyone. Knowledge of the incidence of family violence, like other crimes about which individuals are silent, may never be complete.

Taken from *Family Violence*, Bureau of Justice Statistics Special Report, by Patsy A. Klaus and Michael R. Rand, U.S. Department of Justice.

crowded and substandard housing prevail. "Home" for most inner-city children is often nothing more than a room or two shared by a shifting number of relatives and acquaintances. "Home" means shabby furniture, many children in one bed, faulty plumbing, falling plaster, peeling paint, roaches and rats, dark hallways, and littered stairways. Motivation to change and hope for a better life seem stifled by the foul air. This feeling typifies many delinquents.

The neighborhood is rarely better. Broken bottles, bricks, garbage, and discarded bits of furniture and toys choke the yards and vacant lots. The back alley is the playground, but it too is littered with trash and occupied by vagrant winos. Crooked, callous landlords and cops, gangland kings, dirty politicians, and economic rapists control the turf. They are the adults with power.

Not every delinquent's home or neighborhood is like this, but families who do not battle rats and scrounge for food have other struggles which cross all social boundaries. With money a high priority, there are the demands of holding a job . . . or two. Dad is trying to move up in the company, and Mom also has a job. Work and related social events make increasing demands on the schedule; children are no longer a priority, and they know it. This reversal of priorities often lies beneath the growing disillusionment and alienation of young people. Reared in circumstances where the family could not function, whether slum or suburb, these children react the only way they know how, by being indifferent, callous, unresponsive, and even cruel.

In the urban setting, a great variety of jobs, schools, residences, and facilities are available. For some young people, especially those in the middle class, the problem is one of deciding from too many choices. These options (where to work, how to spend leisure time, what school activities to join, which friends to be with), coupled with the demands and expectations of parents and others, can cause tremendous anxiety. A young person can become immobilized, insecure, and feel like a failure. This can ultimately lead to thoughts of suicide.

In contrast, for those who are economically disadvantaged, options are scarce, with continuous pressure to limit or take away existing alternatives. Very little is available in employment, education, social participation, and "upward mobility." Even knowledge of existing opportunities is severely limited.

WHAT ABOUT FRIENDS?

Friends are the second major influence (after families) on young people, and their peer relationships are important in all phases of their development. In many ways youth seem to function on their own, touching society, yet separate from it. Some belong to gangs, named groups with rigid rules and tight power structures. Most, however, run in loosely organized groups stemming from school or neighborhood cliques, clubs, or activities, a Sunday School class, or a type of youth group.

Regardless of the group, these associations determine the behavioral norms. Peers influence values, how young people relate to others, and even how they talk. In these peer groups, almost every area of a young person's life is discussed, from ideas about themselves, parents, school, and friends, to attitudes about sex, drinking, drugs, and disobeying the law. If the young person has prob-

Gangs

A major difference between juvenile and adult offenders is the importance of gang membership and the tendency of young people to commit crimes while in a group. National crime-survey data show that "personal crimes of violence by multiple offenders rather than lone offenders are more likely to involve juvenile offenders."

Gangs, once thought to be merely a gathering of rebellious teenagers, have grown up to become criminal enterprises in many cities. A recent national survey of law enforcement officers found that while the problem is disproportionately large in the largest cities, gangs are also found in cities of less than one-half million population. Whether in a large or relatively small city, we know that gang members are much more likely than other young offenders to engage in violent crime, particularly robbery, rape, assault, and weapons violations.

Taken from *Report to the Nation on Crime and Justice*, Department of Justice, Bureau of Justice Statistics.

trouble with others, but they can't seem to prove that one boy made another one "go bad." These studies do establish that most delinquent behavior is a group activity. This means that if one young person is caught, the chances are great that he or she was not alone. The following principles will help us better understand peer influence.

1. Young people select friends who are more like them than not, sharing similar values and behaviors. (Don't we all?)

2. Any group of adolescents expects its members to conform to explicit and implicit standards. Troubled youth will participate with others and conform quite naturally to antisocial and illegal behavior.

3. Most troubled youth who don't join gangs will belong to other cliques, and their delinquent activities will vary over time. For example, Joe, Jim, and Steve decide to go drinking and partying. Later, Joe decides to break into an old house and steal some money. Because Jim and Steve refuse, Joe joins with Andy who has been arrested several times for burglary.

4. Troubled young people become highly dependent on each other, especially for acceptance and status and to hide feelings of loneliness.

5. Boys experience more peer pressure to indulge in antisocial behavior than do girls.

6. Male status is determined by physical prowess, aggressiveness, and fearlessness; female status comes from being sexy, attractive, and clever.

7. Most young people do not readily accept those outside their group.

The problem of peer pressure has always existed, but the challenge of confronting *negative* peer pressure has never been greater. Societal

lems at home, these associations become extremely important, often to the point where the family is no longer seen as a reliable source of advice or information. When a young person's needs are unmet at home, the next step is to detach him/herself emotionally from the family and attach to friends. And it doesn't matter what kinds of people these friends are, as long as they accept him or her.

There has been a great deal of interest in trying to determine the extent to which peers influence a young person to get into trouble. Sociologists can show how they get into

changes, media influence, and the information explosion have pushed children to grow up faster and to make difficult and complex moral decisions earlier. Here are some of the choices with which they are confronted.

Sex

An attractive girl, Jane was admired by most of the eighth-grade boys. She always wore beautiful clothes and applied her makeup just right because her mother had often stressed that looks were very important. And she had freedom; her parents never said no. Jane was so attractive, older guys often took notice, and one of them, Joe, asked her for a date. He thought she was a lot of fun, so he asked her to go to a "real party." Jane didn't know the other kids at the party, but they were friendly, and she mixed well. On the fringes, a few of the older couples were "making out." When Joe first asked her to go upstairs, she refused. After a while, however, she realized that she would be left out if she didn't go along. And her friends had said that it was the only way to prove to the older guys that she was a "woman" and not a "little girl."

Drugs

Ted is twelve and lives with his mom; his parents were divorced four years ago. Mom works and often comes home late. One of Ted's jobs is to do the weekly wash at the Laundromat, but one night he was depressed and decided to skip the wash and go out with friends instead. As they were walking along, a "pusher" approached and said, "Hey, any of you guys man enough to sniff some of this?" Ted and his friends decided to give it a try. It was easy, and Ted didn't feel so depressed afterward. Soon his Laundromat trips became

opportunities to continue using cocaine.

Unaware of what was happening, Ted's mother felt better because he wasn't resentful about having to do the laundry. As time passed, he became jumpy and easily excited, and soon he added "yellow jackets" (depressants) to go with the "snow." As Ted kept needing more drugs, the price continued to rise with his addiction. That's when he and his friends decided to break into the washing machines to help pay for what they needed.

Alcohol

Loud music filled the room. Dave, Bob, Anthony, Randy, and their dates had just returned from a rock concert and wanted the night to continue. Dave and Jenni were dancing as Anthony entered the room with a tray of drinks and chips. "Here, have a real drink," he said.

"No thanks. I don't drink," replied Dave.

"You what? Come on! This is Scotch!"

"No, not now."

"What? You gonna turn me down? Don't be a chicken. Have one."

By this time, the tray had been emptied except for Dave's glass, and everyone was trying to convince him to take a drink. Dave felt embarrassed and didn't want to disappoint Jenni or his buddies, or feel rejected by them.

Jane, Ted, and Dave are involved in typical peer pressure situations. Most troubled youth have not developed the values or the decision-making skills needed to confront such pressure. On the contrary, their learned morality reinforces their negative decisions. And many young people may know what their parents want, but their felt needs and present consequences overrule parental expectations.

WHAT ABOUT SCHOOL?

School (or the lack of school) plays a significant role in any child's life, and it is the third major influence on young people after family and peers.

School has not always been so influential. Not too long ago, most families lived in rural areas, and the home was the focal point for socialization and education. Children learned their ABCs from the Bible as Mom read by the light of an oil lamp. Sons followed their fathers' footsteps, working the land, and daughters planned to be wives and homemakers. As industrialization burst on the world scene, however, family members left the farm and ran the machines of production. Cities sprang up, families moved, and schools assumed responsibility for educating the young.

Today, schools are expected to teach much more than the ABCs. Included in the growing list of responsibilities are education, socialization, reform, and physical care. Many believe that the child's *total* mental, social, physical, and even spiritual development should happen in school. And the fact that a school could have a "few" students from deprived and/or dysfunctional homes shouldn't alter its responsibilities.

Schools have also become the great "equalizer." Because "all men have been created equal," education is expected to give every child the opportunity to become a productive member of society, regardless of his or her economic situation, race, parents, background, or neighborhood.

The problem is that lower class children, especially dropouts and delinquents, have no "career" goals for many of the reasons discussed above, and troubled youth see no connection between what is taught in school and what they will do when they leave. They question the need for school, why they have to go, and what good it will do. Then their grades reinforce their feelings of failure, and they hear over and over that they will "never amount to anything" without a high school diploma. From their perspective, however, that diploma is either unattainable or insignificant. The troubled young person feels forced to conform, placed in a mold . . . and being in a mold is the one thing a troubled youth cannot tolerate.

By analyzing a few myths about education, we can better understand how school affects troubled youth differently than other students.

Myth #1. You have to go to school to learn. School teaches facts, figures, and other information, but it doesn't teach a kid how to survive on the streets. Much of what we learn comes from personal experience, and experiences are real to an adolescent. If a young person isn't interested, he or she will not become involved; and if he or she doesn't get involved, the program will have very little value. Troubled youth find full value in school when the content relates to their experience.

Myth #2. Schools will prepare you for the future. Most young people care about today. With troubled youth this attitude is magnified because their present problems are such that just getting to tomorrow is challenge enough. Troubled young people expect immediate rewards and consequences; they will deal with the future when it comes. They need to be taught self-control, decision-making, how to use leisure time, and the most basic social skills.

Myth #3. All children are equal. All children are not equal academically, socially, or economically. For instance, many troubled youth read poorly (with no help at home and no motivation). Often, poor readers are seen as misfits by teachers and fellow students. Poor readers may have an average or above average IQ, but they see themselves as "dumb." They are ashamed in class and want to drop out because of their handicap.

Troubled youth are rarely involved in extracurricular activities. Most students get involved in music, publications, sports, or drama because their parents encourage or push them (and will pay the expenses), because their friends decide to join, or because a specific activity has meaning (career related, etc.). But troubled youth have little parental support and few friends who are involved, and they see no present or future meaning as it relates to their environment. In addition, youthful offenders, truants, and class disrupters are labeled and singled out for special discipline.

Myth #4. School is important to you, and you need to finish. Many troubled youth hear the opposite message at home, and many parents do not encourage attendance or studying. A young person may begin to think, *Mom and Dad dropped out at seventeen and got married. Why should I have to finish school?*

Consider how a father's occupation affects the son's selection of a job and a lifestyle. Often doctors' sons become doctors, teachers' sons become teachers, and ministers' sons become ministers. What does the son of an alcoholic become? What does a child learn from a father who dropped out of school and cannot keep a job because of his drinking?

Both research and practical experience support the idea that a family's socioeconomic situation affects a child's status in the community and influences his or her decision about whether or not to stay in school. Finishing high school is supposed to mean a better job and financial security, but there are few opportunities for this to happen with a disadvantaged young person; therefore, his or her interest in obtaining the coveted diploma diminishes. Frankly, most troubled youth don't care about completing their education. That's why so many drop out. They have already decided that for them, school is not the best way to get ahead.

Myth #5. You can get better grades. The mental ability and the potential may be there, but usually getting better grades involves competition. And competition leads to failure for many troubled youth. Grades, then, become one more negative reinforcement—another reason for giving up and not finishing school.

These five myths represent how many young people with major problems in their lives feel about school. Simply put, schools do not make an impact on troubled youth in the same way they influence other students. Of course, schools do not push young people into trouble, but they do provide the conditions which lead them to drop out and get involved with others on the street. For the troubled young person, school is only an extension of the problems he or she is facing everywhere else.

WHAT ABOUT LEARNING RIGHT AND WRONG?

Most troubled youth do not have a personal relationship with God and do not try to live by biblical principles. Most of their morals and values, therefore, reflect those of their parents and peers. But like most people, the morals they embrace are not necessarily the ones they practice.

Instead, these young people will do whatever is most expedient for their circumstances. As a result, in a specific situation, there may be a vast difference between the moral principle and the action. For example, a boy may say that it is wrong to cheat but will still do it to pass a test. Or he may admit that stealing is wrong but do it to get money for cigarettes.

As the average person enters adolescence, he or she becomes increasingly able to conceptualize and generalize moral rules and principles and is no longer limited to specific rules. Troubled youth, however, find conceptualizing difficult. The concept of honesty, for example, covers everything from speaking the truth and obeying rules to not cheating and not stealing. For a delinquent, honesty just means "not telling a lie." He doesn't see how "honesty" has anything to do with dishonest behavior such as being friendly with a person just to take advantage of him.

Instead of applying abstract, biblical ideals and principles, troubled young people judge the seriousness of an act by its practical consequences and the potential punishment. ("Love," for example, is what he or she feels, not the idea of helping others.) "Right" and "wrong" are interpreted literally. A troubled youth may think, *If stealing is wrong for me, it is wrong for everyone. But if others can steal and not get caught, so can I.*

In contrast, morally mature people consider intentions and the practical consequences of an action. We judge right and wrong differently from the troubled young person. Of course, while we may not admit it, most of us believe there are situations in which it is right to make an exception to our rules. We might argue, for example, that a hungry child stealing a sandwich is not as guilty as a well-fed child who steals a doughnut.

These inconsistencies between right and wrong are difficult for troubled youth to understand and accept

---

The typical delinquent dislikes himself. He has a negative self-concept, especially in regard to his behavior, his moral self, and his family self.

His self-concept shows many of the maladjustments which suggest personality disorder. He suffers from inner tension and discomfort, and is very much at odds with himself, which often throws him into conflict with society. He is also too unstable and immature to withstand stress and frustration. Troubled and deviant, he finds it very hard to cope with life. Seeing himself as bad and worthless, he acts accordingly.

He has an uncertain picture of himself, and is easily influenced by external suggestions and by his environment. He tends to look outward for control and evaluation of his behavior.

He is not defensive and makes little effort to portray himself in a good light. Indeed, he often lacks those psychological defenses necessary for normal self-esteem.

The self-concepts of delinquents are much more negative, uncertain, variable, conflicted, and passive than those of nondelinquents.

Taken from *Delinquents Don't Like Themselves—That's Partly Why They're Delinquent*, printed with permission of Tennessee Institute of Technology.

because they have not been taught to think conceptually (issues must be "black and white"; they can't handle "grays") and they do not see models of consistent morality at home or elsewhere. Most of these young people, therefore, become cynical, reject belief in any general standard of right and wrong, and develop their own moral codes.

WHAT ABOUT SELF-CONCEPTS?

Most troubled youth exhibit very low self-esteem. They have failed at home and at school, with friends and with adults. Because they see themselves as failures, they practice self-defeating behavior and thus reinforce their feelings. Often these self-defeating acts throw them into a *defeat cycle* because their attitudes toward others reflect what they think about themselves. In other words, troubled adolescents will often try to get others to dislike them because they dislike themselves and are afraid to make things different.

In his noted theory of socialization, psychologist Erik Erikson stresses the importance of a positive sense of identity. He states that as the adolescent develops his or her own identity, the question that he or she must answer is, "Who am I?" Adolescents are trying to discover who they are and what they will become. "Am I a child or an adult?" "Will I be a husband and father?" "Will I be a success in life, or will I fail?" Ideally each will develop an identity which will provide future hope and self-confidence. Some adolescents, however, can't seem to "get hold of themselves" or "find themselves." They don't seem to know who they are, why they are, or what their place in life should be. Consequently, they are more likely to

move into delinquent behavior. Unfortunately, according to Erikson, an individual can only risk developing personal relationships and close friendships if he or she has sufficient "ego strength." Avoiding such relationships and experiences because of "self-fear" may result in excessive introspection, worry, isolation, and loneliness which will make the person more vulnerable to getting into trouble and being negatively influenced by peers.[5]

WHAT ABOUT DELINQUENT ACTS?

Why do troubled young people act the way they do? Why do they often steal, vandalize, fight, or try to hurt others? Usually, delinquent acts either express needs or provide unorthodox ways to solve problems. Needs may range from an uncontrollable desire (e.g., stealing a pack of gum) to an irresistible urge to act on a hostile impulse. The motive may be to gain status within the group, to take revenge, or to show off. It may also spring from the frustration of trying to cope. Similar delinquent acts may come from different motives; conversely, similar motives may evoke different acts. It is more important to find out *why* Johnny acted wrongly than to know *what* he did.

Many delinquent acts involve other people. Boys tend to act out their problems overtly by breaking windows, fighting, or wrecking a car, while girls' actions are usually less visible—sexual promiscuity, drinking, stealing. Sometimes punishment for such acts becomes an excuse for young people to take revenge.

Unfortunately for young people in trouble, there is very little in their actions which appeals to kindness or sympathy. It may often seem as if only your God-given love and concern stand between the young person and public spite and cries for punishment.

DEVELOPING YOUR OWN PICTURE

In ministering to troubled youth, the first challenge is to visualize the young person and develop a plan to reach him or her. Your visualization must encompass the factors discussed above and should answer these questions:

● What is the difference between "bad kids" and "good kids"?

● Why do young people get into trouble?

● To which problem areas do I need to give my primary attention?

● How do I concentrate on the *person* as well as the *problems*?

Here is a four-step process to help you summarize your understanding of a troubled young person.

1. Absence of healthy adult models—In this chapter we have discussed parents, families, and homes. Family is the primary influence in a young person's life, and without good adult models, serious problems can develop. To minister effectively to troubled youth, we must provide them with significant relationships and teach them what they have not learned at home about love, values, and morals.

2. Poor self-concept—Many factors contribute to a person's low self-esteem, and a person's behavior usually reflects his or her self-concept. Failure in school, at home, on dates, and with peers will lead to failure in church or in a new relationship with Christ. We must help the young person feel good about him/herself and experience success while we demonstrate that God cares and upholds the worth of all human beings.

3. Dysfunctional peer relationships—We have learned that often the influence of the group and other friends is negative or irresponsible. We must direct troubled young people toward positive friendships with Christian young people who are mature enough to put God first in their lives and who reach out in love to others.

● And whoever welcomes a little child like this in My name welcomes Me (Matthew 18:5).

● Unless the Lord builds the house, its builders labor in vain (Psalm 127:1).

● He said to them, "Let the little children come to Me, and do not hinder them, for the kingdom of God belongs to such as these. . . . And He took the children in His arms, put His hands on them, and blessed them (Mark 10:14,16).

● Fathers, do not exasperate your children; instead, bring them up in the training and instruction of the Lord (Ephesians 6:4).

● Train a child in the way he should go, and when he is old he will not turn from it (Proverbs 22:6).

● The rod of correction inparts wisdom, but a child left to itself disgraces his mother (Proverbs 29:15).

Christian youth groups could play a vital role here.

4. No personal relationship with God— We have not discussed the spiritual hopelessness of the troubled youth because we know that at the root of all of mankind's problems is separation from God. Sin is the root cause of delinquency. We will discuss this later; for now, it is important to note that most troubled youth do not understand that God the Father loves them, has established guidelines for living, and forgives them for their failures. Troubled young people need the help of caring Christian adults who can introduce them to Jesus Christ. This is the most effective way to begin to help a troubled young person change his or her behavior and change his or her life.

CASE STUDY

Work through the following case study and answer the questions on page 46 to practice the principles outlined in this chapter.

Name:	Ruth Johnson
Age:	15
Home Address:	Detroit, Michigan
Natural Father:	Charles Johnson
Natural Mother:	Catherine Johnson
Siblings:	Lisa, age 17
	Donald, age 14
	Robert, age 12
	Joan, age 10
	Kenneth, age 8

At 14 years of age, Ruth was admitted to training school under Section Nine of the Training Schools Act after appearing in court charged with automobile theft.

Previously, Ruth had been placed on probation for shoplifting, and she remained on probation until she went to training school. Her 14-year-old brother, Donald, is presently on probation for theft.

While on probation, Ruth was co-operative about reporting regularly, but she frequently became involved in fights with other girls at the reporting center.

Problems

For several years, Ruth's parents have felt that her most serious problem was wandering away from home. Mr. and Mrs. Johnson say that Ruth is easily led astray and that she would go off with anyone who asked her. At 13, she began staying away from home with a girlfriend, Gina, who was the same age and lived nearby. Often the girls were out very late at night, occasionally overnight.

This became quite frequent, and it was learned that the girls were engaging in a variety of sexual practices with a number of men. Ruth's parents believe that this happened because she was influenced by Gina who introduced her to such activity. Apparently Ruth's mother made several attempts to keep Ruth in the house, but she was able to slip out unnoticed.

While away from home, Ruth sometimes shoplifted. This her parents also blamed on the influence and occasional threats of other children. Ruth never seemed to enjoy satisfactory relationships with her peers. Frequent fights ended friendships just as they were beginning, and Ruth's only long-term friend has been Gina.

As a result of her court appearance for shoplifting, Ruth was placed on probation, and she had frequent psychiatric appointments as well. According to her parents, Ruth did well until just before she went to training school, when she began to steal, cut school, stay out late, and finally, steal the car.

Fate

If you had married and your boyfriend, my father
  came home to us each night to kiss you hello and
    me good night,
      maybe then you would have loved me.

If you had done the little things
  you always spoke of doing
    like going to parties and dancing your worries away
      instead of doing chores day by day
        maybe then you would have really loved me.

But we both missed out in much the same way,
  I had no father and you had no husband.
    You hated yourself for it and in turn you hated me.

I am that child you gave birth to fourteen years ago,
  who cried and no one came,
    who laughed and no one cared.

So I ask you as a troubled young girl who wants her mother
  to fill her past fourteen empty years with new love
    for the future,
to give her the affection you had not from a husband
  and she had not from a father:
to return the love she loaned you when you had none to give
  and to love in order to teach her to love, the living seed
    within her which was lustfully sown into the same long
      miserable life as she.

Author: A Young Probationer

Mrs. Johnson recalls that Ruth has always seemed different from the other children, but she is unable to describe the difference specifically. She says that Ruth is more sensitive and easily upset. For example, Mrs. Johnson was very concerned when Ruth first went to training school that she would think her mother was going to die while she was away. Mrs. Johnson was ill with rheumatic fever as a child, and Ruth believes that she has a heart condition. Mrs. Johnson indicates that this is not the case.

Family

Father: Charles Johnson is about 40, and he works as a laborer full time. He has a second job in the evenings driving a cab, so he spends very little time with the family. Mr. Johnson is a large man with a ruddy complexion and an ever-smiling face.

Born and raised in Nova Scotia, he was the only boy in a family of three children. Mr. Johnson came to the States as a teenager after his father died and his mother remarried. He finds it difficult to talk about his natural father, but he says that he always got along well with all of his family. One does not get the impression that there are very strong family ties.

Apparently Mr. Johnson drank very heavily in the early years of his marriage, but he gradually cut down as his family responsibilities grew. He talks readily of his former irresponsible actions and of how important his family is to him. He admits that he still drinks beer and gets drunk at home from time to time.

Mother: Catherine Johnson looks to be about 35. She does not work regularly outside of the home. She is a short, overweight woman with a pretty face.

Born in Ohio, the middle child of seven, she has one sister (younger) and five brothers, most of whom are living in the Toledo area. Her sister is divorced and lives common-law, and only two of her brothers are still with their wives. There seem to be fairly strong family ties. It is obvious that Mrs. Johnson is particularly close to her father. Her parents are very interested in the family and have been concerned for Ruth. They visited Ruth in training school most weekends with Mr. and Mrs. Johnson. When Ruth first got into trouble with the law, Mrs. Johnson's parents offered to take Ruth to live with them, but Mrs. Johnson would not allow it, feeling that it might be too much for them and also feeling that Ruth should be in her own home.

Siblings: Lisa, age 17, spends most of her spare time at home. In fact, her parents worry that she does not go out enough. Her steady boyfriend is well-liked by the family. At times, Lisa is quiet and seems unhappy; at other times, she is happy and expressive but acts quite immaturely.

Donald, age 14, works evenings selling candies door-to-door and has done quite well. He is said to be a difficult child and has been involved with the police many times, but his parents do not seem particularly concerned about him. They believe that he will straighten up in time.

Robert, age 12, is a quiet little boy who is not nearly as good-looking as the other children. He is not a behavior problem and, in fact, is his mother's willing helper with household chores.

Joan, age 10, is an appealing, outgoing child who looks like Ruth. Mrs. Johnson thinks that Joan is a bit too noisy and excitable, and there is no doubt that she is a difficult little girl to handle. She seems brighter than the other children.

Kenneth, age 8, is small for his age as are most of the Johnson children. Mrs. Johnson is concerned about Kenneth's attitudes lately; he is becoming more defiant of his parents' authority.

During last fall and winter there were several sources of stress on the family. Mr. Johnson was injured at work; and because of his absence from work and delays in receiving workmen's compensation, the family income dropped considerably just when they needed more money for the beginning of school. The two oldest children are in high school and must buy their books and supplies. For two weeks, the Johnsons had to receive welfare. During this time the family pulled together, and there were no major problems with the children. Donald was able to help by using the money he had saved from part-time jobs.

RELATIONSHIPS

The Johnson home is active and noisy. Mrs. Johnson has the responsibility for the children because her husband works long hours. When Mr. Johnson is home, discipline is not the problem it is when Mrs. Johnson is alone with the children. Mr. Johnson insists that his tone of voice makes the children obey. Also, he is less likely to give in to them.

Mrs. Johnson seems to find warm, physical contact with her children difficult, rarely reaching out to them though they constantly seek contact, especially the girls. Her "touching" is quick and rough (e.g., brushing the girls' hair).

The parents give the impression that they are "playing house." They seem to have genuine concern for their children, but they cannot face their serious problems. For example, before Ruth went to training school, there had been many indications of trouble, but Mrs. Johnson didn't report these until Ruth was caught stealing the car.

Mr. and Mrs. Johnson appear to get along well. They say they rarely argue and insist that the plan to have Mrs. Johnson almost totally in charge of the children is mutually agreeable. Donald, and at times, Ruth, try to play one parent against the other; often they succeed. Ruth describes her parents' marriage as very nearly perfect.

Mr. Johnson jokes continually. Apparently he enjoys teasing the girls, especially Lisa. There is a seductive quality about his actions which annoys Lisa and makes Mrs. Johnson uneasy. Also, although 14-year-old Donald was expected to work all summer, Lisa, 17, was not allowed to work until very recently because she "was not old enough." Mr. Johnson seems very protective of his daughters and is extremely demanding of his sons.

The children were expected to do many things for themselves from a very early age. At times, Mrs. Johnson seems overwhelmed with it all, but at other times, she seems to manage quite well.

In spite of the basic feeling of family cohesion, the children spend very little time together. They make friends easily and have their own friends. The parents try to plan family activities that are inexpensive and in which all are eager to participate.

When Ruth first returned home from training school, she spent most of her time with the family, either at home or visiting relatives. Mrs. Johnson was pleased to see a positive difference in the way Ruth and Lisa were getting along. She feels that Ruth has matured and is better able to cope with the daily frustrations of living in their busy home.

Lately, Mrs. Johnson has noticed that Ruth has been fighting more with her brothers and sisters. She is beginning to go out more often and has come in well past her curfew on several occasions. Recently, she was brought home by the police who had found her drinking beer in a parked car with a group of boys.

QUESTIONS

1. Which of the factors discussed in the previous chapter apply to the causes of Ruth's problems? Why?

2. Which family dynamics contribute to Ruth's problems?

3. What are Ruth's present problems, and what is causing each one?

4. How would you try to help Ruth? Which family members would you enlist to help?

5. How have Ruth's heredity and environment merged to cause her to be a troubled youth?

Notes

[1]Gilling, John L. *Social Pathology*. New York: Appleton-Century Co., Inc., 1933, p. 566.

[2]Clinard, Marshall B. *Sociology of Behavior*. New York: Holt, Rinehart, Winston, Inc., 1963, p. 199.

[3]Hirschi, Travis. *Causes of Delinquency*. Berkeley: University of California Press, 1969, p. 94.

[4]Stacey, William. *The Family Secret*. Boston: Beacon Press, 1983, Introduction.

[5]Erikson, Erik H. *Childhood and Society*, 2d ed. New York: Norton, 1963, pp. 247-274.

3. Communicating with Troubled Youth

The church bus groaned to a stop at the gate, and fifty assorted, excited kids poured out for a week of camp. Usually the last to exit, the driver stepped off the bus and called back to a lone figure sitting by the window near the back. She sat silently, staring straight ahead, her eyes fixed on a point in the distance.

"She's been this way since I picked her up at court. Not one word on the way," explained the driver to a camp counselor.

"Let me try," said Mrs. Perry. Slowly walking down the aisle, she placed her hand on the silent girl's shoulder and said quietly, "Come on, Sara."

Without a word, the girl got up and followed Mrs. Perry to her cabin.

For two days, Sara spoke to no one. And Mrs. Perry went about her business of being a camp counselor; she didn't even try to talk to her silent counselee. Sara was obviously different from the other girls in the cabin.

On the third day, Sara slowly pushed open Mrs. Perry's door. She stood there for a moment and then said, "Hi," in a friendly but tired voice.

"Oh, Sara. I knew if I waited long enough you would want to talk! We all have things that trouble us, things that gnaw at us inside and build like volcanoes until we can't bear them a minute longer, and we have to tell someone. When a girl wants to open up, there's no one to talk to like her counselor, and that's me, Sara. You're really home now, you know. We love you and know how much a girl really wants to go to camp. We have a church home for you too, just as long as you need one,

Darling. Don't forget that."

"I need an aspirin," responded Sara.

During dinner, Mrs. Perry decided that it was time for a heart-to-heart talk with Sara; so she sat next to her and began. "Sara, we are adults, and we know that the best way to help others become adults is to treat them like adults. Now, you are only 14, but we believe that you, like everyone else, just need the chance to discover who you really are. We want you to have that freedom, Sara; therefore, our rules are very few. All we ask is that you trust us, depend on us, and confide in us. Now then, that's enough about that. I'm sure we will get along just fine. Have some squash and pass it on."

"I hate squash!" Sara answered. She stood up and left the dining hall.

The next few days were filled with activities, but Sara tried to get out of most of them and dutifully went through the motions when she had to participate. She ate very little at mealtimes but munched on candy at night. When Mrs. Perry confronted her with her negative attitudes, Sara gave an insolent look and retorted, "So?"

One morning, a strange odor wafted from Sarah's room. When Mrs. Perry questioned Sara about it, she snapped, "Who wants to know? It's my room, isn't it?" Mrs. Perry didn't know what to say and remained silent. Sara smiled.

At breakfast the next day, things exploded. Sara had been awake until 3 A.M. and had refused to get up. Only with verbal threats and nagging could Mrs. Perry "pull" her out of bed and out of the cabin. Now Sara was sitting at the table, cross and irritable, mumbling about how her head ached and how much she hated camp. Suddenly Mrs. Perry shouted, "Look here, young lady, this has gone far enough! We pick you up at court and bring you to this beautiful camp. You eat our food and sleep in a bunk that another girl could have used. Yes, and we loved you too. Then you stay awake all night, won't eat dinner, stuff yourself with candy, smoke drugs, and won't get up in the morning. I tell you, this has got to stop, and it's going to stop right now!" The volume rose, and her face grew red, but she went on, "This is a good Christian camp.

"We have always tried hard with the girls here, and none of them has ever behaved like you. You will not be the first one to spoil the camp for everyone else. If you think that you can come here and behave like this, you are wrong! Now get up and clear the table. Then get ready for chapel and quit whining. If you'd go to bed at a decent time, you wouldn't have a headache."

Sara went to chapel. When chapel ended, she walked straight to her cabin and was quiet and polite with everyone. That afternoon, while the others were swimming, Sara ran away. She did not leave a note.

Beginning to reach out to troubled youth is never easy. How would you try to get through to Sara? There are many skills which will help you effectively communicate with any troubled young person. In this chapter, we will focus on the most important of these skills.

Effective communication is built on trusting relationships. "Communication" is a broad topic and includes learning how to craft words, how to develop verbal techniques, how to listen, how to read nonverbal messages, and other important abilities. If all we do is learn how to use words, however, we will miss the mark. Remember the lesson of 1 Corinthians 13:1, "If I speak with the tongues of men and of angels, but have not love, I am only a resounding gong or a clanging cymbal." Our flood of carefully crafted and chosen words, delivered with great technique and skill, will only be so much noise. As was emphasized in chapter one, our communication foundation *must* be trusting relationships.

Dr. Ernest Shelley, formerly with the Michigan Department of Corrections, has stated, "Our biggest job is to convince the probationer he is not a different breed of cat. We must show him he is like others in that his needs for recognition, accomplishment, pride, and love are basically the same as everyone else's." Dr. Shelley then cites the example of a prisoner who was considered to be incurably disturbed. Every psychiatrist agreed. One night, a guard began to talk with this prisoner. The guard did not have a high school education and presumably was not educated enough

to know that the prisoner couldn't be helped. After several months of having the guard just listen to him and be his friend, the prisoner was determined to be rehabilitated. Soon he was released from prison. Without a friend, this man would still be incarcerated.[1]

Dr. Shelley's illustration underscores a truth which is confirmed in our own experience. Whether a bank executive, single mother, college-bound high school senior, or street person, each one of us needs others. We need their presence, acceptance, and support. How we relate to others, therefore, is very important, and it can change lives!

UNDERSTANDING YOURSELF

Before we can build trusting relationships and effectively communicate with troubled youth, we must have a good understanding of ourselves—our Christian maturity and commitment, abilities and gifts, values, and motives. In short, we must recognize our limitations and strengths and actively rely on the Holy Spirit.

Imagine your phone ringing at one in the morning. You are hardly in the mood to talk to anyone, but Cathy's on the line, and she is confused and afraid. Her parents have kicked her out of the house, and she needs your help.

Imagine the youth group meeting where Jim says he wants to talk. After a few stumbling sentences, he confesses a serious drinking problem. He wants to know what you think he should do to stop and how he can salve his guilt.

Imagine your regular monthly trip to Juvenile Hall for Bible study. You have talked with tough kids before, but this time you meet Jason, who has just been indicted for murder. His mother and stepfather don't seem to care; he needs a real friend, but he acts cool and aloof toward you.

Imagine this is your Sunday School class: Usually a relaxed group of high schoolers, on this Sunday, tension fills the room. Cindy, Terry, Debi, and Lynn are angry with Teresa who gets on their nerves. They are tired of her pushiness and insensitivity and have decided to isolate her from the group. Their actions are tearing the class apart, and you wonder whether to confront the problem head on or to let it work itself out. Teresa is your next-door neighbor, and you know about her problems at home.

These are typical situations in any ministry with troubled youth. Each of these young people needs a relationship with a person who has his or her life together and can lovingly and carefully share some answers. Let's take a closer look at the real you.

What are your prejudices?

At age nine, when asked what he would be when he grew up, Henry David Thoreau responded, "I'll be myself." And he was—the most independent mind of his time. Too often, however, adults are unable to be "themselves." Instead, they are preoccupied with their pasts, jobs, social positions, and roles (parents, voters, homeowners, etc.). It is easy to become locked into our prejudices, opinions, and concerns and never break out of our little worlds and reach out to others.

Take a "self-inventory" and list your presuppositions about life and about others. What possible barriers could keep you from "being yourself" with a troubled young person? . . . race? . . . nationality? . . . certain sins? . . . part of town? . . . some other disapproved or disliked characteristic? Or perhaps an incident in your past colors the way you look at life in general (e.g., domineering father; racial incident in school; family's work ethic; lack of physical affection at home; and so on). After identifying your particular prejudices, ask God to help you break free of them and accept those who don't fit your idea of "acceptability."

What are your needs?

Another important area for introspection is "needs." In other words, what hidden "personality baggage" do you carry into relationships? Many adults, for example, work with young people because they enjoy the praise of others or they like having kids depend on them. Others may be driven by feelings of inferiority as they "minister" to those with whom they can feel superior. And there are those who are trying to prove that they can succeed where others have failed. (These are the "reformers.") Before you begin to work with troubled youth, ask, "Whose needs are being met?" We dare not use young people to make ourselves feel or look good or to support our sagging egos.

What are your motives?

This question flows from the previous one because of the possibility that a desire to help others may mask a deeper desire to meet one's personal needs. Having settled that issue, however, it is still necessary to think through your reasons for choosing this type of ministry. What do you hope to accomplish . . . and why? Your answers will reflect the depth of your desire and your theology.

Troubled youth usually will not be "likeable," especially at your first meeting. But your ministry with them should be based on "love," a commitment to reach out to them with the love of Christ, no matter what they look like or how they respond. This "love" lasts and can endure setbacks, disappointments, and personal rejection.

The Bible has much to say about the necessity for helping those in need and the urgency for telling people about Christ. If you truly believe the Bible, you will be motivated by a deep concern for these unique, invaluable creations of God, persons for whom Christ died and who need to know Him personally.

Take a closer look at your motives.

What is your "Christian maturity level"?

No Christian has "arrived" this side of heaven. Each of us has plenty of growing and maturing to do. But there is a vast difference between an immature, baby Christian and one who is learning and stretching his or her faith. Those who expect to share the Good News with others must be applying it to their own lives. Troubled youth will push you to the foundation of your faith and will continually test the strength of your commitment.

In addition, the troubled young person will trust and grow with the help of the mature person who demonstrates a lifestyle guided by biblical truth, who is growing in his or her identity because of Christ, and who has the wisdom to both listen and speak the truth in love. On the other hand, immaturity and untrustworthiness will signal danger to the person seeking answers.

Here are the characteristics of the

> ## Christ is looking for men and women with character, not perfection, to minister to troubled youth.
>
> 1. *Knowledge of the Word (2 Timothy 2:2 and 2:15)*. The leader provides personal direction from the Bible.
>
> 2. *Courage as a decision maker (Luke 22:42)*. The leader makes the right decisions, no matter how unpopular.
>
> 3. *Availability to people (Luke 19:1-10)*. The leader gets involved with youth.
>
> 4. *Priorities in order (Luke 9:57-62)*. The leader knows and does what is important.
>
> 5. *Kindness and humility, nonjudgmental attitude (Mark 10:42-45)*. The leader of young people is someone who is real, who feels free to be himself or herself.
>
> 6. *Compassion for people (John 15:12-13)*. The leader really cares.
>
> 7. *Truthful in dealing with people (John 21:15-19)*. The leader is honest and consistent.
>
> 8. *Faithful (John 13:2-14)*. The leader has stick-to-ittiveness.

maturing Christian—the basic spiritual qualifications needed by an adult seeking to communicate with troubled youth.

1. *Be quick to listen and slow to speak (James 1:19)*. Effective communication begins with careful listening. If you listen to what a person says with an open mind and without presuming what he or she is going to say, you will discover real needs and hurts—the starting point for your input.

2. *Depend on the Holy Spirit for guid-*

ance (John 14:26). Jesus promised His disciples that the Holy Spirit would teach them all things. It is not enough to collect data. You must understand and interpret what you have seen and heard in the young person's life; therefore, you must depend on God for insight and guidance to be able to speak with wisdom (1 Corinthians 2:11-16). But remember that the Holy Spirit works through you, using your skills, gifts, and mind. Depending on Him, then, is not an excuse for lack of study and preparation.

3. *Show wisdom by your good behavior (James 3:13-18).* The source of our wisdom is God, and His wisdom is marked by

● *purity (v. 17)*—This is in direct contrast with wisdom that flows from selfish ambition (v. 14). It reflects God's nature and values with the clear ring of divine authority. Your counsel should reflect God's values and behavioral standards.

● *peace (vv. 17-18)*—Christ brings peace, and He imparts a peaceful spirit. Your insight should lead to healing, not conflict, and young people should sense in you a relaxed, peaceful attitude.

● *gentleness, with consideration, submission, and mercy (v. 17)*—You have been a recipient of God's loving forgiveness, and you should be able to exhibit these qualities toward others. "Gentleness" does not dominate, force a person to change, or confront someone with his or her "wrongs." Paul carefully instructed Timothy that, "the Lord's servant must not quarrel; instead, he must be kind to everyone, able to teach, not resentful" (2 Timothy 2:24). Confrontation is often necessary, but it must never be done harshly.

● *impartiality (v. 17)*—Someone has said that "to know all is to forgive all," and this is nowhere more true than with troubled youth. When you understand the environment and background of a person, you can better understand what is behind his "outrageous" statements and reasoning. His or her mind may be cluttered with a multitude of fears, feelings, tears, anger, anxieties, and expletives. When you reflect God's wisdom, you will filter through the bluster and "baggage" and hear the real problem.

● *sincerity (v. 17)*—This means having genuine concern and being without hypocrisy. You must enter the relationship with an understanding of your own weaknesses and problems but without the need to dump all of them on the young person. It also means that you should serve others regardless of their level of desirability. Every person you contact, youth or adult, deserves your attention and service without any hint of partiality.

As a Christian, you can be a vital link in helping a troubled young person change, but this process begins with a life well-lived and not just well-taught. Young people must be able to see Christian maturity in you. Technique is important (and will be discussed later), but your lifestyle is crucial. Young people need living, flesh-and-blood examples of the truth. You can be an example, a person who consistently reflects Christ.

What are your values?

Any person committed to being a change agent in the lives of troubled youth will quickly become aware of a great gulf between his or her values and those of the young people with whom he or she works. Perhaps the greatest values clash occurs between middle-class, Christian adults and lower-class, minority youth. Often the evangelical youth worker believes that his or her middle-class value system is part of the "truth" which he or she is attempting to impart. Before we go further, therefore, two principles must be underlined: (1) Middle-class values are not synonymous with biblical Christianity; (2) the "provider/consumer" dichotomy which elevates the "missionary" above the "heathen" is inconsistent with the servant role of Christians and will evoke resentment and opposition. With these "givens," here are some of the cultural myths which can be unconsciously woven into our values.

● *The "Horatio Alger" Myth*—Anyone can follow the footsteps of Abraham Lincoln; our system provides equality and equal opportunity for all.

● *The "Justice Is Blind" Myth*—Our legal system administers justice fairly and equally to everyone.

● *The "Crime Never Pays" Myth*—Sooner or later, all offenders will be caught and get what they deserve.

● *The "Key to Success" Myth*—The only way to achieve and move up in the world is through hard work, perseverance, and sweat.

● *The "Face-Value Idealism" Myth*—Persons or groups with the ideals of service and commitment (e.g., Hippocratic oath, academic freedom, "liberty, equality, and fraternity") will act consistently with those ideals.

These concepts are called myths because they are not true. Instead, they are like folk wisdom, legends handed from generation to generation. The problem comes when we believe them and act as though they really are true. Let's consider one, the "Key to Success" myth.

A commonly held middle-class value is *ambition*. This is the success-oriented belief that if people work hard, they will get ahead in life and be somebody. But to lower-class adolescents (especially older ones), ambition is an unproductive fantasy. They have seen parents and others begin with high ideals and enormous effort only to be denied the opportunity to succeed and become trapped in the status quo. Thus, many decide to live by manipulating the system, since there is much evidence to indicate that they will get more that way than by hard work.

Middle-class young people are given increased responsibility to prepare them to "make it on their own." Many lower-class youth, however, place much less importance on individual effort. Instead, his family or "his kind" will stand behind him, the government will supply his needs, and his gang will defend him. He is much more group-dependent and believes that by himself, he has very little potential for survival.

Most people in the middle class believe that there is virtue in developing one's personal potential. If a person has musical ability, for example, she owes it to herself to develop this gift. In contrast, lower-class adolescents learn that there is no point developing skills unless they are marketable immediately. They know that there is very little potential for making a living by developing anything other than practical abilities and that very few of them will get the "big break" necessary to make it on the basis of talent.

"Gratification postponement" is the idea that people should save or invest *today* for greater benefits *tomorrow*. This is a philosophy held by most college-bound, middle-class youth. Lower-class young people develop a much more *now*-oriented outlook on life. Because their needs are tied more closely to survival, they live with an ethic which says, "Spend it while you have it, for tomorrow will not be any better than today."

Middle-class adolescents learn to control their aggression, releasing it by playing sports like hockey and football (or vicariously by watching) or through sophisticated verbal assaults. In contrast, lower-class youth express their hostility immediately and physically. Street gang fights and X-rated epithets are common.

Despite the popularity of criticizing police and other authority figures, middle-class young people learn that law and order work for their benefit, protecting life and property. But lower-class youth hold little of the traditional respect for law and order. They have seen police protect the property of the rich landlords while ignoring the poor people living on and in those properties. Soon they believe that the police are more interested in their own success than in serving people. Most inner-city, minority youth believe that the police will use them to promote themselves or to improve their image.

Value systems are adaptive. That is, a value is held because it is thought to work. Middle-class values of budgeting time and resources, for example, work well for those who have sufficient time and money to budget, but not for those who have insufficient resources to meet their daily needs.

Unfortunately, these cultural myths affect the way we look at life in general and how we evaluate others. We must dispel them with a strong dose of reality and a close look at the Bible. Our values are part and parcel of us. We live by them and, to a large extent, we expect others to live up to them as well. It is easy to impose our values on others, whether or not the values are needed or valid. After identifying *your* values, think through those of the young people with whom you are or will be working, and don't allow your values to become a barrier in your relationships with them. Then, if a change is needed, be sure that you have something much better to offer as a replacement for what these youth know and believe. Of course, it is vital that all of us, youth and youth workers alike, discover and live according to a value system that is truly biblical.

UNDERSTANDING RELATIONSHIPS

You can develop a good relationship with a troubled young person by understanding basic interpersonal principles and then by practicing, practicing, practicing! None of us is born with great communication skills; instead, we learn how to relate "on the job." This is why who we *are* is much more important than what we *say*.

Of course, an intellectual understanding of relationships will not automatically provide you with the skills necessary to communicate love and acceptance. These skills can only be developed through repeated interaction with real people, but knowing solid communication and relationship-building principles will provide the foundation. These principles are explored through the following questions.

What is the purpose of relationships?

Relationships are vital for effective communication. This is especially true with troubled youth whose lives are crammed full of failure, terrible role models, neglect, abuse, and a base understanding of love. You can discuss and write and preach about values, God, life's meaning, and love, but your words will be unheard and unheeded. Your life, however, can speak volumes. When young people see you respond under pressure, they learn about your values; when they see you react to tragedy and hardship, they learn about your relationship with God; when they see you unselfishly serving others, they learn about love; and when they know you as a friend, they listen to what you have to say.

Relationships are a critical part of the overall "helping" process. They are the vehicles through which we can help young people solve problems and mature as whole people. The Apostle Paul's goal was to continue "admonishing and teaching everyone with all wisdom, so that we may present everyone perfect in Christ" (Colossians 1:28). This means that we should see the bigger picture, viewing each young person in terms of his or her total growth and discipleship, considering every dimension of his or her life.

Because each person is unique with his or her own set of potentials, problems, and pressures, our relationships will serve different purposes, depending on the individual. In communicating with a young person on probation, for example, you may be trying to motivate him to stay in school or to support him emotionally during a very difficult time. With a pregnant teenager, your relationship will serve as the springboard for answering questions about being an unmarried mother, abortion and adoption, and where to get financial aid. With a person who doesn't fit in at church, your friendship can be the bridge to her involvement in a Sunday School class or the youth group.

It is important to understand that relationships are not ends in themselves; they are bridges and vehicles for effective communication. Because all youth are not alike, your relationships will address a variety of needs, but lives will be changed for the better. Relationships result in changed lives.

How do you begin to build relationships?

Building relationships starts with accepting troubled youth as they are with all of their problems and difficulties. That is, instead of approaching the person with ideas of how you want to remake or reform him or her, you must come as viewer and receiver, ready to participate with the young person in his or her world. God accepts them, and so must you. God created this person; He loves him and sent Jesus to die for him. He has value and worth to God.

This is an exciting way to relate to people. If you view each young person as a *discovery*, you won't force him or her to conform to your idea

Ten Commandments for Working with Troubled Youth

THOU SHALT not allow sin to build up in thy life.
THOU SHALT have a sense of humor.
THOU SHALT be able to flex.
THOU SHALT do anything thou tellest thy youth to do.
THOU SHALT be committed and consistent.
THOU SHALT keep in touch with those who understand thy youth's problems.
THOU SHALT give thy youth responsibility.
THOU SHALT help thy youth grow as whole people.
THOU SHALT consult the parents of thy young people on a regular basis.
THOU SHALT pray for thy young people because of thy love for them.

of the typical *or* ideal adolescent. You won't feel the need to analyze and answer; instead, you can accept, learn, and grow together. Remember, God accepted us "while we were still sinners" (Romans 5:8). He didn't place any behavioral criteria on us. He accepted us and sent Christ to die for us *in our sin.*

Of course, this may be easier said than done. Several years ago, Bill was struggling to "stick it out" with one young man. After six months of trying everything imaginable to demonstrate his acceptance and love, Bill found the boy still refusing any help whatsoever. Bill felt frustrated and rejected, and he poured out his story and feelings to his pastor. He had invested six months of time and emotional energy and had sacrificed much to reach one needy boy named John—with no results. He felt like giving up.

After listening for a few minutes, the pastor quietly asked, "Why did you go to the dentist last week?"

"An abscessed tooth," replied Bill.

"What were you thinking about as the dentist treated you?" said the pastor.

"Me . . . my tooth. Why?" asked Bill.

"Exactly," the pastor replied. "Bill, you are just like John. Right now, John is thinking about himself. He is hurting, and this is how he reacts. Just like when you're hurting, you think about 'Bill.' "

Bill got the point and agreed to continue working with John and, eventually, John began to understand Bill's care and concern. It wasn't easy to accept John for who he was, but it made all the difference. The turning point in the relationship was Bill's realization that John was engulfed by his own needs and not able to return Bill's love.

Bill also learned a basic concept in building helpful relationships, a concept called "empathy." Defined as "feeling *with* someone else," empathy is an attitude of putting yourself in the shoes of the other person, feeling his or her hurts. It means asking yourself, "How would I feel if I were in his situation?" When you empathize with young people, you see life from their points of view, and you can begin to accept them . . . as they are.

What's next in building relationships?

As you accept young people and empathize with them, you will see their real needs and be able to help them. In *Life-Style Evangelism,* Dr. Joseph Aldrich makes the point that the Gospel becomes "Good News" only as it speaks to another person's needs.[2] It is only when the message of Christ touches a troubled youth's needs that he or she will recognize its importance and validity.

What a great way to demonstrate God's love—empathizing with the needs of a hurting young person and then reaching out to help. Dr. Anthony Campolo in *The Power Delusion* highlights the tremendous effects that our selfless service can have.

> Many of us think we must love people first and then, because we love them, do good things for them. In reality, the opposite is true. The more good we do for people, the more we love them. The Bible says, "Where your treasure is, there your heart will be also" (Matthew 6:21). This means that what a person invests in, he loves. If a person invests in a relationship, makes sacrifices for it, provides every consideration for the other person who is part of the relationship, he is creating love.[3]

The Bible tells us to invest in others and to meet their needs (read again Matthew 25:31-46), and it shows us how to relate. Jesus provides the best example, but He did not employ just one style. With the Pharisees, He was direct and confrontive. With the adulterous woman in John 8, He was indirect and nonconfrontational. Jesus' relational style depended on the needs of those to whom He was ministering.

We accept, we empathize, and we meet real needs with a style tailormade for the individual. These are the relationship building blocks.

What about feelings and attitudes?

Any relationship involves the interaction of feelings and attitudes. We can assume that at first the young person being helped will feel somewhat uncomfortable. This feeling inevitably accompanies social needs or problems. Sometimes it is easily recognized. A girl shouts, "Damn you, get out of here! Leave me alone!" Or two boys slug it out. Fights, vandalism, and refusing to accept discipline are ways of acting out the emotions. At other times, however, troubled young people will refuse to express any emotion and appear to be "hard," hardened to love and hardened to communication.

Emotional expressions, social struggles and their effects, problem coping abilities, emotional maturity levels, and personality strengths and weaknesses differ widely with individuals. But within these differences there emerges a pattern of feelings and attitudes common to all troubled youth, springing from basic human needs.

Here is how the pattern progresses.

1. The young person has a conscious or subconscious *need*.

2. This need creates a *feeling* in the young person.

3. The feeling is *expressed* toward you because you are there and have developed a relationship with him.

According to Dr. Gary Chapman, the most effective way to communicate your love for someone is to do it in their "love language." Love languages are the "primary method that a person uses to express love for another person." They are also "the way that person most prefers to receive love." In becoming the best helper that you can, answer these questions. Consider *first*, what is *your* primary love language? *Second*, what are the primary love languages of your group members? The five love languages are:

1. *talk*—Saying, "I love you," "You look nice," "Nice job," "I'm proud of you," etc.

2. *time*—Spending a few minutes of quality time together over coffee or Coke, just walking together, being in an uninterrupted environment.

3. *actions*—Doing things for people: washing the car, doing dishes, building, cleaning.

4. *gifts*—Giving gifts: anything that takes some thought and a little effort, and is from the heart.

5. *physical touch*—Touching: patting, hugging, etc. "Personal space" is small if not nonexistent.

Taken from Dr. Gary Chapman's book, *Building Relationships*, Winston, N.C.: Marriage and Family Life Consultants, 1983.

4. Because of your relationship with the young person, he must begin to *reveal* his problem and "weakness."

5. The young person is *afraid* of how you will respond.

6. These needs, feelings, and fears may be expressed through his *actions*.

The troubled young person may never verbalize his or her deepest needs, but they will emerge through emotions, attitudes, or actions. For example, if a girl has a strong need to express herself, she may talk for an hour about all sorts of things without allowing you to squeeze in a word. If a boy wants to be recognized as an individual, he may dress and act to attract attention. If a person wants to feel "worthy" of your love, he may go to great lengths to be available to you. As you build relationships and learn to communicate, you will learn to recognize these symptoms and respond appropriately. This won't happen immediately; it takes time, and no one is able to understand everything about another person's needs, emotions, and motives. But God does! He cares more about these young people than we ever will, and He will help us put the pieces together.

LEARNING INTERPERSONAL SKILLS

How should you respond to the basic needs of troubled youth?

As has been stated above, each troubled young person is an individual with unique and special problems, personality, and emotional design; therefore, each one requires a different response from the helping person. And no single need stands alone; it is an integral part of the whole person with whom you seek to relate. Felix Biestek in *The Casework Relationship* has identified seven areas of need which interrelate in the lives of troubled youth. As we understand these areas, we will see how loving relationships can help meet their real needs.

Need Area #1. To be treated as individuals. This means recognizing each person as a unique creation of God with special, God-given qualities. He or she is different from everyone else, with his or her own likes and dislikes, problem-solving procedures, and social style. You must be careful to accept and empathize with the individual and help him or her make decisions from his or her special point of view.

Need Area #2. To be recognized as persons of worth. Everyone needs to be seen as someone special—a person of value, regardless of abilities, appearance, associations, or accomplishments. Accepting a person does not mean approving all that he or she does; his or her way of life may differ radically from anything you have ever known. It does mean loving him or her no matter what, with no strings attached.

Need Area #3. To not be judged. This means not drawing conclusions about a person without all the facts, simply on the basis of how he or she dresses, looks, or acts. You must go beyond the outward appearance and relate to the real person inside. Try to understand his or her behavior and background, but don't judge because of the surface data.

Need Area #4. To make their own choices and decisions. Every person has the right to determine his or her own life path. This applies to you and to troubled youth. The best course of action will not always be chosen but, unless absolutely necessary (to avoid tragic consequences), you should not interfere. This does not mean that you should have no involvement. Your counsel and advice are very important. But they should come in the form of constructive alternatives and helpful questioning to allow the young person to decide for him/herself.

Need Area #5. To have secrets kept for them. No one wants to be a "window," with all his deepest desires and struggles exposed for everyone to see. We need to keep some things to ourselves, revealing them only to those whom we trust. At the very beginning of a relationship with a troubled youth, you must decide with him or her what is personal and what is general information. After this has been determined, stand by your decision or trust will be shattered. Of course an immediate response is, "What about serious problems like abortion, suicide, or violent crime? Can't we then break a confidence?" Here is a general rule: The only confidence that you should break without a child's permission is one that will result in physical harm to someone. At most other times, breaking the confidence will hurt the relationship.

Need Area #6. To receive "controlled emotional responses" to problems. Sometimes a relationship becomes so strong that the helping person becomes too involved with the troubled young person and his or her problems. When this happens, objectivity is lost, and very little real help can be offered. You must be sensitive to the young person's feelings and empathize with him or her, but not be so involved that you take over his or her role in problem-solving. Never allow the relationship to become one of dependency rather than support or become so immersed in the young person's life that you neglect your own responsibilities.

Need Area #7. To express their feelings. Everyone needs a person with whom they can express deep, real feelings. This is especially true with troubled youth. For many, you will have little doubt about how they feel, but sometimes you may want to actively encourage and stimulate them to tell you what is going on inside. In either case, listen carefully without discouraging or condemning the expression of their emotions.[4]

How you remember these areas of need and respond will greatly determine how well you communicate with troubled youth. Solid, positive relationships form the foundation for effective communication, and these are built through spending time with young people, accepting and empathizing with them, understanding and responding to their real needs, and listening carefully.

How should you listen to troubled youth?

To respond correctly to the seven basic needs discussed above, you must know how to listen. Good listening provides valuable information about a person, giving us clues and cues for verbal input, and communicating care and concern.

Good listening is active; it requires you to think through what a person is saying, look for facts and feelings, and try to empathize with his or her situation. Listening does not mean hearing hours of mundane comments or an uninterrupted string of words. It is simply a way of approaching the problems which arise in the daily events of a person's life. In *How to Help a Friend,* Paul Welter states, "A response no longer than 12 seconds is usually an effective length in counseling or helping situations. In 12 seconds one can say two sentences or a total of 23 words. A consistent response of over 20 to 30 seconds pre-

Communication

To effectively communicate, we must find ways to get an individual to listen to what we are saying, to understand what we mean, and to act appropriately after receiving the message. When the communicants come from different segments of our society, as is often the case with the troubled youth, we can anticipate communication problems.

Two mistakes are often made. One is to attempt to speak a language with which we are unfamiliar. The other is to speak "over the head" of the young person. Both of these deserve some discussion.

It has been said that if youre going to help people, you have to get down on their level and talk their language. But one does not easily go to another level and speak another language without being considered phony. To attempt to use a subcultural language when you are not familiar with it is to invite disaster.

It is important that our language be simple and clear. There is a common language that can be understood by everyone in our society. To attempt to converse in a subcultural language suggests that the young person cannot communicate outside of his "jargon."

If we were to tell someone, for example, that we thought he had done a good job, we could say to him, "You performed that task in an exemplary manner," or "You're where it's at." Or we could say simply, "You did a good job." The third would be understood by everyone and would be preferable.

sents a major problem. What we communicate is 'I want to talk to you rather than with you.' "[5]

Certainly Job felt the need to have someone listen to him when he cried out to God, "I loathe my very life; therefore I will give free rein to my complaint and speak out in the bitterness of my soul" (Job 10:1). Instead of listening, however, his friends talked too much. Three chapters later we read: "If only you would be altogether silent! For you, that would be wisdom" (Job 13:5).

To be effective, active listening must be firmly grounded in your attitudes. You cannot pretend to listen. And at times, it will seem as though the young person is saying, "I know you think you understand what I said, but I'm not sure you realize that what you heard is not what I meant."

It takes work to really hear what a person is saying. Here are some barriers to effective listening:

● *Lack of time*—Our schedules are packed with obligations and appointments, and often we are thinking about what we have to do instead of concentrating on the person in front of us. If you don't have time to listen to someone at a particular moment, set up another time when you can deal with him in depth.

● *Preoccupation with own needs*—Pressures from job, home, school, or personal emotional problems can block us from hearing others. If this is the case, or if you are struggling to solve the same problem, commit your needs to Christ right then and table them until you can deal with them later. Make a conscious decision to work on the young person's needs first.

● *Emotional immaturity*—Sometimes our fears and insecurities can come between us and those whom we are trying to help. If this happens, identify it as such and remember that you can help even if you don't have all the answers. A problem in one area of your life does not disqualify you from being a helping person.

● *Language*—Subculture cliches or jargon can be difficult to understand. If you don't understand a troubled young person's words, ask him or her to clarify: "I'm not sure I understand what you said. Will you explain what you mean?" or "Let me see if I can summarize what I hear you saying." Sometimes, of course, the choice of words may shock you—profanity, vulgarisms, or threats. When this happens, try to accept what is said without negative reactions, listening to what is meant, not just to the words.

● *Disinterest*—Much of what people tell us will not be interesting per se; that is, it may not relate to our interests. But if we really care about people, we will be interested in what concerns them. If you find your mind wandering, take a close look at the person and focus your thoughts on your love for him or her.

● *Disturbing content*—Often people share problems or struggles which hit us in areas of our weakness—present conflict or past failure. If this happens, honestly share the details of your own failure and how you are working toward a solution. Together, then, you can tackle the problem.

What do you achieve by listening?

You may be thinking that listening is too passive and that in order to be helpful, you should be directive, telling the troubled young person what to do. Clinical experience and research evidence, however, clearly show that sensitive listening is an excellent method for affecting personal-

ity change and family or group development. Effective listening can help bring adjustments in values, attitudes, and outlook on life. People who have been carefully listened to become more emotionally mature, more open in revealing their true feelings (without defensiveness), more democratic, and less authoritarian.

When we listen sensitively to young people, they tend to hear themselves better and to have a stronger grasp of their feelings and thoughts. When they have shared their ideas openly with a person who does not criticize or judge, they are better able to evaluate and are more likely to feel that they can make worthwhile contributions.

All of us have self-concepts through which we evaluate our experiences. Those experiences which fit our mental self-portraits we readily accept, but we struggle with those which do not fit. Sometimes, of course, the experiences are too painful, and so we deny them outright. *Listening* does not threaten the troubled young person's self-picture because he or she does not have to defend it. An accepting atmosphere gives a young person permission to express his or her self-concept, explore it, and compare it to reality. Then he or she is in a position to change. An interpersonal climate of equality, freedom, understanding, acceptance, and warmth allows the young person to feel safe enough to incorporate new experiences and values into his or her self-concept.

How do you communicate caring?

One of our communication goals is to let the young person know that we really care about him or her. This is a vital link in the whole communication process and an important piece of the content which we are attempting to communicate. At times, it will seem as though a particular young person is oblivious to our genuine love—our actions and words bounce off, unable to penetrate his hard exterior. For those who have been hurt and hardened by past experiences and present realities, accepting love is very difficult. It will take time to get

CYCLE OF REJECTION

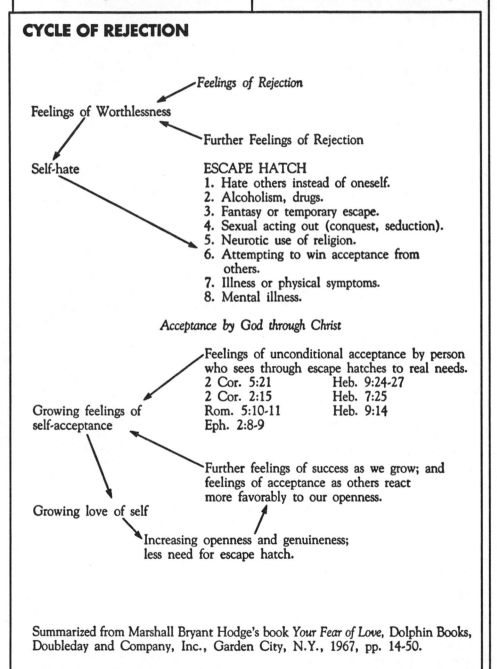

Feelings of Rejection

Feelings of Worthlessness

Further Feelings of Rejection

Self-hate

ESCAPE HATCH
1. Hate others instead of oneself.
2. Alcoholism, drugs.
3. Fantasy or temporary escape.
4. Sexual acting out (conquest, seduction).
5. Neurotic use of religion.
6. Attempting to win acceptance from others.
7. Illness or physical symptoms.
8. Mental illness.

Acceptance by God through Christ

Feelings of unconditional acceptance by person who sees through escape hatches to real needs.

2 Cor. 5:21	Heb. 9:24-27
2 Cor. 2:15	Heb. 7:25
Rom. 5:10-11	Heb. 9:14
Eph. 2:8-9	

Growing feelings of self-acceptance

Further feelings of success as we grow; and feelings of acceptance as others react more favorably to our openness.

Growing love of self

Increasing openness and genuineness; less need for escape hatch.

Summarized from Marshall Bryant Hodge's book *Your Fear of Love*, Dolphin Books, Doubleday and Company, Inc., Garden City, N.Y., 1967, pp. 14-50.

through. Here are four principles to remember, however, when discussion opportunities arise.

1. Listen to everything that is being said. Every message has two components: the content and the feelings underlying the content. Both give the message its meaning, and it is this total meaning which we must attempt to understand.

A young person may come to you and say, "I've finished raking the leaves." His meaning is fairly obvious: he has completed the job and is probably looking for your approval. He may also be asking for your help in finding out what to do next. Suppose, however, he had said, "Well, I'm finally finished with that damned job of raking leaves!" The surface content is the same as before, but the total meaning of his message has changed in an important way for both of you. Here is where sensitive listening can facilitate the relationship. Suppose you simply responded by giving him another job to do. Would he feel that you had really heard him? Would he feel free to talk to you again? Would he feel better about raking leaves, anxious to do a better job next time? Of course not. If, on the other hand, you responded with, "Glad to get it over with, huh!" or "Had a pretty rough time with it?" or "Guess you don't feel like doing anything like that for a while!" or another empathetic statement, the young man would know that you heard what he meant and would be more open to additional conversation.

Extra sensitivity on your part can transform an average relationship into a good one, and this type of communication demonstrates your care and respect.

2. Respond to feelings. Often the verbal content is much less important than the underlying feelings. To catch the full flavor of the message, you must respond to the emotional component. If, for example, the young man says, "I'd like to break this rake and make toothpicks out of it," responding to the verbal statement would be absurd. Instead, you should speak to his disgust, anger, and/or frustration at trying to rake leaves. This would recognize the true meaning of his message. Get into the habit of asking yourself, "What is he really trying to say? What does this mean to him/her? How does he/she see this situation?"

When you respond to feelings, you tell the young person, "I am interested in you as a person, and I think that what you feel is important. I respect your thoughts, and even if I don't agree with them, I know that they are valid for you. I feel sure that you have a contribution to make. I'm not trying to evaluate or change you; I just want to understand you. I think you are worth listening to, and I want you to know that I am the kind of person with whom you can talk."

By listening for and responding to feelings, you show the young person that you care about who he or she really is on the inside.

3. Look for nonverbal clues. Not all communication is verbal. A person's words alone don't tell us everything about his or her message. It is important, therefore, to look for the nonverbal statements.

The way a person hesitates in his or her speech can tell you much about feelings. So too can voice inflection, stressing certain points loudly and clearly while mumbling others. The young person's facial expressions, posture, hand movements, eye movements, and breathing should also be noted. All of these are important.

By being sensitive to the nonverbal messages, you will be better able to respond to feelings and communicate effectively.

4. Be aware of the total communication environment. How you appear to the young person is very important. First of all, if possible, you should get rid of anything that might distract you from giving your total attention to the young person (especially in a counseling setting). The physical environment can be too beautiful (e.g., expensive pictures on the walls, windows with picturesque views) or too uncomfortable and ugly (e.g., cold room, uncomfortable furniture). The setting should allow both of you to give full attention to each other.

Your appearance is also an important consideration; not the clothes you wear, but the fact that you are comfortable and relaxed. Your body language can hinder or help communication. You should

● *Face the youth squarely.* This is the basic caring posture. It says, "I am available to you."

● *Maintain eye contact.* Look directly at the person to facilitate deeper involvement with him or her.

● *Keep an "open" position.* Crossed arms and legs often signal less involvement and a "closed" attitude. An open position is a sign that you are open to what he or she has to say.

● *Lean forward.* This is another nonverbal sign of availability and involvement.

● *Remain relatively relaxed.* When you are relaxed, you give yourself the room you need to listen and respond fully. The young person knows that he or she can feel comfortable with you. If, however, you are tense and tight, he or she will feel uneasy.

Don't adopt a rigid formula; just be yourself, allowing the helping process to flow naturally. The point is that you should be aware of what you are saying with your body. Your nonverbal messages can communicate that you really care.[6]

IN PRACTICE

Our purpose, of course, is to help real, live, troubled young people. None of what we have learned will make any difference unless it is translated into the lives of young men and women. It is time, therefore, to discuss how this happens.

How do you meet troubled youth?

You probably already know a troubled young person or two. They certainly are not hard to find. In fact, they may have already found you. If, however, you are among those rare adults who does not know a troubled young person, making contact is very simple. Here is a process to follow.

1. Think through what you hope to accomplish. This is as easy as saying, "I want to get to know Joe, next door." ... "I am going to help Cindy with her daughter." ... "I would like to minister to the young people down in the park." Get the idea?

2. Position yourself to make contact. Here, the informal, casual approach works best. Find out where the person hangs out and go there. This sounds simple (and it isn't very difficult), but it will take courage. You may feel out of place in a strange environment. Of course, it may be that the place is common to both of you: next door, the park down the street, your church.

3. Meet the young person. Walk up to him or her, introduce yourself, and strike up a conversation. Talk about those subjects in which he or she is interested. Try to discover common ground—similar likes and dislikes. The main purpose is to find out enough about the person so that you can begin a relationship. Eventually you will want to know his or her hobbies, friends, subjects at school, family makeup, and schedule. Involving the young person in an activity is a great way to break the ice.

4. Remember what you have learned. After your initial contact with the young person, review what you learned about him or her. You may even want to keep a written record. Don't think that you will be able to identify and solve a person's problem immediately; relationships take time. At this early stage, all you are trying to do is to earn the right to talk with the person a second time. If he or she is willing to see you again, no matter for how long, you have begun a relationship . . . you have opened the door.

What about relating one-to-one?

We have stated continually that effective communication and building good relationships go hand in hand. In fact, you can't have one without the other. And the real "stuff" of relationships happens one-to-one.

Much can happen in group settings, but it is in the personal, individual times where young people begin to let you look beneath their protective masks. As they get to know you, sensing that you care enough to spend time with them and trust them, they will learn to trust you. Consistency in this area is worth at least a dozen of the most creative, articulate, and poignant group meetings.

Spending time one-to-one with a troubled boy or girl makes him or her feel special. Whether it is having a Coke, going shopping, or just hanging out in the park together, the person begins to realize that someone is interested in him or her as an individual and cares about what is happen-

ing in his or her life. By listening to an adolescent share joys, fears, disappointments, frustrations, hopes, and concerns, you build a relationship that will make an impact on a life.

One-to-one times will have other effects. Those youths who cause trouble so that they will be noticed will begin to simmer down as they realize that they have an adult's attention and love. Those who are shy or inarticulate in a group will discover an outlet for expressing their thoughts and feelings. Those who are lonely or feel rejected will realize that they have a friend.

One-to-one times are conducive for counseling about personal problems. Without the distractions of other group members, it is not difficult to hear what a young person is really saying. And you can take the initiative in encouraging them to open up. You could say, for example, "When we were talking about parents the other day, I noticed that you suddenly got very quiet. I hope I didn't make you feel uncomfortable. Was there something wrong?" If you have shown that you care and are willing to listen, most young people will respond straightforwardly.

The most important and exciting result of one-to-one experiences is sharing the Gospel with a boy or girl and seeing him or her trust Christ as Saviour. It is important to explain (and interpret) the Gospel to each person individually because of the varying levels of comprehension and the multitude of questions. But this is when communication is most effective.

When you spend considerable time with young people individually, they can see a positive picture of maturity and adulthood. Your life, as a model, will be a powerful learning tool. By getting to know you and watching you in action—relating to your family, worshiping, or reacting to stress—they pick up your values and priorities. For some troubled youth, you may be the only good model they have.

One-to-one times can center around a variety of activities including going out for ice cream, playing tennis or another sport, attending an athletic event or a concert, doing something in your home (baking, painting, washing your car, watching television—most young people will enjoy the opportunity to help you with a project), or a multitude of other options. Determine the person's interests and build your one-to-one times around them whenever possible.

What do you do when it gets tough?

To be perfectly frank, building relationships and communicating with troubled youth will not be easy. There will be setbacks and obstacles, and you may wonder why you ever decided to get involved. For a few moments, let's compare the process of relating to a typical troubled young person with a typical "normal" person.

Consider the pattern of most relationships. You meet someone in the neighborhood, at work, at church, or another neutral setting. You don't know each other, but you realize right away that you have something in common, and you begin to converse. Over time, as the two of you continue to relate, you share what you think, feel, value, love, hate, and fear, depending on the amount of time you spend together and your "like" for each other. Quite naturally, as you continue to get to know each other, trust develops. You two are no longer strangers. You are friends, persons who trust each other.

Let's suppose, however, that there is a fifteen-year-old boy who needs help. He is afraid of adults because they have always hurt him. He doesn't share your values or believe in very much and is only committed to surviving in a world that doesn't care about him. And he feels like God makes impossible demands. In addition to the relationship barriers already mentioned, when you tell him that he has sinned, that Jesus paid the price, and that God wants to be his loving Father, he doesn't care; he doesn't hear you. He knows that he has blown it all his life. He feels like a failure and doesn't want another "loving father"—the one he has comes home drunk, beats him up, and tells him what to do. That father is more than enough.

Do you see the picture? We may expect to build relationships with troubled youth and have them work out just like "normal" kids. We may even believe that they should appreciate the chance to get to know us, respect us as adults, have likes, dislikes, and values like ours, and behave a certain way. The truth, however, is that usually none of those expectations are realistic. Troubled youth are so wrapped up in their own needs that they won't meet ours; they won't return love or change overnight. These relationships are long-term investments, not quick cures. Relationships with troubled youth must be built on trust, and trust takes time.

Building relationships with troubled young people is also difficult because it requires us to change. We will have to adjust our schedules and spend time, energy, and money. The toughest part is changing our expectations.

Some time ago, a Youth for Christ staff member had the opportunity to help a young couple at his church begin to build a relationship with their niece. Jennifer was fourteen. She was very normal and had not been in a lot of trouble. Her biggest problems were at home. Mom and Dad were divorced, Dad had remarried, and Mom was living with a boyfriend. Neither parent wanted Jennifer, so, for all practical purposes, she was without a home when Greg and Sue agreed to take her into their home as a foster daughter. They felt strongly that this is what God wanted them to do.

Before long, however, Jennifer began to act as you might expect. She did poorly in school, came home late, tried to manipulate the other children in the family, and "conned" whenever she could. Finally, Greg and Sue began to feel the pressure and wondered whether they were in over their heads. Both began to question how long they could keep helping Jennifer without hurting their family.

As they talked with the staff member, it became evident that they were learning how to relate "on the job." Sue said that after the first month, the honeymoon was over, and that after two months, things were getting worse. Greg said how difficult it was to work with Jennifer; she didn't appreciate what they were doing for her. She didn't show any interest in changing, and she wouldn't accept the family rules. Furthermore, trust was nonexistent. Greg and Sue began to understand the four factors which make these relationships tough.

1. They cost—time, energy, family, money, emotions. This is an expensive price if you don't want to give them up.

2. They push your needs into second place. There is little reciprocity; it feels like you receive a lot less than you give.

3. They take a long time. Conditions will probably get worse before they get better. To be effective, the relationship must be long-term.

4. They require you to change your expectations. Usually things will not turn out the way you thought they would. Here are some expectations which must change:

- a troubled youth will appreciate you
- a troubled youth will trust you
- a troubled youth will obey you
- a troubled youth will be honest with you
- a troubled youth will be open to the Gospel
- a troubled youth will want to change
- a troubled youth will accept your values
- a troubled youth will accept your advice
- a troubled youth will become responsible
- a troubled youth will want to be loved

Building relationships and communicating with troubled young people is not easy, but we really shouldn't expect it to be. First Corinthians 13:7 states that love "always protects, always trusts, always hopes, always perseveres." This kind of love involves paying the price, trusting, having realistic expectations, and commitment. It *will* be tough, but God calls you to nothing less than selfless love over the long haul.

Effective communication with troubled youth, then, begins with having a realistic understanding of yourself, knowing the ingredients of successful relationships, and learning interpersonal skills. Next, however, you must make contact with young people and begin to relate one-to-one. It won't be easy, but over the months and years, God will use you and your loving concern to change lives.

Notes

[1]Shelley, Dr. Ernest. *Dynamics of Individual and Group Counseling by Volunteers,* Book #5 of Teaching Module Booklet for Juvenile and Criminal Justice Volunteerism. Produced by "Volunteers in Probation," National Conference on Crime and Delinquency, 1981, p. 28.

[2]Aldrich, Dr. Joseph C. *Life-style Evangelism.* Portland, Ore.: Multnomah Press, 1981, chap. 4.

[3]Campolo, Dr. Anthony. *The Power Delusion.* Wheaton, Ill.: Victor Books, 1983, p. 159.

[4]Biestek, Felix P. *The Casework Relationship.* Chicago, Ill.: Loyola University Press, 1957.

[5]Welter, Paul. *How to Help a Friend.* Wheaton, Ill.: Tyndale House Publishers, 1984 (1978), p. 208.

[6]Adapted from *Interviewing and Counseling* by Barbara O'Keen (Belmont, Ga.: Duxbury Press, 1976) and *The Skilled Helper* by Gerald Egan (Monterey, Calif.: Brooks, Cole Publishers, 1975). Both works will assist you in developing effective verbal and nonverbal skills.

4. Disciplining Troubled Youth

"**A**nything wrong, Roger?" asked Don McKloskey. "You're muttering to yourself."

Roger Smythe looked up at his coworker. "Oh, was I? It's just this report on Richard Erbbe. You know, that kid tells some unbelievable stories. I don't know what makes him think he's going to get away with them. They're such obvious lies."

"What does the report have to say?" asked Don.

"Well, his soccer coach from last year seems to think that Richard is one of those kids who has a lot of guilt feelings about something or other, and so he lies so he'll get caught and punished. It says here that he probably feels better when he's punished." Roger laughed, "It's always nice to have the latest bulletin from Freud and company, but I have to get to the church. I have a program to run."

Don glanced at his watch and nodded. "Yeah, and I better put this stuff away too. The guys will be out of class and ready for practice in a few minutes."

Half an hour later, all the boys had checked in for soccer practice and were heading to the field. Noticing Richard Erbbe among them, Don called him back. "Hold on, Richard," he said. "You know you're still on restriction for stealing that money. You can't play until tomorrow."

The boy turned and spoke quickly to his coach. "Whaddya mean? I got permission from Mr. Boulten. We made a deal. Barney's sick, and I cleaned out the equipment room, so Mr. Boulten lifted my restriction one day early."

Don was puzzled. It was true that Barney, who had the equipment room to clean, was out with a sore throat; and it was also true that sometimes the boys were allowed to work off certain punishments. But Harv Boulten hadn't mentioned it earlier.

Sensing Don's hesitation, Richard pressed him, "Come on, let me go. The guys are ready to play, and we don't have much time. It gets dark early now."

"You can go," replied Don, "if you're telling the truth. I'll check with Mr. Boulten when he gets back."

Richard ran to the field, leaving Don still feeling uncertain. He didn't want to interrupt Roger by calling him, but then he thought at least he would take time to check out the equipment room. With one glance, he knew he'd been conned. The room was a mess; obviously Richard's restriction had not been lifted. Thoroughly disgusted with himself for being so gullible, Don decided to wait until later to confront him.

After practice, in the locker room, Don called Richard to the side and asked him again about his story. Richard grinned and shook his head. "You're my friend, man," he replied. "Would I lie to you?"

Don was livid. "Listen, Richard," he seethed, "you do this all the time, and it only buys you trouble. Don't you know by now that you can't get away with it?"

"OK, Coach, OK," soothed Richard, motioning with his hands as if to calm troubled waters. "Let's cool it. Punish me if you want, but I really wanted to practice. Is that a sin? Besides, you'd be surprised how many times I do get away with it. The way I figure, it's worth the chance."

Angelina removed the necklace from the envelope hidden under her mattress. She had never seen anything so beautiful. She held it up to the light streaming through the cabin window, and its crystal angles captured the colors of the rainbow. Absorbed in the necklace, Angelina didn't notice Cheri enter the room. Angelina pushed the necklace under her leg, but it was too late.

"Angelina, what have you got there?" Cheri asked.

"Nothing," Angelina answered with an innocent tone and look.

"Come on. You may as well let me see it," said Cheri.

Angelina pulled out the necklace, which seemed to have lost some of its luster.

"Why that's Karen's necklace!" Cheri cried. "We've been looking all over for it. How could you think you'd get away with stealing it? You know stealing will get you into trouble!"

"But Cheri," Angelina pleaded, "Karen has so many pretty things. She would have forgotten the necklace in a few days. I don't have anything, and it would've made me very happy." She started to cry.

Washington stood over the boy and glared at him. With nostrils flaring and between heavy breaths, he growled, "Maybe that'll teach you, you son of a bitch!"

Mr. Johnson grabbed Washington's arm just as he was about to hit Bill again. Washington pulled away.

"What do you think you're doing, Washington? You know fighting's is not allowed here. Everybody in Brigade hates fighting, and we've never had a fight before. None of the other kids ever fought." He ran out of words and just grabbed Washington again, his own face contorted with anger. He really didn't know what to say or do.

By this time, Bill was on his feet. "You tell him, Mr. Johnson. Tell him we don't allow no fighting here. Everybody's against it. I tried to tell him, but he wouldn't listen. He just hit me instead. He's a troublemaker. Kick him out!"

Taking a deep breath, Mr. Johnson replied in a steady, calm voice, "Go get cleaned up, Bill." And then he turned to Washington.

"OK, Washington, why? You know you can't go against what everybody else thinks is right. God doesn't want you to fight. That makes it wrong."

Washington turned silently and began to walk out of the church. Then he turned back and said slowly and evenly, his face revealing the intensity of his feelings, "No one calls my mom a whore!"

These cases represent typical young people with discipline problems. In each situation, the person broke a societal rule and was confronted with his/her guilt. But their wrong actions and responses when confronted are symptoms of deeper discipline issues.

As adults attempting to minister to troubled youth, we will meet many Richards, Angelinas, and Washingtons, young people who need discipline in their lives. And our response to this challenge becomes a vital part of ministry.

Discipline Prevents Punishment

Discipline is the act of stretching the mind and body of a person so that when the performance comes, it can be a pleasure because of the pain a person faced in the practice.

As I define it, discipline comes *before* the act, and punishment comes *after* the act, if the act isn't done well. If you consistently discipline well enough and thoroughly enough, there isn't any need for punishment because children have learned how to act.

Most parents live on the basis of reaction and response rather than initiation. That's the whole name of the ball game.

In *The Effective Father*, I have a chapter about a canoe trip through white water. There are two ways to paddle a canoe through white water. You can wait until you get into the rapids and then decide what you're going to do. But you'll probably end up falling into the water. Or, you can keep your eyes fifty yards downstream, picking out your route so you know exactly how you're going to act before you get there. Many parents make their errors by failing to plan ahead.

Gordon MacDonald

Taken from *Parents and Teenagers*, Scripture Press, 1984, used by permission, p. 425.

Effective discipline is a skill with many elements, and it must be learned. Throughout our relationships with young people, we will need to employ discipline to affect necessary behavioral changes. This chapter deals with the elements necessary to discipline effectively.

WHAT IS DISCIPLINE?

When most people speak of "discipline," they mean "punishment," but the two words are not synonymous. According to the dictionary, *discipline* is "training that corrects, molds, or perfects the mental faculties or moral character."[1] "Correcting" or "molding" may involve punishment, but that is only one of the elements.

The purpose of discipline is to teach. If we discipline troubled youth effectively, they will learn to accept and live within certain limits. Discipline, therefore, shows youth the correct path to follow and then guides them until they are able to walk the path on their own.

Our broad understanding of discipline must include positive direction and leadership, corrective action, valid rules and standards, and personal affirmation.

WHY DO WE NEED RULES AND STANDARDS?

A contemporary misconception of freedom is the "absence of rules or boundaries." In reality, however, rules are necessary for life and for order. In fact, without limits and boundaries, real freedom cannot exist.

The natural order of the universe is based on rules and principles. The planets orbit the sun and the moon orbits the earth, and our days, nights, seasons, and tides result. Gravity and other physical "laws" govern our lives. Without these "rules," there would be no life, let alone freedom. Thinking human beings live within God's natural laws and plan their lives accordingly. Certainly these laws restrict, but without them, we would die.

There are also societal, or interpersonal, boundaries. Human beings are created in the image of God and have infinite worth and dignity. It is *wrong*, therefore, to use or abuse another person. When we ignore this "law" and violate another individual's personhood in the name of freedom, we hurt ourselves and become less than human.

From a purely secular point of view, society needs regulations for order and protection. Consider, for example, highways without speed limits, lights, or signs. Drivers would have total freedom for a while . . . until the accidents. Chaos would result.

Rules, regulations, boundaries, and limits are vital for real freedom to exist. Within the right boundaries, throughout society and as individuals, people are free to grow, mature, live, and enjoy life. *Discipline*, therefore, involves teaching a person to recognize and respect the right boundaries. This is "finding the path" mentioned above.

Standards are also important. These are the goals or ideals toward which we strive. Every person needs a reason to live, a purpose bigger than him/herself.

Standards are also the measurement of life. That is, when we know what is good, healthy, productive, superior, and important, we can move in that direction and avoid the bad, unhealthy, counterproductive, inferior, and unimportant. The proper goals motivate us and keep us moving in the *right* direction. So discipline also involves acknowledging and understanding the right goals and standards.

Most troubled young people fall woefully short in their understanding of both rules and standards. In their homes and neighborhoods, they have been taught only to survive, regardless of which "rules" are broken. And their role models, parents and other adults, too often exhibit no discipline at all.

Our task is critical because we touch their lives while they are still young. They can learn and change, and they have most of their lives to live.

We can teach discipline through our words, our actions, and the standards and rules we clearly communicate and lovingly enforce, one-to-one and in groups.

WHY DO YOUNG PEOPLE BREAK RULES?

It is important to answer this question if we are going to teach troubled youth to live within certain boundaries and to accept someone else's rules.

Young people break rules because of one or a combination of the following reasons.

● They do not know the rules.

● They do not (or refuse to) understand that the rules apply to them.

● They do not understand the need for the rules.

● They are struggling with other, "internal" problems.

All of these reasons, except perhaps for the first (which can be corrected through clear communication), are determined by

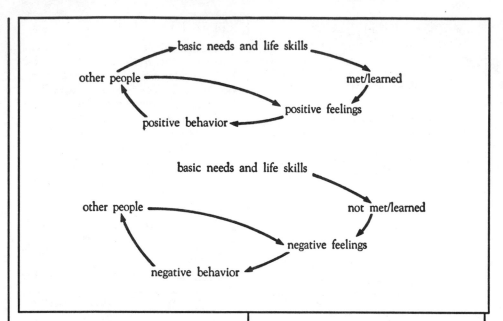

their individual backgrounds, emotional maturity, and self-concepts. Let's look for a moment at the development of the *self-concept*.

Personal Development

Developing one's identity is a lifelong activity. The self-concept is influenced by many factors which interweave and overlap throughout a lifetime. One of these is *basic needs*. All of us are trying continually to meet our needs, and our success or failure in this effort affects how we see ourselves.

Another factor is our *life skills*. These include caring for ourselves physically, building relationships, communicating, and solving problems. The degree to which we learn these skills will have a direct effect on how we feel about ourselves as good, competent persons.

The third factor is *unresolved feelings*. Feelings carried from the past like excess baggage eventually find their way into our actions, thoughts, emotions, and reactions. They often surface in our self-concepts.

Then there is the factor of *how people respond* to us. What our parents, siblings, neighbors, teachers, friends, and others affirm in us (behavior, talent, appearance, etc.), we assimilate into our identities.

Finally, there is our placement in the whole *developmental process*. That is, how does our stage of personal development match with where we should be or are expected to be? This will have an impact on how we feel about ourselves.

The diagrams above illustrate the relationship between basic needs, developmental tasks, feelings, and behavior.

According to our diagrams, the success or failure of meeting basic needs and learning life skills impacts directly how we feel about ourselves, lives, families, friends, jobs, associates, youth with whom we work, etc. Our feelings, then, determine our behavior, and as we "act" toward other people, they respond and reinforce the feelings about ourselves . . . and the cycle continues.

Building a Firm Foundation

If a firm foundation in discipline has not been laid, one struggle parents can expect is in the area of faith. Children who have not been disciplined are not going to believe their parents. Discipline creates trust and respect. Without discipline there is no basis for trusting the parents values or faith, and no respect for their viewpoints.

Discipline is important in helping our teens feel loved. In fact, discipline is a fruit of love. In some cases, parents are never able to show outward affection or verbal affirmation, but the kids discover love in their discipline. I am not talking about the rules here, but the kind of strictness that produces respect. I have heard many young men say that their fathers never took them anyplace, but they cared for their fathers because they were strict and the sons knew the strictness came out of love. Discipline without love is not going to be effective. The love might be buried underneath, but it has to be there.

The person who helped me the most with this aspect of life was a stepuncle. I was afraid of him. I don't recall that he ever "whopped" me, but I never wanted him to. He didn't express much outward love, but he created an environment where I had to respect him.

John Perkins

Taken from *Parents and Teenagers*, Scripture Press, 1984, used by permission, p. 410.

It can be a positive, upward climb or a negative, downward spiral.

The diagrams also show the significant points at which the cycle can be interrupted—meeting basic needs, teaching life skills, becoming a significant person in their lives.

Basic Human Needs

Simply by being human, we share the same basic needs. Abraham Maslow, in his classic volume *Motivation and Personality*, summarizes these in six categories. Of course, whether or not these needs are met is quite subjective; only the individual can know for him/herself. He or she must feel that the need(s) has been met, regardless of what others think or say. Here is Maslow's list.

1. Physical needs—These are the requirements for survival (common for most living creatures). They include food, water, rest, protection, sex, etc.

2. The need for safety—This means feeling safe. Many studies have shown the detrimental effects of living in situations of constant fear. These may be temporary, as in war, or long-term, as in living in a heavy crime area of a city.

3. The need for love—Love is so important that babies have been known to die from the lack of it. This need continues throughout life. Its subdivisions are friendship, parental love, brotherly love, and sexual love.

4. The need to belong—People need to be part of something greater than themselves—a place and an affirming group. Forming relationships is one way to expand one's self, and *belonging* implies an extension of the self into identification with others. Consider all the clubs and social organizations in the world; they were formed in response to this need.

5. The need for self-esteem—Everyone

needs to feel worthy and worthwhile. We need to know that we can do something important and significant, to make a contribution. These "somethings" may include talents, hobbies, personality characteristics, etc. Whatever they are, we must feel inside that we can do them well.

6. *The need for self-actualization*— This is the drive for success or fulfillment. It means reaching our potential both in terms of our accomplishments and who we are as people, becoming the best that we can be.[2]

Experiencing success in meeting our basic needs will help build positive self-concepts which will give us freedom to develop healthy relationships with others because we will not be obsessed with our own needs. Because of this, other people will accept and "love" us, which will encourage us to feel worthy of love and successful as persons.

But the flip side is also true. If our needs are not met regularly and legitimately, we will seek alternate ways to meet them. Our actions, then, will most likely lead to negative encounters with others who stand in the way or whom we must "use" to get what we want. When they react in anger or disgust, our feelings of worthlessness are intensified, and the pattern is reinforced.

You can readily see what happens with troubled youth. We have already described their situations as "survival," and that is exactly what they often are (for food, shelter, safety, love, etc.). If these young people are focusing their attention and energy on meeting these basic needs, especially the first few on the list, they will have very little regard for society's laws, rules, and limits or for your behavioral suggestions. Instead, they will do what they must to live another day.

Life Skills

In a sense, *life skills* are no more than what must be done to successfully meet one's needs. In other words, as we grow and mature, we learn how to satisfy our needs for food, shelter, and sex in socially acceptable ways; we learn how to build good relationships with people and experience their love and acceptance, how to develop our talents and abilities, how to use education, how to solve problems, and how to plan, dream, set goals, and make things happen.

Once again, if troubled youth have learned how to meet their needs in socially *unacceptable* ways (e.g., stealing, lying, forcing, etc.), they will find it very difficult to obey new rules to the game of life. And there are many of these skills which they may have never learned at all (e.g., how to study, set goals, get a job, communicate feelings and ideas, etc.). Then if others expect them to perform in a certain way, they feel inadequate or incompetent, and they refuse.

Personal Feedback

We receive continual feedback from others. They smile at us and are happy to see us, and we feel good; or perhaps they scowl, get angry, and lecture, and make us feel ashamed or guilty. Adults are a very important source of feedback for young people. They are the authority figures, and they have the power to enforce their desires. For troubled youth, the number of adults with whom they come in contact is quite limited, so the feedback received is very significant. This is especially true in determining right and wrong.

As a person grows, he or she learns by doing. Acceptable, or "right," actions have good consequences, and unacceptable, or "wrong," actions have bad consequences. These consequences determine what is right and what is wrong, and values and morality are taught.

Responsible Christian parents determine to teach values and moral standards consistent with biblical principles and societal norms. They may use praise and reward to reinforce good actions and scolding and punishment to help deter bad actions. At the earlier ages, no act is good in itself—only if it brings praise or reward. But the children develop good habits and learn to respect authority. Then, as children mature, they are taught the importance of God's approval and how to develop and internalize values and priorities.

Again consider the troubled young person. The significant adults in his or her life may provide little or no verbal feedback and a very laissez-faire approach to parenting. In single parent homes or those where both parents work, the schedule may be too crowded for personal attention. In both these situations, usually the only feedback is negative—and physical—and the cycle continues. Young people reared in this environment will resist anyone telling them what to do, and they will consider your feedback very cautiously.

In summary, fulfillment of basic needs, knowledge of life skills, real feelings, involvement of significant adults, and other factors all work together to form the self-concepts of troubled youth and determine to a great extent how they will respond to discipline. We cannot understand them without knowing about their backgrounds.

This does not mean, however, that you must know *everything* about young people before you can discipline them. It does mean that the more time you give to understanding them, the better the job you will be able to do.

The necessity for quick action

When troubled young people break the rules, the reasons are deeper than disobedience. Usually, these are "hurt" children, and forcing them to conform will not be effective. They need to discover and deal with the inner feelings that drive them to behave as they do. You may be their only outlet.

Sooner or later, you will have to confront the problem of broken rules. Then you must act quickly and decisively and in a calm and loving manner. (We will discuss this thoroughly in the next chapter.) The first step to solving the problem, however, begins with prevention—establishing fair and enforceable rules.

HOW DO I ESTABLISH FAIR RULES?

A fair rule for an *individual* is a guideline, boundary, or limit which takes into account his or her background, experience, age, and personality, and which helps him or her mature, moving toward becoming a *whole* person.

A fair rule for a *group* is similar, with the very important exception that more than one person is involved. A group rule must take into consideration the various individuals involved (their uniquenesses, needs, backgrounds, histories, etc.) *and* the special personality of the group as a whole. It is also important to consider the purpose of the group and the fact that the rules must be consistently and uniformly enforced. Remember, too, that there are special group dynamics whenever two or more people are together. With every person added, the number of relationships multiplies, and the personality of the group changes. This reality

Using Authority

When we think of authority, we are inclined to think negatively. However, authority can be a major tool in problem solving. How it is used will determine whether discipline actually occurs.

The *implicit* authority of your personal strength as evidenced by the fact that you are a successful person will be most helpful. If nothing else, you know how to get along in this world without breaking the law. In addition, you have the authority to reward and commend. These two are powerful factors. The rewards and compliments which we take for granted are unknown to troubled youth. They must live without clear definitions of what is good.

The enforcement aspect of authority should not be overly emphasized. As a volunteer, you are really not being asked to be an enforcer. The power of society to enforce will continue whether or not you are working with a young offender, and he or she knows what being an offender means. Emphasize, instead, what must eventually govern the lives of all of us—an inner discipline to do what God wants.

should also be in the rule-making grid.

Your rules should be those which your young people can accept; therefore, knowing their backgrounds is crucial. If you are aware of their needs, you will find it easier to decide on limits to set. Let's assume that a boy wants to smoke. Should you allow it? Of course, it would be in his best interest physically not to smoke. But consider how hooked he might be and what role smoking plays in his life. Instead of prohibiting smoking altogether, it probably would be better to allow it in certain places and at specific times. It would be helpful to ask yourself, "Is this a rule which can be reasonably enforced?" and "Will this rule benefit or harm the purpose of our relationship?"

Here are six questions which will help you determine which of your rules are fair and which of them are not.

1. Is it important (or just a personal preference)? In other words, does your rule reflect your ministry priorities or does it merely reflect your personal biases?

2. Will it help or hinder your relationship? For example, telling the individual above that he could not smoke would probably hinder the relationship more than it would help.

3. Will it help the young person mature as a "whole" person? Consider how the rule affects the mental, social, physical, and spiritual areas of the individual's life.

4. Is it reasonable? Understanding where the person is developmentally and socially, can you expect him or her to accept this rule? Is it consistent and within his or her ability to obey?

5. Is it specific and clearly stated? In other words, does the young person understand what you really mean and what the limits are?

6. How will you enforce it? Consider the consequences of noncompliance and how you will enforce the rule. Often it is helpful for the young person to participate in deciding the consequences (when the rule is made, of course).

Rules (limits, boundaries, and guidelines) are an important part of discipline, but discipline is more than setting rules. *How* you communicate the standards and boundaries and how you enforce the rules is crucial. And that leads us to a look at discipline methods.

WHAT DISCIPLINE METHODS SHOULD I USE?

Remember that the purpose of discipline is to teach troubled youth how to act, and it is virtually impossible to do this without becoming actively involved in the process. There are discipline methods which do not require your involvement (e.g., assigning the task to someone else), but they are much less effective. Determine to do the teaching yourself and not to "pass the buck."

Approaches

Here are four ways to approach young people. You will probably use a combination of these depending on the individual and the situation.

1. *Person-to-person*—a personal, private conference with the young person.

2. *Casual conversation*—an informal discussion at almost any time and in almost any place.

3. *Group decision*—consensus by the group for certain behavioral standards.

Occasionally a person can be disciplined best by group or peer pressure. For example, you begin to tell a story to your group, but a girl continues to cause a disturbance. Instead of continuing with the story, you stop talking and do something else (write a note or whatever). When the rest of the group asks why you have stopped, you answer, "Since Sue didn't want to listen, I thought you would all rather just rest. Any interruptions will ruin our story." The group will quickly inform Sue that she should be quiet, and they will agree to listen without interrupting.

Group pressure should be the *exception*, not the rule, but it can be effective in certain situations.

4. *Touch control*—singling out a person for immediate, personal attention in the midst of a discipline situation.

This is an important discipline tool. It is helpful to speak to the whole group, but it means much more to speak to *one* person. For example, in your cabin, a boy continues to whisper to his friend after lights out. You could make a general "let's keep quiet" announcement or even mention his name from your bunk . . . and accomplish very little. If, however, you get up, walk quietly to his bunk, put your hand on his shoulder, and speak to him firmly and personally, he will usually shape up.

Rewards

In working with troubled youth, an easy trap to fall into is assuming that most of what they do is bad. But rarely will you meet a troubled young person who does "bad" things all the time. As a matter of fact, most of what you will experience with young people probably will be very enjoyable and desirable. It is important to recognize these desirable behaviors and to reinforce them, encouraging the person to continue to act in that way. Rewarding good behavior, or positive reinforcement, is based on two very simple principles.

1. *Behavior is influenced by what happens immediately afterward—the consequences.* In other words, what a person does in the future is influenced by what happens after he or she does something now. Behavior that is rewarded tends to be repeated. Behavior that is not rewarded is less

likely to be repeated.

2. *Your behavior influences the young person's behavior.* When you respond to a youth's behavior by smiling, scowling, praising, criticizing, punishing, rewarding, loving, or avoiding, you are communicating approval or disapproval. By being intentional with your responses and providing certain kinds of consequences for behavior, you can increase the number of good actions and decrease the number of bad ones.

Intentional, positive consequences are called *rewards.* They can be as simple as smiles, attention, verbal approval, special privileges, loose change for candy, or something more elaborate. It is important to remember that what is reinforcing to one person may not be for another. For example, one young person may think it's a treat to have lunch at McDonald's while another may consider it no big deal. Here are some "rules of thumb" regarding positive reinforcements and troubled youth.

● Keep it simple. Most troubled young people just want your love. A smile, a word, an arm around the shoulder are more valuable than money. Each person's needs will dictate the best reward. Use the most simple one that works.

● Watch the timing. Timing is very important. The more immediate the reinforcement, the more effective it will be. When you praise a girl for showing up on time or compliment a boy for refusing to fight, right away, you let them know you appreciate what they have done. If you wait until later, the effect will not be very strong, and you may even forget altogether. It is important to reward every time until the behavior has been established. Then you can switch to a more varied timetable (such as every third or fourth time).

● Take it gradually. Don't demand immediate change. It just won't happen. Instead, remember that a "big" behavior is made up of many "little" behaviors. Take schoolwork, for example. When a young person does poorly in school, he may have to correct his attitude, learn how to read, learn how to study, learn how to get along with others, learn how to respect authority, and attend classes before he can do well as a student. Watch for those "small" actions, reinforce them, and use them as the first steps toward the major change.

Incentives

Using incentives is a practical way to facilitate behavioral change. An incentive is something worth working for, something the young person likes to do or to have.

Motivation is one of the most difficult obstacles faced by those working with troubled youth. The typical troubled young person has a short attention span, a lack of stability, very little support at home, and short-range goals at best. It is a real challenge, therefore, to persuade him or her to continue with a program after the novelty has worn off.

Your success in motivating troubled youth to be involved consistently and to continue to work toward changing their behavior will be directly related to what they believe is in it for them. Simply stated, incentives are the "something in it for them." Incentives help you get their attention long enough to show them that you care and that you can be trusted. It is a system, however, which requires discipline and consistency on your part if it is to work effectively.

The use of incentives is not magic, nor is it a quick and easy solution to deep personality problems; it is a tool which can be used in the whole discipline process. In most cases, incentives will work when the behavior to be changed is specific and simple. Complex problems must be broken down into smaller pieces.

Here are some suggestions for using incentives.

1. *Use a variety of rewards.* The rewards do not need to be elaborate or extravagant; be creative and keep them simple. Find out what the young person likes, and go for it. Also, remember that the rewards you need should be available when you need them. Using reinforcers that you can't deliver is worse than using no incentives at all.

2. *Reward good behavior quickly.* This has been discussed previously.

3. *Watch out for competition.* Competition can be harmful to certain young people. Troubled youth need to succeed in defeating problems, not each other. Encourage them to compete with themselves, not with others.

4. *Clearly define the behaviors and the rewards.* For example, the desired behavior could be, "Stop running around during Sunday School." The reward might be a Coke and hamburger at Burger Chef. Keep the guidelines concise, simple, and on their level. If it can't be understood easily, don't use it.

5. *Begin with short-term rewards.* Remember that troubled youth have short-term goals. They need immediate gratification, and they will not work on changing their behavior today if the reward doesn't come for three months. As you continue to work with them, however, they will become increasingly patient, and you can use longer-range incentives.

6. *Use less "sophisticated" rewards with younger youths.* "Carrots" are easier to use with younger children. As they get older, their "hot buttons" become more difficult to find. Incen-

tives work best for late elementary and early adolescent youth.

7. *Keep a record.* Don't trust your memory. When you offer a reward to someone, write it down. It will be very embarrassing and counterproductive to admit later that you forgot. This also will eliminate any argument with your young people over what was promised.

8. *Remember that "love" is better than money.* Material rewards have their limits, and research shows a definite correlation between the length of behavioral change and the use of "social" rewards. Your approval can be a powerful incentive.

Confrontation

Effective discipline helps young people face their situations realistically. Remember that good discipline teaches, but it is up to the youth to learn. They will have to make choices along the way; you cannot do the deciding. Instead, you must stand apart from the decision and help them evaluate the consequences of their decisions.

This "help" very often involves confrontation. To confront is not to attack or to preach. Quite the opposite is true. Effective confrontation is tenderly, firmly, and honestly bringing a person face-to-face with the reality of his or her actions. If you fail to confront the young person, you will miss a most crucial step in his or her growth.

We sometimes fear confrontation because we do not understand it, believing that we will lose their friendship or break the relationship. Proper confrontation, however, is not threatening and does not involve conflict. It is a natural, helpful activity.

Proper and effective confrontation begins with your attitude. Analyze your feelings and the kind of attitude you are projecting. If, for example, you are angry or hateful, those feelings will overshadow your confrontive words, and the person will not hear what you are saying. He or she will simply react to your attitude. If, however, your attitude is one of genuine concern for the person's well-being, he or she will see your attitude, sense your concern, and listen to your words. *How* you confront is as important as what you say.

Also remember that effective confrontation takes place in the context of a relationship. Think of how you would respond to correction from a stranger. Young people are no different. It is true that you must "win the right to be heard," and we have already discussed the dynamics of relationship building. Your friendship with a person will be the bridge for effective communication, including confrontation.

There are two key aspects to confrontation which must be balanced: *supporting without condoning* and *confronting without condemning*. Basic to effective confrontation is the assurance of the support you have already established for the person and for your friendship. Before they respond positively, young people must be able to sense that you are for them and concerned about what happens to them.

The problem with being supportive, however, is that young people can believe that you are condoning or will overlook their actions and attitudes. But for real change to take place, they must assume full responsibility for themselves, understanding that they are part of the problem as well as the solution. Consequently, you must verbally explain the truth about their actions. This is confrontation.

Being supportive without condoning means identifying with the youth's feelings while telling him or her firmly, softly, and straightforwardly about their behavior. The young person must take the responsibility for his or her actions.

When considering confronting young people without condemning them, there are several points to remember.

● *Your motives must be pure*. Do you have the person's best interests at heart? Decide whose needs you will be meeting.

● *Confrontation is a way of helping*. To confront is not to be unloving or unkind; in fact, it could be the most loving thing you could do.

● *Your words must be spoken in love*. The person who knows that you are speaking out of love for him or her will receive your message.

When Paul confronted the Corinthians (2 Corinthians 7), he caused them sorrow; but he was glad because the confrontation "led to repentance" (verse 9). Jesus confronted the woman at the well with her sin and her need for eternal life, but He did not condemn her for having had six husbands (John 4). These examples illustrate the results of proper and effective confrontation and the necessity of "hating the sin" while "loving the sinner."

Often confrontation can begin with a question. This will help ease into the conversation and help the individual see the problem for him/herself. Here are some confrontational questions which you can use with young people.

● "How did you feel when that happened?"

● "Are you having trouble feeling you can trust anybody?"

● "How has it been going with the problem we discussed?"

A Question of Discipline—When and How Often?

One of the toughest problems for parents of teenagers is the question of discipline. We know they still need it, but they're too big to spank. Obviously there are no easy answers, but here are some guidelines.

1. There is a difference between punishment and discipline, though they are tied together. "Discipline" is the means of moving someone toward *positive* goals.

2. Learn to know when enough is enough, and look for the deeper reasons for bad behavior. Punishment becomes useless if you are constantly punishing repeated problems. The teens action is a symptom of a deeper problem which needs attention.

3. Punishment should not be an exercise in anger or an expression of frustration. Try to calm down before meting it out.

4. Be specific about possible consequences of the youth's behavior. Help him or her explore a positive alternative to the negative behavior.

5. Enlist the teens help in designing discipline. Ask him what would be a fair and motivating punishment (and reward) in specific situations.

Adapted from *Parents and Teenagers*, Scripture Press, 1984, used by permission, p. 431.

● "What happened when you said/did that?"

● "How's it going between you and God?"

● "What are you doing to help the situation?"

● "What problems might your parents be facing in their lives which would cause them to be tense at home?"

● "How are you feeling right now?"

● "How much of the problem would you say is your fault?"

● "When is this feeling most intense?"

● "What solutions have you tried so far?"

Actions and reactions

There is one response in confronting situations which Scripture indicates is always appropriate—the spirit of gentleness (Galatians 6:1-2). And this response is always effective. It indicates self-control and an inner calm and strength given by the Holy Spirit that protects us from unguarded and inappropriate reactions to the person and his or her behavior. To react responsibly, keep these four counseling principles in mind:

1. Be aware of facial expressions and body language. Did your eyebrows raise when that titillating incident was revealed? Did your mouth turn down as a secret sin was shared? Be careful that your actions do not belie your words. This is not to suggest a blank, unfeeling face; rather it means not expressing shock or condemnation which would block a young person's listening and honest speaking.

2. Avoid making premature judgments. Adolescents will often seek approval for their behavior. Take for example, a boy who comes to an adult counselor asking for advice on how to deal with his parents, hoping that the counselor will take his side in the situation. You must be mature enough to wait until all the facts are in; then you can judge the rightness or wrongness of behavior. One way to do this is to ask questions.

3. Avoid interrupting. If our young people need anything, they need to know that there are adults who will listen to them. Instead, what they often encounter is an unthinking person who "butts in" with advice or examples. Because of your maturity and experience, you will be tempted to jump in and solve the problem instead of letting the person explain and work through the situation. Sometimes letting the person squirm is the best medicine.

4. Speak in terms of "I, . . ." not "you." This principle is true for all interpersonal relationships and especially appropriate for confrontation. When telling a young person about his or her mistakes, disobedience, or other wrong behavior, be sure to describe your feelings—don't attack them. For example, you might say, "I heard what you said to John, and I was very disappointed. It seems to me that that violates our agreement. What do you think?" Even in anger, try to describe your feelings and the situation. Instead of yelling, "You idiot!" you can yell, "Look at that! Now what are we going to do?" This does not remove a person from personal responsibility for his actions; but it does focus on the *actions* and their results and not on your *judgments*.

Negative reinforcement vs. punishment

Punishment is often used to deal with undesirable behavior; however, there are several problems connected with this approach, especially with physical punishment.

Punishment may eliminate bad behavior, but it may also have negative side effects, causing stress or a severe emotional response such as fear or anger.

For many troubled young people, punishment makes the situation worse. The effects are temporary and soon wear off. At other times, what is thought to be punishment turns out to be positive reinforcement for the wrong action. The child who tries to get attention is a good example. He may enjoy being punished because your attention is more important than his fear of the other consequences of his acts.

Many troubled youth come from physically abusive homes. If you punish them physically, you reinforce their terrible worldview and may cause deep emotional scars.

There are several alternatives to punishment. One is to ignore the undesirable act. Believe it or not, sometimes just pretending that it doesn't exist can be an effective way to decrease its occurrence. Almost any behavior which doesn't threaten the safety of the child or others can be ignored. This approach is most effective when combined with positive reinforcement, especially when positive behavior can be substituted for negative. Remember, to get rid of a specific bad behavior, you must give the child a good one. Sometimes, on their own, young people cannot think of other ways to act.

Another alternative to punishment is "time out." You cannot ignore annoying or obnoxious behavior or fighting, especially in a group setting. "Time out" is similar to the parental reaction of sending a child to his or her room. It means having the young person go off by him/herself to cool down and think things over for a while. Time out periods should not be too long. In some cases, five or ten minutes is sufficient. This amount of time helps the person think about how a problem situation might be handled more effectively.

Other alternatives relate to positive reinforcement and incentives, which we have already discussed.

HOW CAN I MOVE THEM TOWARD INDEPENDENCE?

We began this chapter with case studies about showing troubled youth the right path and helping them walk down it. This is what it means to discipline them. There comes a point, however, where our direct intervention ends, and we must leave them to make their own way down the path. This is *self-discipline*, and it is our goal.

We have already covered (and implied) much of what should be done to move young people toward becoming mature, self-sufficient people, and much more will be discussed in subsequent chapters. The key concept in this process, however, is *trust*. That is, the degree to which we are able to trust young people on their own will determine how quickly they move toward true independence. This is not easy; there are fears and risks. But if we never trust them, they will never learn to make it.

It was Saturday afternoon, and a party was scheduled for the church activity center that night. A shiny, late-model car pulled to a stop in front of the church, and two middle-aged mothers, bearing cookies and other refreshments for the party, entered the foyer. As the women looked around, they spotted two boys busily putting up decorations. These young men hadn't been attending the youth group very long and everyone knew that several months before, they had been caught burglarizing the store down the street.

The women put the food beside the door and looked around briefly for someone to receive their contributions. The youth pastor entered the room, and one of them said, "These are for the party tonight. I guess it will be all right just to leave them here. They won't be stolen, will they?"

The pastor responded, "Well, maybe we'd better set them inside until party time," and he unlocked the kitchen door. It was one of those subtle interchanges that usually escapes unnoticed.

In effect, the woman's query was, "Can we safely leave this food in the hall with those two kids in the room?" And his words and actions meant, "No, we'll be missing a few bottles of pop if we do."

But the subtleties were not lost on the two boys, who glanced at each other. Seeing this, the woman hastily attempted to gloss over the situation by saying, "Oh, I'm sure these refreshments will be all right here. I'm sure you can trust these boys."

Now the problem was out in the open. In attempting to ease the situation, she had brought it to a head. The boys said nothing, but their reactions to this quick switch were obvious in their expressions. In effect, they were saying, "Lady, you've never seen us before in your life. How do you know whether you can trust us? You've already shown how you really feel; no cover-up will get you off the hook now."

The pressure was on the youth pastor as the boys stopped decorating to see how he would handle the situation. Would he reverse himself to try to look "open" and "trusting," or would he put the refreshments under lock and key and talk his way out of it?

Without batting an eye, he simply said, "Mrs. Smith, we're not quite ready to trust these boys yet." You could see the boys glance at each other, nod, and return to their task. This time there was no disdain for the stated position. The pastor was straightforward and honest. What he

said was consistent and real. It did not attempt to evade a most difficult subject—trust.

As your relationships develop with troubled young people, you will continually think about trust. "Can I trust this kid? How much can I trust him?" "What happens when I trust her and she lies or disobeys behind my back?" "How should I respond when trust has been broken?" And how will you respond when he says, "Please let me go into the store. I won't steal anything," and you realize that he has three candy bars hidden under his coat when he comes out? Or when she says, "I need to leave the group for a minute. I have to go to the john," and you learn later that she really only wanted a cigarette.

Inevitably the decision to trust or not to trust will be yours. And the tension is between building confidence and fostering independence in the individual.

Because trust is so important, here are some principles which will help you decide who, when, and how to trust. These are adapted from "The Mother of Trust" by Dale G. Hardman.[3]

1. Trust is essential to any good relationship. A troubled young person needs to be trusted and needs to fulfill that trust just like you. Teaching him or her to fulfill your trust is worth the risk. It will help him or her mature.

2. Permitting a young person to "con" you is not good. Knowingly allowing a troubled youth to con you is not helpful to anyone concerned. Everyone is fooled from time to time, so don't be surprised or overly upset when it happens to you. Instead, say to the person, "Evidently I trusted you and gave you some responsibility before you were ready for it. You are going to have to earn it before I can trust you again."

3. Troubled youth violate trust because they are socially immature. Don't interpret a violation of trust as a personal affront. There are all sorts of

---

Can You Be Too Trusting?

As a youth worker, you cannot be too trusting—in fact, you have everything to gain as you trust a teen's integrity. Mutual trust is a blessing, if you feel that your teen trusts you, you really value that, and vice versa. Trust breeds responsibility. Give teens the opportunity for independence, and communicate your trust to them by saying yes as often as you can.

Trust that is earned by good judgment increases as children learn to make decisions. Don't trust teens too soon in areas where they are likely to fail; don't give trust where direction or more maturity is needed; don't trust when there is not enough knowledge or experience or confidence to make a good decision. A young person's repetitive bad choices are sending a message that your help is needed in learning to make positive and constructive decisions.

Teach your children how to make wise choices; then as they become teenagers, allow them frequent chances to make their own decisions. As you encourage their independence, give yourself and them to the Lord. Can you trust God too much?

Taken from *Parents and Teenagers*, Scripture Press, 1984, used by permission, p. 438.

factors in the person's background that led to his or her behavior. Without condemning the individual, explain your thinking and describe your feelings, holding up the goal of *trust*. For example, don't ever tell a young person no without giving a reason based on his or her level of maturity and your relationship. "Judy, how long have we known each other? Two weeks? That's not very long for me to get to know you, is it? You may be really dependable, but I don't know yet. When I get to know you better, I'll trust you with my radio."

4. *Trust lightly rendered is lightly held.* If you give your trust too quickly, it will not be taken very seriously. If, on the other hand, your young people know that trust must be earned, they will not be very likely to break it.

5. *Trust must be rooted in truth.* How well a young person matures in matters of trust relates to your personal integrity and honesty. Everyone believes that they are basically honest. For example, we would never tell an outright lie or cheat or steal, but there are more subtle attempts to rationalize our mistakes and to conceal our weaknesses.

We may use the transparent excuse, "I didn't forget our appointment, John. Something came up"; or "I didn't really lose my temper; I was just trying . . . " or "I made this decision because I thought it was best for you." Young people know when we are conning them.

It is difficult to maintain total honesty throughout a relationship, but when you are dishonest, you are saying, "I can't trust you, so I had to lie to protect myself."

6. *Trust is a two-way street.* The degree to which a young person values the trust you place in him is directly related to how much they trust *you*. Can you be trusted to keep appointments, to do what you promise, to keep confidences? You may be the first person they have ever known who they feel can truly be trusted.

Effective discipline is a skill with many elements. It means correcting, molding, and perfecting the young people in our charge, moving them toward the goal of self-discipline. Discipline is never quick or easy, but it is a vital part of ministering to troubled youth.

5. Handling Problem Situations

At 5′ 11″ and 200 lbs., Julio Sanchez was 15, going on 25. At their first meeting, Brian Barton was not very impressed. Julio had come to the shop looking for work at a time when Mr. Barton was busy and didn't have time to sit and chat. And when he learned that Sanchez was a dropout, Barton knew that there was no way he could hire him. But Sanchez persisted, and as they talked, Brian began to see that he was very sincere.

Maybe Julio could do some of the odd jobs around here to give me more time, he thought. "Sanchez...you ever had any work experience?"

"Sure, man. I can do anything if the money's right," Sanchez replied.

"Well, I need a man to clean the shop and work in the storeroom."

"When do I start?"

"Come in tomorrow at 8 A.M., and I'll show you what I need."

During the next few weeks, Barton found himself regretting his decision to hire Sanchez. He was more trouble than he was worth. He couldn't clean the shop without help, and every time he was approached about a new job to do, he stalked off without even trying. After several weeks, however, they seemed to settle into a routine with both Barton and Sanchez making the necessary adjustments. Julio was doing his job and even accepting correction.

One afternoon, a neighborhood boy who would hang out around the shop from time to time told Barton that Julio had been smoking in the bathroom despite the no-smoking fire regulation. Brian confronted Sanchez with this accusation, and Julio apologized and promised to change. He seemed sincere, and Barton let it drop.

Twenty minutes later, the alley behind the shop echoed with sounds of a fight. Sanchez's voice filtered through the thumps, bangs, squeals, and shouts. Putting down his tools, Barton ran to the rear door and looked outside. He stood, frozen by the sight of the two boys struggling. When he approached them, the smaller boy broke partially free and began to kick. Sanchez blocked the first kick but caught the second one in the stomach. Furious, he grabbed the boy and hit him in the face. Blood began to flow from his nose, and Sanchez backed away. Barton stopped just short of Sanchez, looked him squarely in the eyes, and asked, "What's going on here?"

As Sanchez began to answer, the boy seized the opportunity and ran away. "The little rat got me in trouble, and I'm gonna kill him. Almost cost me this stupid job. He made me mad," he said evenly through clenched teeth. He was white with rage and close to losing control completely.

Barton knew he had to tread very carefully to defuse the situation. As they returned inside, he spoke softly, asking Sanchez the identity of the other boy, what caused the fight, and who started it. After hearing the answers, Barton replied, "You're telling me that you started that fight because you didn't want to lose your job?"

"Yeah, that's right," said Sanchez.

Sensing things had calmed, Barton said, "First of all, don't worry about the job. I think I know how you feel, and I'm glad you want to keep working. But you know you were wrong to smoke in here. The inspector was right to make that rule because of all the chemicals and solvents we keep in the shop. It has to be obeyed; you know it, and I believe you when you say you'll keep it. Now, the kid's gone. Let's just calm down and talk for a few minutes. Forget about that boy, and I'll see what I can do to keep him out of your hair. But I want you to do two things for me. First, don't think about getting even and, second, remember not to smoke around here. Can you do that? If you can, we'll go for pizza after work on Saturday."

Sanchez nodded and answered, "I'll try, but if that kid makes any more trouble for me, I ain't makin' no promises!"

For the rest of the week, life at the shop ran smoothly. Sanchez worked hard to please Mr. Barton, and he kept his word about not smoking. He even managed to ignore the "offending" boy, who returned to the shop on Saturday. That night, after work, Barton invited Sanchez to his house for some "three-wheeling" and pizza. While they were riding, Brian expressed his gratitude for Julio's good work and for his self-control in the shop.

Then, while walking back to the house, Brian explained how everyone loses his temper from time to time and that there are some good reasons for getting angry. "I used to get angry all the time until I understood what the Bible says and decided to do it. Let me show you what I mean."

Barton took out his pocket Bible and turned to Proverbs 14:16-17, "A fool is hotheaded and reckless. A quick-tempered man does foolish things." "Of course," he added, "it's pretty tough to do what the Bible says if you don't have a relationship with God. . . ." And he continued to share the Gospel in terms Sanchez could understand.

One of the challenges of working with troubled youth is learning how to deal effectively with problems as they arise. But there are no prepackaged, easy solutions to every situation. The kind of problem faced by Brian Barton was not unique. He was confronted with resolving an interpersonal conflict and with teaching Julio Sanchez how to control his temper. Mr. Barton did not choose the time or the participants; he had to react quickly, instinctively, and immediately.

Often, adults beginning to work with young people think they have all the answers, that they will know exactly how to respond in every situation. But those attitudes only apply in the classroom. When you deal with real people, troubled people, you realize very soon that each person and each problem is unique and that the easy answers simply don't work.

The shattering of this "youth-work idealism" can lead in two directions. The person may decide that he or she is just not cut out for this kind of ministry and perhaps God is leading to another area of service.

But there may also be the opposite response—the caring adult deciding to learn how to cope, respond, and help. For this person, the commitment to the ministry takes precedence over personal difficulties.

In our last chapter, we discussed *discipline*—showing young people the correct path to follow and then guiding them along that path until they are able to walk alone. This means that *rules and standards must be established.* It is impossible for any person to function, let alone grow, if he or she does not know the boundaries of right and wrong conduct.

Discipline means that young people must be taught to live up to the standards and within the limits imposed. Eventually these *external* rules will be *internalized*, but this process happens differently according to the individual. His or her background, personality, abilities, and other factors all come into play. Rarely will this internalization of rules occur quickly, and in the interim, there will be much pushing against the limits, testing of the leader's resolve, falling back into old lifestyles, and dealing with crises as in the case of Barton and Sanchez.

Though discipline is not just punishment or responding to negative behavior, the crises (problem situations) which you will face will usually involve an emotional explosion and/or rule breaking. We have already discussed why troubled youth break rules. Their reasons are usually more than simply willful disobedience. Other unconscious forces work beneath the surface. Your response, therefore, to a problem situation is very important in helping a young person learn and grow, not just in "keeping the peace."

THE COMPROMISE PRINCIPLE

The first skill to learn in handling problem situations is compromise. This means understanding that there is the young person's "side" to the story and so *negotiation* is appropriate and necessary. You may begin to feel like a diplomat for Christ, negotiating in order to keep the relationship alive and to develop friendship and trust.

This does not mean compromising biblical absolutes, but it does mean reconsidering adult and middle-class perspectives. If Mr. Barton had simply reacted firmly and dogmatically to Sanchez's problems, he probably would have lost the opportunity to help him. Instead, he saw the confrontation as one step in the lengthy process of helping Sanchez change.

Willingness to negotiate and compromise also says that we understand that no one is perfect and we all make mistakes. We must make room in our social theory for temporary setbacks. Consider for a moment how you like to be treated when you falter or really blow it. Undoubtedly empathy and forgiveness top the list of your most appreciated responses. The bad situations you encounter are not the end but merely opportunities

to teach the troubled young person to become everything God wants him or her to be.

Compromise means not taking the hard line, but it does not mean being a "pushover." Rules and their enforcement are necessary. Troubled youth need to have limits and to have those limits taken seriously. And those young people who find it easy to bend the truth will try to con you continually; always be alert for this. Compromise means responding *in light of the rules*—working on meaningful incentives and punishments.

Compromise also means approaching troubled youth with an attitude of hope. It is easy to think that those who have learned self-defeating behavior will respond that way regardless of what we do. The truth is, however, that young people, just like everyone else, change and mature. As a caring adult, you can have a powerful influence in their lives, simply by conveying your expectations that they can and will change for the better. Your hope for them will foster hope in them.

Fortunately, as Mr. Barton discovered, there is life after a crisis. Usually the problem is not as difficult to handle as is thought initially, but you must learn the steps to take to turn a bad situation into a good one. The following is a simple, generic model for dealing with these problems. It includes the four basic steps you should take.[1]

STEPS FOR DEALING WITH PROBLEMS

Think again of how Mr. Barton responded to the problem with Sanchez. What was going on in Brian's mind? Was he happy? Was he angry? Did he expect Julio to fight? How would you have handled the situation?

It is difficult to predict problems. There was really no way that Barton could have known how Sanchez would react when confronted with his smoking violation. Because starting a fight with the boy was unexpected, Barton could not anticipate his own reactions.

You will also be confronted with the unexpected. Usually these situations occur between two or more young people, but even one youth can create a problem which is difficult to resolve. Boys fighting, a girl drinking, a child stealing, someone smoking in the church restroom, or vandalizing, are a few of the problems which could arise. Whatever it is, be ready.

Step #1–React

In all situations there are natural reactions, and the way you react usually will show how the problem affects you. If two girls begin to fight, and you have never experienced this before, you may be shocked, surprised, or even amused. If, however, you catch a boy burning a hole with a cigarette in the upholstery of your new van, your reaction will be much different! In other words, your reactions will be based on the specific problem and your frame of reference. Learning how to react involves more than experience-it means taking four substeps: position, observe, listen, act. Let's consider them one at a time.

Position

Positioning means putting yourself in the right place. In the Barton/ Sanchez interchange, we know that Mr. Barton probably did not expect the fight between the two boys to occur. But if he was expecting a flare-up of some type, his timing was way off. When he did finally arrive, however, he positioned himself so that he could hear and see what was happening. He did not like what he saw, but he was wise enough not to intervene without knowing what was happening. He saw that he could not force Sanchez to stop fighting without placing himself in danger and possibly losing control of the situation entirely. Therefore, he stood where he was far enough away to be safe but close enough to see and hear.

Positioning requires placing yourself at a safe distance but close enough to understand what is really going on.

Observe

The second substep in reacting is "observing." This means looking at behavior, appearance, and environment.

Observing was not too difficult for Mr. Barton; he could see what was going on. Sanchez wasn't trying to hide anything. He had been "ratted on," and someone was going to pay. Barton could watch Sanchez act (behavior); he could see his angry expressions (appearance), and he was very familiar with the environment.

In many situations, however, observing is not so easy. Imagine yourself, for example, leaving church after a midweek program and walking toward your car. You notice several young people smoking behind the building. Because of the dark, you can't really tell what they are doing, but as you continue to look, you see that they are huddling around the basement door and fiddling with the window. As you approach them slowly, they walk away.

What did you learn? Were they planning to break in later, or just hanging around? Was their behavior out of the ordinary? (What were they

Responding to an Angry Youth

Some of the following suggestions for dealing with an angry young person are based on *The Aggressive Child* by Fritz Redl and David Wineman. These suggestions should be considered helpful ideas and not seen as a "bag of tricks."

1. Catch the young person being good. Tell him or her what behaviors please you.

2. Dont ignore inappropriate behavior that cannot be tolerated.

3. Provide physical outlets and other alternatives.

4. Use closeness and touching.

5. Express interest in the youth's activities.

6. Be ready to show affection.

7. Ease tension through humor.

8. Appeal directly to the young person.

9. Explain situations.

10. Use physical restraint.

11. Encourage young people to see their strengths as well as their weaknesses.

12. Use promises and rewards.

13. Say no!

14. Tell the young person that you accept his or her angry feelings.

15. Build a positive self-image.

16. Use punishment cautiously.

17. Model appropriate behavior.

18. Teach young people to express themselves verbally.

with basement windows?) What about their appearance-how did they look? Consider the environment—should they have been behind the church?

In every situation, you must observe and draw conclusions about behavior, appearance, and environment. You must decide whether what you see is normal or abnormal, comparing the present with what you know about similar instances in the past. At first, of course, many of your experiences with troubled youth will be new, so you will have to withhold judgment for a while. Fortunately young people are usually quite consistent with their behavior patterns and easy to read. After you have worked with them for a short time, you will recognize whether or not their acts, looks, and settings are normal.

Listen

The third substep of reacting effectively is "listening." This is important because *who* is talking, the subject of the talk, and *what* is said will all provide valuable clues. Listening carefully will also reveal the emotions and feelings involved.

Positioning and observing are prerequisites to listening. When you are in the right position, you will be able to hear better; and when you are observing carefully, you will better understand what is being said.

Often we think we are listening; but, in reality, we hear very little. This may happen because we prejudge the person who is speaking. The young person's looks, behavior, accent, sentence structure and grammar, choice of words, etc. may turn us off to his or her real message. Or we may prejudge because our values are different. Our language reveals these values, and we don't appreciate slang and four-letter words and can't

doing? Do young people usually hang around behind the church and play

understand the intensity of their rebuttals. To listen effectively, we must avoid prejudgments.

Another listening problem is concentration. It is very difficult to listen to someone when you have a thousand other things on your mind. Concentration becomes especially difficult when you are involved with more than one person at a time. Every parent knows that listening to one child while caring for another is almost impossible. To listen effectively, we must focus our thoughts and attention on the speaker.

Because of our inability to listen effectively, we don't hear what is really being said, and we miss key words. A young person, for example, can be yelling at the top of her voice, "I love marijuana. . . . I love booze." A typical, quick, first reaction would be to tell her to be quiet and not say words like "marijuana" and "booze." But besides the fact that she is being obnoxious, there may not be a behavior problem at all. If, on the other hand, a boy whispers through clenched teeth to another child, "I'm going to kick your $%#&$•@!! when we get out of here, you little •&%#$%!!" If your reaction to this interchange is, "I'm glad they're quiet for a change," the real message is lost because feelings and key words are not heard.

How does a person identify key words? Experience plays a major role. You will find, for example, that verbal threats are often voiced without emotion and are rarely followed through. It will not take a lot of experience, however, to recognize words like "fight," "kill," "get out of here," "leave me alone," "get lost," "chicken," and a smorgasbord of four-letter choices.

Failure to listen effectively also deafens us to underlying feelings and emotions. Is the person happy or sad? Does he wish for something or demand it? Has she been rejected? Are they angry and losing control, or rational? Feelings are a very important part of communication, and we must hear them.

When we do not listen effectively, we also miss *verbal signals*. These are like conversational signposts which tell us where the person is going. They can include threats, overstatements, desires, needs, problems at home, tensions at school or with friends, etc. These signals may be very loud and filled with emotion, or they could be quiet, given with very little feeling.

Sanchez was sending loud and intense signals. Mr. Barton, of course, realized this even before he positioned himself at the door and observed what was taking place. He knew that Julio was serious and not just fooling around.

Explosive situations, which escalate in their difficulty to be defused, often begin with loud and emotionally packed conversation. Many troubled youth get attention by speaking loudly and "acting out." On the other hand, rarely will a loud voice or an emotional mood alone lead to serious problems.

As you listen to words, listen also for strong differences in voice levels—when quiet talking becomes loud or when a noisy conversation suddenly becomes silent. You need to find out what has caused the change. Usually, verbal threats plus a drastic change in noise level and emotion equal danger.

Listening, then, means hearing the signals, picking out the key words, and catching the emotions.

Act

Acting is the last substep of reacting, and it involves two responses.

First, you must *stop* the behavior that is causing the current problem. For example, Barton had to stop Sanchez from fighting. If he had not, someone would probably have been hurt badly.

Your first responsibility in handling any problem situation will always be *physical safety*. You must protect yourself, bystanders, and those directly involved. Safety concerns supersede all others.

Most problem situations will not involve aggressive behavior like fighting, but often there will be the possibility of someone getting hurt. Young people can be hurt in many ways.

There are other behaviors which should be stopped. For example, a young person may be shouting at you. Before you can solve his problem, you will have to lower the decibels. In another case, a girl is planning to run away. By the time you get involved, she is out the door and walking down the street. You must stop the "running" before you can help her see another course to take. Or you see a boy stealing a bike. You must stop the stealing before you can help him learn that stealing is wrong. In these examples, specific actions had to be interrupted or stopped altogether before help could be given.

The second "acting response" is to *prepare* the person for further help. Ministering to troubled youth is a long-term process. Simply stopping present behavior does not deal with the underlying causes, so *preparation* follows *stopping*. Preparation means "turning the corner" or "leaving the door open" for the next step in the process. It may involve asking a question or telling how you feel about what you have just observed and heard. In either case, preparation, by definition, is getting the person ready for what comes next.

Returning again to the Barton-Sanchez scenario, we know that Mr. Barton recognized that there was a problem. He positioned himself close

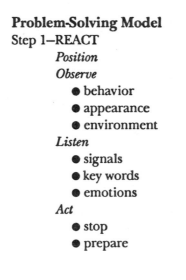

Problem-Solving Model

Step 1—REACT

Position

Observe
- behavior
- appearance
- environment

Listen
- signals
- key words
- emotions

Act
- stop
- prepare

enough to see and hear, but far enough away to be safe. He observed Sanchez's behavior, appearance, and environment. He listened to what Sanchez was saying, picking out the key words and assessing the emotions. His next step was to determine how to act.

Brian could have had several different responses. He could have called for outside help; yelled in anger at the boys; threatened Julio with "Sanchez, stop fighting or you're fired"; or tried to control the situation physically.

He understood, however, the importance of handling the situation in such a way so as not to jeopardize his future relationship with Sanchez. His real concern was to see Julio change, and he knew he could help.

His action, therefore, was to approach the boys and to ask, "What's going on here?" He used no verbal threats, no anger, no outside reinforcement; he just asked a simple question. Barton knew how to act. He decided that there was trouble and got involved. He stopped Sanchez from fighting but left the door open so that he would be able to continue to help. Now he was ready to move to the second step.

Step #2–Find out

Finding out means gathering information. The more you know about what is going on, the better you will be able to understand the situation.

Mr. Barton's "What's going on here?" was an excellent question to prepare for "finding out." He did not ask it, however, to gather information. If that had been his method for learning about what was really happening, he would have learned little. It is important to follow up with good questions which help us discover what we need to know. Like a re-

porter, we want to get the facts, so good questions try to uncover the who, what, where, when, why, and how.

● *Who* is involved? Who was with you? Who else was in on it? Who don't you like? Who did this to you?

● *What* are you doing? What are you going to do? What happened? (These questions also include "How?")

● *When* did this happen? When will it happen? When do they plan on doing it?

● *Where* did this happen? Where is it going to happen? Where are you going? Where are they?

● *Why* were you there? Why did you do this? Why is it going to happen? Why did they do this?

These questions should be asked in an atmosphere of love and help, not fear and interrogation. The way

Anger Covers Up Fear

Hostility or anger may also be expressed by the troubled young person. It is important for you to realize that much of the anger expressed by the young person actually masks fear—fear of not measuring up, fear of someone getting too close, and fear of change. If you can react to the fear rather than the anger, they will be much less intimidated and able to withstand the anger. The life of a troubled young person has been filled with anger which has usually been met with angry responses. What the young person desperately needs is to see mature responses and alternatives to anger. He or she needs to know people who can "keep their own cool" or regain it.

you ask the questions makes all the difference as to the information you receive.

As a young person answers your questions, watch his or her appearance and subtle actions—the nonverbal clues. This will help you understand the physical, social, and emotional state and assess motivation. It is true with troubled youth that "You can lead a horse to water, but you can't make him drink." If a person wants help, he or she will be more willing to answer your questions. For long-lasting results, the person must want to change and must expect that things will get better as a result of your questioning, even if the present experience is uncomfortable or painful.

As you ask questions in these five areas, you must also evaluate the answers: What was said or not said. Look for gaps in the story, and ask yourself whether it makes sense.

Remember, many troubled young people have learned how to stretch the truth. They know that the person who knows why they acted a certain way will probably judge them and make demands of them. Ironically, even when they have been hurt deeply, they will often withhold information. By telling the truth, they risk rejection.

Your challenge, therefore, is to learn as much as possible while reassuring the young person that you really care for him or her. The value of the information you receive will vary in direct proportion to how well you relate to the person. If a young person doesn't trust you, he or she won't tell you what you want to know. Finding out means learning "Who?" "What?" "When?" "Where?" and "Why?"

Step #3–Identify With

We have discussed reacting and finding out in a problem situation. Both of these steps are designed to help us collect information and to gain control of the situation before it gets out of hand. But we must do more; we must take the initiative and help the young person learn and change.

Unfortunately, many adults stop after the second step, content to halt the negative behavior and to figure out what has happened. Then they tell the boy or girl what to do, using familiar refrains such as, "John, you did the wrong thing. I don't ever want to see you do that again" or, "Sue, I know you disagree with me, but remember, this would not have happened if . . ." or, "Andy, we all have problems, but it is wrong to . . ." or, "Tyrone, here's what you have to do." Perhaps the *lecturer* feels better, but the speech does little good.

When we simply stop the behavior, gather facts, and then give young people our adult advice, they lump us with all the other adults in their lives who give familiar "should" and "ought to" messages. Advice giving doesn't create a positive, learning atmosphere, teach self-discipline, or let them know that we know how they feel. Steps three and four move beyond this and are the most important steps in the process.

To *identify with* means communicating your understanding of the facts and resulting feelings, helping young people explore the facts, feelings, values. Step two ("find out"), involves learning certain facts. Now, in step three, you report to the young person what you heard.

Identifying facts

Here it is important to "get the facts straight" and to repeat them accurately to the person. You could say

The Angry Youth

Handling young people's anger can be puzzling, draining, and distressing for adults. In fact, one of the major problems in dealing with anger in youth is the angry feelings that are stirred in us.

To respond effectively to overly aggressive behavior, we need to know what triggered the outburst. Anger may be a defense, shielding the person from painful feelings; it may be associated with failure, low self-esteem, and feelings of isolation; or it may be related to anxiety about situations over which the young person has no control.

Angry defiance may also be associated with feelings of dependency and closely linked to sadness and depression. In youth, anger and sadness are very close to one another, and it is important to remember that much of what an adult experiences as sadness is expressed by a youth as anger.

Before we look at specific ways to manage aggressive and angry outbursts, several points should be highlighted:

● We should distinguish between anger and aggression. Anger is a temporary emotional state caused by frustration; aggression is often an attempt to hurt a person or destroy property.

● Anger and aggression do not have to be dirty words. In other words, in looking at aggressive behavior in children, we must be careful to distinguish between behavior that indicates emotional problems and behavior that is normal.

● In dealing with angry young people, our actions should be motivated by the need to protect and to teach, not a desire to punish.

something like, "Ted, you're saying that Tim has been picking on you because he hates you. Is that right?" or, "Mary, what I hear you saying is that you can no longer talk to your mom because she is always fighting with your dad" or, "Sarah, I hear you saying that you don't want to get into the car because the others always make fun of you" or, "Joe, are you saying that you broke the window because Lou dared you to do it?"

Identifying the facts is rephrasing and summarizing in your own words what you hear the other person saying. Then, when you ask whether or not your summary is correct, you let the person know that you are trying to understand.

Identifying feelings

Even more important than identifying facts is knowing what the young person is feeling because

1. Feelings are more personal and immediate than facts, and they provide an inside look at the young person.

2. Feelings are a powerful motivator; young people act on what they feel. The more intense the feeling, the more likely they will do something about it.

You must deal with *feelings* to be fully effective.

Identifying feelings means communicating your understanding of what is going on inside the person emotionally; and it is important to get these feelings out in the open. You could say something like, "Cathy, it sounds like you're angry with your mom" or, "Dave, you are upset with the judge's decision" or, as Mr. Barton told Sanchez, "Don't worry about the job. I think I know how you feel." (He could have added, "Sanchez, you are angry because somebody told on you, aren't you?")

"Identifying," then, means finding out and verbalizing the correct facts and feelings. "Identifying *with*" means communicating your understanding of those facts and feelings.

Step #4—*Give direction*

Giving direction is the last step in handling problem situations effectively, and it could be best described as the bridge between insight and personal action. In this step, our goal is to help the young person

● understand what the situation means in relation to his or her real problem,

● see the problem in its most concrete terms,

● know why it is important to solve the problem,

● want to make the necessary changes in his or her life.

"Giving direction" involves five substeps, each of which builds on the others. They are (1) decide; (2) ask; (3) reinforce; (4) teach; (5) check up.

Decide

Your first decision is how best to control the behavior. More than just *stopping* a specific behavior, this means preventing the negative or unwanted act from *reoccurring* in the future. Your decision will be based on rules which you have already established with the group or individual, his or

her behavioral pattern, and the information that you have learned. Of course, if your expectations and rules are "unwritten," or even unspoken, now would be a good time to discuss them. In other words, let the offending person know how he or she has violated an expectation or rule.

You must also decide *how* you will ask the young person to do what you want, how you will enforce and reinforce your request, and how you will follow up in the future.

Ask

After you decide the best course of action to take, you must ask the young person to do what you want done. This is a natural part of any relationship, but *the way a person asks* is crucial. How you ask depends on the situation and the specific young person.

Sanchez, for example, was not ready to be told directly what to do. Because of his intense emotions, he would not have heard the directives.

You can speak mildly ("Would you please . . .?" or "I would appreciate it if you would . . .") or more emphatically ("I want you to . . ." or "I need you to stop doing that now"). Use the mildest method that will get the job done; you can always get stronger and more direct. Notice also, that in all of these statements, the focus is on "I." In other words, the statements are not impersonal nor are they judgments. Instead, they are statements from a caring authority to someone who needs direction and help.

Reinforce

Young people are usually motivated by consequences. They will do what brings them good results and avoid what hurts or brings bad results. Most troubled youth rarely have been rewarded for doing right and feel like they are only punished for doing wrong. They will have a difficult time understanding that being corrected is in their best interests because in the past this hasn't been the case. The main reason for using reinforcement is to heighten young people's awareness of the importance of their actions by making the consequences of certain acts (and failures to act) more clear and real.

"Reinforcement" falls into two categories: *verbal* and *physical*. Verbal reinforcement could be a warning, declaration, or proposition:

● *Warning*—"If you do not *(behavior)*, then *(consequences)*."

● *Declaration*—"Because you *(behavior)*, then *(consequences)*."

● *Proposition*—"If you will *(behavior)*, then *(reward)*."

Physical reinforcement can involve touch (positively) or a material or activity reward (something tangible) given or withheld.

Teach

This is the fourth substep to "giving direction." Teaching means

● determining the skill that they need to learn,

● demonstrating how to do the skill,

● helping them practice the skill.

Troubled youth lack the skills which allow them to handle problem situations effectively, and this lack of "life skills" leads to behavioral problems. It is necessary, therefore, to determine the individual's weaknesses which have been leading to his or her problems. Then you can help him or her learn that important skill.

Avoiding Mistakes

When encountering people with problems, often our response is to try to change their way of looking at things, to get them to see the situation as *we* see it. We plead, reason, scold, encourage, insult, prod—anything to bring about the desired change to the direction we want to travel. What we forget, however, is that we are usually responding to our own need to see the world in certain ways. It is always difficult to tolerate and understand actions which differ from our standards and norms. If, however, we can free ourselves from the need to push troubled youth along our own paths, we will be able to listen and to understand them.

A common dilemma is when you are asked to make decisions, judgments, and evaluations, to agree or disagree with someone or something. But the person's question frequently hides a real need which he or she is far more anxious to communicate.

Passing judgment, negative or positive, makes free expression difficult. And advice and information are often interpreted as efforts to change a person. Thus, both judgments and advice can be barriers to the development of a good relationship. Moreover, advice is seldom taken and information hardly ever used when it has not been sought by the young person.

In other words, some of the techniques and devices most often used in relationships are of little use in establishing open communication with young people.

In Sanchez's case, Mr. Barton would have to determine that Sanchez did not know how to control his anger. Then he would know where to emphasize his teaching. Most troubled youth learn best by seeing and then doing, and so Barton would have to do the skill with Sanchez. He could teach Sanchez to do something as simple as counting to ten before reacting or a more complex problem-solving method—whatever would help him control his anger. Then Mr. Barton would need to help Sanchez practice what he was learning. Youth learn by doing, so Barton could role play a specific situation or ask Sanchez to teach his new skill to another person. The practice would help the skill become an important part of Sanchez's life.

Check up

This is the last substep of "giving direction," and it means following through with what you have done so far and looking for other opportunities to teach.

It would be great if all problem situations would end with young people taking the initiative in solving their own problems, but that is very unrealistic. Instead, there will be setbacks, and at times, progress will seem very slow indeed. You must be prepared, therefore, to work hard at helping the young person translate this experience into future action. By checking up, you will be helping him or her develop an action plan to move from the present reality to where he or she should be. This means providing young people with enough direction and support so that they will resolve future problems on their own.

This happens one step at a time, helping young people see that by doing *A*, eventually they can do *B*. Each step, then, is a checkup and reinforcement of the previous one.

Checking up also means just taking time to ask individuals how they are doing in specific areas on which you are working together. By looking the person in the eyes and saying sincerely, "How's it going with _____," in a few seconds you can determine if the person is doing well or if help is needed. In either case you have let that person know that you care, that you are thinking about him or her, and that you are holding him or her accountable.

A checkup can also be an "extended review" where you sit and talk through the progress over the past few months, emphasizing the positive and reminding him or her of the incentives.

This process of working with an individual over an extended period of time will give you the opportunity to share how God and the Bible fit into his or her situation. He or she could be "ripe" for the Gospel.

THE SUM TOTAL

This, then, is the basic problem-solving model, illustrated on page 105.

Learning how to use this model will take practice. For a while, you must walk through each step as you go along; eventually, it will become second nature to you.

Along the way, you will discover some special situations which you will learn to handle only through experience. One such situation involves *defiance*—active rejection of your authority as the leader.

The symptoms of defiance include repeated rule breaking, stubbornness, and verbal retorts. Most adults find defiance to be very threatening or even frightening. When faced with

GIVE DIRECTION

Decide

Ask

Reinforce

Teach

Check-up

IDENTIFY WITH

Facts

Feelings

FIND OUT

Who

What

When

Where

Why

REACT

Position

Observe

Listen

Act

Is It Wrong to Get Mad?

Many people ask, "What should I do if I become angry?" When we hold out expectations and demands, we lay ourselves open to disappointment and anger when our expectations are not met. When we invest ourselves deeply in a person, we expect to see some return on our investment. This is only natural.

But we should be honest with youth when we are angry or disappointed in them. To attempt to conceal real anger would be dishonest. When we care about someone, we become angry when their behavior doesn't serve their best interest. Rather than try to conceal our feelings, it will serve the relationship much better if we openly admit our anger, express it, and proceed from there. This will serve to clear the air.

We must demonstrate the maturity, however, to recover from this emotion and resume the relationship. Young people who have received much anger will assume that anger equals rejection. They must be taught that rejection need not follow anger.

change from aggression and anger to fear and contrition. Also, your immediate silence to the challenge will alert the group that this is a serious matter; they will be watching to see what the consequences are.

3. Be decisive when you act, but in a calm and quiet manner. ("Speak softly, but carry a big stick.")

4. Refuse to "have it out" publicly when a young person wants to fight you, verbally or physically.

5. Let the person speak everything that is on his or her mind before you respond, and accept what is said as worthwhile, even if it attacks you or other staff members. Though many environmental and personal factors have influenced the person's actions, staff members are almost always part of the problem.

6. Admit when you are wrong.

7. Give firm and specific consequences for the person's actions.

Poor Self-concept

Another problem-solving situation that requires special handling involves helping a young person with a poor self-image. Troubled youth often believe that they are worth nothing and can accomplish very little. The following steps may help you bring down the barriers of poor self-concept.

a defiant young person

1. Remain calm so as not to be drawn into a power struggle with the young person. Avoid the natural tendency to strike back with a show of force. Force may succeed in suppressing the immediate problem, but it will probably involve losing your temper and/or humiliating the youth.

2. Pause for a few moments before responding. This will give you time to control your temper and to think about your next action. During this pause, the person's mood could

1. Try to identify the main source of a youth's negative feelings. It may be a parent who has always denigrated him or her, or there may have been a bad experience at school, etc.

2. Build a strong relationship with the person. Your acceptance and approval will demonstrate that not everyone thinks he or she is worthless.

3. Provide success experiences, building on his or her strengths and helping others notice. Praise him or

her publicly.

4. Place the person in a group and help him or her speak to others.

5. Share the fact that God loves the individual for who he or she is, not for looks or accomplishments and regardless of what others think.

Underachieving

Here are some tips for helping an underachiever—the person who does not perform up to his or her capabilities in school, at work, at home, or in your group.

1. Discover the area in which he or she works best.

2. Encourage development of that area of strength.

3. Extend his or her achievement to other areas related to the original strength or interest.

4. Reinforce the achievement—everyone needs praise.

5. Reinforce the positive verbal expressions (when they feel good about what they have done).

Discouragement

When the young person is trying to complete a very difficult task and is not succeeding, try the following:

1. Break up the task into small, manageable parts.

2. Offer rewards for accomplishing each part.

3. Communicate continually about his or her progress.

Lack of Motivation

Often troubled youth will not want to do what they should. Then your task is to motivate them.

1. Understand the person's background—why the specific task is not appealing, and what really "turns him or her on."

2. Use social rewards such as "points," awards, group memberships, special jobs, leadership responsibilities, and privileges.

3. Provide information. Discuss his or her abilities, interests, and vocational goals. There are many helpful tests available, but be sure that the personal information acquired is related to growth and understanding and will not be too threatening to the person.

4. Build on the individual's inter-

Depression

Problem situations often stem from adolescent depression. The two factors that characterize adolescent depression are "social abandonment" and "acting out."

Research suggests six core factors in depression. These are:

1. *Lack of self-confidence*—including guilt feelings, lack of energy, brooding, and sadness.

2. *Social abandonment*—including emptiness in life, death wishes, and social frustration.

3. *Loss of interests*—including difficulty in interpersonal communication.

4. *Sadness*—including weight change, grouchiness, frequent crying, and feelings of hopelessness.

5. *Somatic symptoms*—including disturbed sleep and feelings of loneliness.

6. *Acting out*—including desire to run away from home, aggressiveness, and lack of self-confidence.

Refer to chapter 11 for additional helps on dealing with adolescent depression.

ests. When you discover what he or she enjoys, use those interests as motivational tools. That is, provide rewards related to them or define the task in terms of them.

5. Include the person in the planning process. This will give him or her ownership of the task.

6. Provide counseling and guidance, using professionals and others.

7. Model with your life what you want your young people to become. Are your achievement standards realistic? Do you complete difficult tasks regardless of how you feel? Do you handle responsibility well?

8. Enlist the aid of others, establishing a supportive environment.

9. Use the family in this supportive environment. Parental discussion

---

Empathizing

A difficulty which many of us face is that of being unable to put ourselves "in the shoes" of the person who is facing difficulty adapting to society's demands. In addition, we can be overcome by the youth's situation once we begin to feel with him and recognize his problem.

Our task, as the helping person, is to develop the capacity to feel with him while retaining our objectivity. Everyone has experienced hurt during a lifetime, so it is difficult to avoid overidentification when we see other people struggling with similar situations.

Knowledge of ourselves is an important factor in helping. When we offer to help, we must be psychologically stronger than the person being helped. If we are not, we will be dismissed very quickly.

---

may help produce more positive attitudes.

Procrastination

When a young person habitually puts things off until the last moment (or doesn't do them at all), he is a chronic procrastinator. It's a good idea to establish rapport with the young person and then to help him or her define the problem. If he or she agrees to work on the procrastination problems, suggest the following:

● List the tasks which you are putting off right now.

● Identify the most pressing one.

● Prepare a plan for doing this as soon as possible; set the date and time.

● List the possible distractions which could prevent the on-time completion.

After you've worked through the previous steps, bring the person to the point of commitment to do the most pressing task. Draw up a contract if necessary. Then help him or her design a schedule for the next week.

Be sure to follow through with this person. Use incentives if necessary and work out further action programs together.

Slow Learning

Whether through the lack of education or mental ability, these young people consistently fall behind the group in learning content or skills.

1. Start a special group for those in this category so they can proceed at their own speed.

2. Accept the slow learner by finding as many ways as possible to say yes or to affirm him or her for what has been done.

3. Include the person in the plan-

ning process. Discuss what he or she can do and at what level.

4. Use simple contracts awarding progress, however small.

5. Avoid competition with peers.

6. Adjust the curriculum to fit the individual.

7. Remember that short-term goals are most effective.

8. Provide individual attention—tutoring (e.g., help with reading).

9. Recognize that the slow learner is a potential dropout from school. Make available vocational guidance.

10. Adjust your standards of achievement.

11. Find suitable materials and methods. This may include movies, stories, etc.

Minor Inattention and Misbehavior

When young people disrupt the group or disobey occasionally or in a minor way, take action quickly.

1. Make sure you can see the whole group. Arrange the seating so that this is possible (no one should be sitting behind a couch, etc.).

2. Ignore the very minor incidents. It is neither necessary nor advisable to intervene every time something occurs.

3. Establish individual eye contact. Look right at the offending party.

4. Touch the person gently or use a soft gesture to get his or her attention. Then, after establishing eye contact, get your message across by nodding, shaking your head, putting a finger to your lips, or pointing.

5. Move closer to the person.

6. Ask for a "task response." Having young people do something specific will command their attention while avoiding any mention of wrong behavior.

7. Praise desirable behavior. Instead of calling attention to the person who is causing the problem, praise a person near him or her for doing the right thing. When the offender changes, praise him or her too.

Showing Off

Some young people continually seek attention from their peers and leaders by trying to impress or entertain them. Now and then they may be talented and funny, but often their behavior is frustrating and disruptive.

1. Look for ways to give them attention and approval tied to good behavior. Inappropriate behavior should be ignored.

2. Be specific with the person about what you are praising. This will reinforce positive behavior and discourage showing off.

3. Reassure them constantly that they are liked and respected by you and the other leaders.

4. Be careful not to do or say anything that will call attention to the misbehavior or to make the person feel rejected when the show-off is too disruptive to ignore. A comment like, "We're having our small group now," would be better than, "Stop acting like a silly clown."

5. Delay attention rather than refuse it when the person seeks it at an awkward time.

Aggression

A basic principle of behavior modification is that desirable behavior should be rewarded and undesirable behavior ignored. This is very difficult to apply to the aggressive young person because he or she may hurt others or damage property. You will have to intervene.

Being Accessible

Being available to troubled youth means much more than being physically present. It means demonstrating your willingness to let him know you as a human being. We may be reluctant to become involved with the people we are supposed to help. Behind this reluctance has been a fear that if we become involved, we would be conned or disappointed. But a troubled youth will only learn to find his way in the world as he can see love in action.

Letting young people know you as a person starts by setting a positive example. Just as you have learned from positive examples in your life, so must your youth.

As a caring adult, you have a vital interest in the young person. Let this come through naturally, and you will find that youth will pick up these signals and respond to you.

1. Count to ten when the aggressive behavior appears (to make sure you are under control and to give you time to decide how to respond).

2. Don't hesitate to restrain the person physically (if possible) if the behavior persists. If he or she responds by straining to get away, making threats, or staging a temper tantrum, hold the person until he or she regains self-control.

3. Speak quietly but firmly while restraining the young person. Tell him or her to calm down and get control. Reassure the person that his or her concerns will be heard, but only after calming down.

4. Restrain the most belligerent person when two or more are fighting and they don't respond to your demands that they stop. Again, talk to the combatants until they calm down. *Do not get between two fighting young persons.*

5. Move the aggressive person to the side after he or she has calmed down. If the two who were fighting have stopped, they too should be removed from the scene.

6. Talk to the young person. Listen to what is said. It is important to help the aggressive person see the difference between feelings and behavior. Feelings should be accepted as legitimate or, at least understandable. Misbehavior is not acceptable. State clearly that he or she will not be allowed to hit others, destroy property, etc.

7. Remember, most fights are two-sided and rarely have similar causes. Sometimes conflict is better resolved if not interrupted. Also, look for teachable moments—many opportunities have arisen out of conflict.

Notes

[1]The problem-solving model in this chapter is based on principles from *The Art of Helping* by Robert R. Carkhuff (Amherst, Maine: Human Resource Development Press, 1977) and *Interpersonal Communication Skills for Correctional Management* by Robert R. Carkhuff, Tom Keeling, Richard Pierce, and John D. Blakeman (Amherst, Maine: Human Resource Development Press, 1977).

6. Communicating the Gospel to Troubled Youth

Now we come to the heart of the matter! We know who troubled young people are, we have learned the right steps to take to reach out to them, and we are prepared to handle special problem situations. So the question is, what do we do with this information? In other words, how can we effectively communicate the Good News of Jesus Christ to these very needy young men and women? Consider these situations.

Barry knew the time was right. A young professional and a volunteer youth worker, he had built a good relationship with Tom. Over the past several months, they had spent a great deal of time together, and Tom had begun to change. Barry was pleased and excited that Tom trusted him. They had even attended church together, and Tom seemed to enjoy it. Tom knew that Barry was "religious," and he would play some of the Christian "rock" tapes in Barry's jeep when they drove together.

So this is it, Barry thought as he picked up Tom for lunch. Afterward, Barry explained the Gospel while Tom listened. He tried his best to help Tom understand sin and the fact that Jesus had died a substitutionary death for him. Because of their friendship, Tom listened politely . . . and also declined politely to respond to Barry's Christ.

Barry was frustrated. He really thought Tom trusted him and that he would accept Christ as Saviour.

As the weeks passed, Barry found himself spending less and less time with Tom. He decided that perhaps he had "cast pearls before swine," and that he might better spend his time working as a youth sponsor for the church.

Barry invited Tom to attend the youth meetings, but Tom had drawn a few conclusions too. He had met enough of these "do-gooders," social workers, counselors, teachers, and now a preacher. They were all the same. If you don't buy their "bill of goods," they move on. With all that talk about being concerned for him as a person, he had hoped that Barry was different. Obviously he was wrong.

Ed was a good Sunday School teacher. He had a great group of very normal eighth-grade boys. For the most part, they were eager to learn and a lot of fun.

Dave Smith was the one exception.

Ed had met Dave through his mom, Evelyn Smith, who worked in the same office. During the six months of working together, Ed and Mrs. Smith had discussed many subjects, from the weather and sports to politics and young people. Eventually their discussions covered deeper topics such as spiritual matters and her personal struggles. Ed learned about her divorce, about the problems of being a single parent, and how Dave had been ignored by his father. And now Evelyn was struggling with alcohol.

After Evelyn decided to get help with her drinking problem, Ed became involved with her son, agreeing to take care of him so she could attend the outpatient program at the local hospital. At first, the relationship between Ed and Dave was a real struggle. They didn't click, and nothing Ed did to try to establish a friendship seemed to work. One day, however, Ed invited Dave to a party for the Sunday School class and to church on the following Sunday, and Dave said yes. Just having Dave attend was a success.

Often Ed would think about how he could share Christ with Dave. He would pray and prepare his Sunday School lesson well, only to have it fall on Dave's seemingly deaf ears the following Sunday morning.

One evening, as Ed was studying, he realized that this particular lesson would provide an excellent opportunity to present the Gospel because the subject was sin. He wondered how he could explain it in a way that Dave would understand. Then he got an idea.

Ed began his lesson by placing a chair on the table in the center of the room. Then he asked one of the boys to sit in the chair with the sign "God" hanging around his neck.

Next, he asked Dave to run slowly around the table. After a few times around, Ed told Dave to choose someone to get on his back. Ed labeled the piggyback rider "sin" and instructed Dave to continue running laps with his new load. A couple of minutes later, Ed told the boy in the chair (labeled "God") to get down and run alongside Dave and his "sin" burden. He had "God" offer Dave a drink of water (which he did). By this time, Dave was just about ready to collapse with "sin" on his back. Then Ed told the boy labeled "God" to offer to carry "sin" for Dave. Dave stopped running and "sin" climbed on the other boy's back. The second boy realized quickly that Dave had good reason to be tired.

After restoring order, Ed asked the class what they thought everything meant. It didn't take long for them to answer. Then Ed asked, "Do you ever feel that sin drags you down and makes life difficult?"

Class: "Uh . . . sometimes."

Ed: "What did you notice about sin?"

Ed watched Dave's face light with interest as he answered, "When 'sin' got on my back, it really slowed me down. I could hardly run."

Ed: "What did it mean when 'God' got down and offered help?"

Class: "Dave got the weight off his back."

Ed: "What did 'God' do that 'sin' didn't do?"

Class: "He helped Dave and didn't take a free ride like 'sin.' "

Ed: "How does this change the way you look at God?"

The class had never been so attentive—even Dave was listening. Ed looked at Dave and told the class this story. "Imagine yourself walking out in a field, and you suddenly come across a big anthill. You sit down in the dirt and begin watching those ants, fascinated by them. All at once, while watching the ants, you hear a tractor in the distance. A farmer is starting to plow the field, and you know that in only a few minutes, the sharp plow blade will rip through the anthill killing some of its inhabitants, scattering others, and leaving all of them homeless. You start yelling frantically at the ants, telling them to leave while they still have time; but they ignore you and go on with their work. They don't understand you because you are not speaking their language. You are just a large, noisy, wild 'thing' hovering over them. The only way that they would listen to you at all would be if you could somehow become an ant and talk their language. As you live with them and get to know them, they would learn to trust you. Then, in an impending disaster, they would listen to you.

"God loves us so much that He sent Jesus, His Son, to become a human being (like you becoming an ant) so He could tell us about God's love. God became a person like you and me. In John 14:6-7, in the Bible, Jesus says, 'I am the way and the truth and the life. No one comes to the Father [God] except through Me. If you really knew Me, you would know My Father [God] as well. From now on, you do know Him and have seen Him.'

"God 'came off the table' in the form of His Son in order to show us His love and to take our sin on Himself. Jesus has come to help us get to know God personally."

Ed continued to explain what it meant to give one's sin and heart to Christ. After class, Dave prayed and gave his life to Christ.

Both Barry and Ed wanted to communicate the Gospel to their young people. Both spent the time and paid the price to show that they really cared. Ed succeeded, but Barry did not.

In this chapter, we will discuss how to share the Good News of Christ with young people like Tom and Dave. The concepts and skills will be transferable and will make you a better witness for Christ. We will examine the *message*, the *listeners*, and the *communication process* including concepts, skills, and tools.

THE MESSAGE

The Gospel is Good News. It is not a negative pronouncement, a book of laws, or a funeral eulogy; and it isn't an argument or an apology. The Good News of Jesus Christ is the promise of eternal life and the only hope for personal change and abundant life.

Every person who responds positively to the Gospel does so through the work of the Holy Spirit in his or her life, not the clever technique of the presenter. But God has chosen to use people to share His message with other people. The Holy Spirit wants to work through us. Effective and responsible evangelism involves the balance of the following:

● *Proclamation*—verbal communication of the message

● *Relationship*—personal communication, winning the right to be heard, being a significant person in another person's life

● *Incarnation*—living demonstration of the message

Simply stated, the facts of the Gospel are as follows:

1. God is good, He is love, and He loves us (1 John 4:16; John 3:16).

2. Man has broken fellowship and friendship with God through self-centeredness and rebellion (sin) (Romans 3:23; 1 John 1:8).

3. The natural result of this break with God is death, eternal death (Romans 6:23; James 2:10).

4. In spite of our attitudes and actions, God continues to love us, and He sent Jesus to earth to rescue us from sin and death. (1 John 3:5; Romans 5:6-8).

● Jesus is God (Philippians 2:6).

● Jesus is man, but He is perfect (1 Peter 2:22).

5. Jesus died on the cross, in our place, taking our penalty on Himself (1 John 4:10; 1 Peter 3:18).

6. Jesus rose from the dead and lives today (Acts 17:2-3; Romans 8:34).

7. We can restore our relationship with God and have new, eternal life by renouncing our sin and believing in Jesus—accepting what He did on the cross and giving our lives to Him

(John 1:12; Acts 3:19; Ephesians 2:8-9).

● God forgives us and declares us "not guilty" (Ephesians 1:7).

● God gives us life (John 10:10).

● God makes us His very own children (1 John 3:1-3).

● God guides our lives through the Holy Spirit (John 16:13; Romans 15:13).

● God promises us heaven when we die (John 14:1-4).

You Are a Message
by Dr. Joseph C. Aldrich

Made any referrals lately? I should have a dollar for every person I've sent to a Honda dealership. I'm convinced my Honda Accord is a first-class winner. I'm more than satisfied; I'm delighted with it. Without a doubt, a satisfied customer is the best salesman.

Satisfied with Jesus Christ? How are sales? Referrals? You don't like the analogy? Well then, how's fishing?

Perhaps you're the strong, silent type. You really believe that "silence is golden." But is silence golden if boy or girl goes to hell because of it?

Is silence sin? You be the judge. If silence about Him is the same as "putting a light under a bushel," then that silence is a wrong silence. If the command to love a neighbor involves referring him to the One who is love, silence is wrong. If harvesting whitened fields has anything to do with talking about the saving grace of Christ, silence is wrong.

And if the Great Commission means what it says, if communicating is part of being a fisher of men, then silence for the Christian equals disobedience.

Hondas, Jesus Christ. Any comparison as to what value, worth, satisfaction? Buy a Honda, save a few dollars on gas, enjoy a fun car, share the good news. Jesus Christ? The way, the truth, the life. And the only answer to the longing of the human heart for peace, forgiveness, cleansing, life, hope, eternity. You'll talk about Hondas, but not about Him, the Wonderful Counselor, Mighty God, Everlasting Father, Prince of Peace? Under a bushel we hide the One who "took up our infirmities and carried our sorrows?" Should the One who was "pierced for our transgressions . . . and crushed for our iniquities" be our "secret Saviour"?

If He is a secret Saviour, your "God in a box," I'd suggest you start working on an explanation to give the One who said, "He who disowns Me before men will be disowned before the angels of God" (Luke 12:9).

Taken from *Life-style Evangelism*. Multnomah Press, 1981, Portland, Oregon.

Communication
by S. Rickly Christian

1. People don't know how to communicate today. This is due to the influence of television, etc. Studies show that the average father spends three minutes a day with his children.

2. Communication is the most important factor in the success or failure of interpersonal relationships. A child once cried, "I just need someone to talk to."

3. Five keys to communication:

- Be honest and open.
- Be positive and encouraging.
- Be clear so that you are understood.
- Communicate your feelings.
- Listen.

4. Lack of communication is the major factor in the two basic mistakes of young people:

- letting loneliness overwhelm,
- being content with surface relationships.

Taken from "The Big Ten," *Campus Life* magazine, February 1981, used by permission.

Effective communication begins with knowing the message. But this is just the beginning. This message must be translated into the individual language of the listener-the troubled young person.

THE LISTENERS

Every person is a unique blend of personality, talents, abilities, and needs, and so it is difficult to generalize about the "typical" troubled youth. But these young people *do* have special problems which we must overcome if we are to successfully communicate the Gospel.

Understanding needs

The troubled young person is a complex package of needs. Unlike average young people, he or she has social, physical, mental, and emotional needs which are not being met and which have little hope of being met in the future.

Typical evangelical approaches to sharing the Gospel are usually inappropriate and ineffective with troubled youth because their needs and other limitations become obstacles to understanding and knowing God. Consider the following:

- The young person who has learned not to trust anybody will find it difficult to trust God.

- The young person who models his or her life after self-centered parents and other family members will not understand Jesus giving His life for that person's sin.

- The young person who believes that love is for self-gratification will not comprehend God's love. This includes those who equate "love" with "sex"—a message prevalent in their music and peer group, and probably with their parents too.

- The young person who lives in emotional and material poverty will find it difficult to respond to an offer of "abundant life" from someone he or she cannot see.

- The young person with an underdeveloped or weak conscience will experience little guilt or sorrow for sin.

- The young person who does not trust the "establishment" will find it difficult to trust the God who is so often associated with the status quo.

- The young person who only

knows retribution will find it difficult even to consider the significance of God's forgiveness.

Because of these problems, the central concepts of the Gospel are foreign to most troubled young people. The communication challenge grows when you couple their emotional makeup with the learned art of superficial response (a form of "conning").

Breaking down barriers

How people learn is determined by their mental abilities, emotional makeups, and environments. We are born with capacity to learn, or "brain power" (and even this can be affected by diet and other environmental factors), but feelings and how we deal with them are, for the most part, learned from our parents and others.

Perhaps the greatest influence on how a person learns is his or her environment. This includes the motivation and climate for learning (Is education a high value in the home and culture?); the educational level of parents, siblings, and peers (Are they college graduates? Or high school dropouts?); the family's communication pattern (Do they think conceptually and talk in sentences?); and the nature of the schools (What are the qualities of the buildings, classrooms, and teachers, and what is the teacher-to-pupil ratio?). Because of deficiencies in all of these areas, most troubled youth will

● have very poor reading skills,

● have a limited vocabulary,

● have little biblical knowledge,

● learn by experience,

● need to meet pressing physical needs before they can really listen.

In short, troubled youth usually learn best in an informal, unstructured setting where the "teacher"

One Very Powerful Tool Is Active Trust

In some cases, trust can be a natural part of your day-to-day relationship with a young person—loaning him your car, letting him handle your money, giving him a key to your house. There are also some exercises that can help you manufacture trust situations with young people.

For instance, the "trust fall" is an effective demonstration of your trust in a person. Stand rigid, with your back toward your partner, and fall back into his or her arms. Of course, if you weigh 220 and your partner weighs 120, perhaps he or she could bring a friend to help. The idea is to learn trust through trusting. A troubled youngster is more likely to trust you and God when he himself feels trusted.

uses simple language and illustrations with which they can identify. This is quite different from those young people who have been reared in homes which value education and who have attended schools with innovative administrators and excellent facilities.

These differences and barriers to learning can be overcome by remembering the following:

● You will communicate better an hour after a good meal rather than an hour before it.

● You can compensate for poor reading and vocabulary by reading aloud to them, paraphrasing and explaining even marginally difficult words, using children's Bible stories, and never assuming that they understand.

● You can overcome their lack of Bible knowledge by sharing Bible stories as if you were speaking to a child of five or six (without talking down to them), keeping your language simple and using concrete terms that they understand.

● You can teach "love" and "trust" by helping young people *experience* love and trust, not just talking about them.

● You can teach concepts by using examples and everyday life experiences, as in the following example.

CASE STUDY

Beth is fourteen and lives on a farm with her divorced, alcoholic father. She has felt a need for love for a long time, and just recently, she has discovered that her maturing body has attracted attention, if not love, from a group of boys at school. One of Beth's neighbors is a Christian. The woman is concerned for Beth and has tried to build a friendship by bringing over a meal once a week.

"Love," the neighbor would say, "is different than lust." But Beth didn't understand. Then one day when they were out at the barn, a man from the

city drove into the farmyard looking for what he called "compost." Beth and the neighbor chuckled as he picked up some dried straw and manure and rubbed and sniffed it while commenting on what a fine mixture it was.

After he left, the neighbor had an idea. She shared with Beth that the kind of love Beth would receive from offering her body to the boys was a lot like the man who just left with a truckload of manure for which he paid $20.

She continued to explain to Beth that the boys' "love" seems attractive, but it really is only manure compared to the quality of love that God offers.

Beth understood her neighbor because the example hit her where she lived. She had just experienced a foolish "city slicker," very serious about a truckload of cow manure, and so she could see herself in the same light.

Correcting misconceptions

In addition to *needs* and *barriers*, we must be aware of the wrong ideas which troubled youth have about life, adults, and God. These misconceptions must be overcome if we are to effectively communicate the Gospel.

1. Adults can't be trusted. The experience of troubled youth is that adults take and don't give. Parents beat, abuse, drink, and don't love. Since God is often seen as the ultimate "adult," this is where your relationship as a caring, committed, and loving adult is basic to effective communication of the Gospel. If you bridge this gap of mistrust, perhaps the source of your love, God, will be trusted.

2. Authorities can't be trusted. In the eyes of troubled young people, teachers, deans, police, and other authorities seem to be looking for ways to "get" them. Often their fears aren't

---

Use the Teachable Moments

If you'll keep your eyes open, God will provide opportunities to present the Gospel very naturally. In the midst of the crisis of being kicked out of her house, one youngster was led to the Lord through John 14:1-3, "In My Fathers house are many rooms." By the way, it is tough to use the teachable moments if you aren't there for young people. Again, the relationship is the foundation.

entirely unfounded. Once youths are labeled "troublemakers," the worst is expected from them. Authorities, then, are seen as trying to make them look bad. If you are seen primarily as an authority figure, you will have to prove that your motives are sincere and that you really want the best for the young person.

3. *The "Christian system" can't be trusted.* Most churches that they know are run-down buildings or out-of-touch institutions. Troubled young people are very pragmatic; they believe in what works. For them to accept the Good News, they must see that the Gospel is valid and that it really works.

4. *God can't be trusted.* Much of a young person's mistrust of God comes from bad experiences that he or she has had with religious people (the aunt who is always on his back about church, the neighbor who is threatening God's judgment for her behavior, the "Jesus nut" preaching on the corner, etc.). They think, *If these are examples of what God does to people, He can stay away.* Another source of their mistrust of God comes from the terminology used to describe Him. If God is seen as an authority figure, a father, or an adult, He will be tossed into the mix of mistrust described above. (If a boy's earthly father comes home drunk and abuses his mother and him, he won't be too interested in getting to know a bigger, more powerful Heavenly Father.) And, of course, there are also the other misconceptions of God represented by popular songs and movies.

In our consideration of the "listeners," we have already suggested how to overcome obstacles to the Good News caused by needs, barriers, and misconceptions. Let us now take a closer look at how we can effectively communicate the Gospel.

THE COMMUNICATION PROCESS

Winning a troubled young person to Christ involves three basic steps. The first requires *building a friendly relationship*. This is the foundational step that God uses for sharing the Gospel. The Holy Spirit wants to work through you, so ask God to make you a channel of His love, to help you be consistent, to cover your mistakes, and to give you bold sensitivity. When you spend time with young people, getting to know them, allowing them to know you, and showing a genuine interest in them, you will begin to build trust. And when they trust you, they will listen to what you have to say.

Troubled young people often have

"While holding meetings in Egypt among some soldiers, I asked a big sergeant in a Highland regiment how he was brought to Christ. His answer was: 'There is a private in our company who was converted in Malta before the regiment came on to Egypt. We gave that fellow an awful time. One night he came in from sentry duty, very tired and wet, and before going to bed he got down to pray. I struck him in the head with my boots, and he just went on with his prayers. Next morning I found my boots polished beautifully by the side of my bed. That was his reply to me. It just broke my heart, and I was saved that day!" (Rev. J. Stuart Holden)

Taken from *Campus Life Guide to Student Leadership*, Youth for Christ, 1985, used by permission.

Good Samaritan

A class of seminary students was assigned a sermon on the Good Samaritan. They spent weeks studying the Scripture and commentaries to prepare their message about a Samaritan who had helped a man who had been beaten, robbed, and left to die. What they didn't know was that the professors "planted" a man along the path they would take to the lecture hall, and made up the man to appear to be beaten, robbed, and left to die. One at a time, they came to deliver their sermons, and one by one, they all walked around the man on the sidewalk. All of them flunked the exam that day, because the test was not to see if they knew the story or could communicate the story, but whether or not they would put into practice what Jesus was teaching.

Taken from *Ministry Resource Manual 5*, Youth for Christ, 1984, used by permission.

not received the emotional nourishment from their parents that they need. They may not have experienced consistent and unconditional parental love, and they very likely don't know what it feels like to be accepted and loved. If you say, "God loves you," they won't understand what you mean. But by demonstrating real love and forming meaningful relationships, you will provide a living example.

As we have discussed in previous chapters, relationships take time and personal commitment. Don't expect troubled young people to like and trust you immediately.

Sharing ideas is a second basic step to communicating the Gospel. As the young person accepts you, he or she will begin to accept your message about life and God. Your values will become sensible as you become what sociologists call a "significant other." Your consistent expression about what makes you "tick" and the advice you give about life will take on new meaning. It is during this step that the content of the Gospel is shared.

When sharing the "facts" about Christ and salvation, it is vital to speak in terms that young people understand. Watch out for multisyllable words and tired clichés. Your task is similar to that of a foreign missionary who must translate the Gospel cross-culturally, so be sensitive to cultural mores and language. And, as mentioned earlier, because these young people tend to think in concrete and pragmatic terms and not in concepts, you must communicate in ways they will appreciate—using stories, examples, and illustrations. Keep the message simple and personal.

The third basic step to sharing the Gospel involves *encouraging personal commitment*. This is the decision by the troubled young person to relate him/herself to the Christ seen in your life. You have presented God's Word to this confused mind and heart through your personal relationship, but his or her commitment to Christ will only take place after you have been a consistent example of a believer.

Remember that you must reach the point of confronting a young person with his need for Christ and the necessity of receiving Christ as Lord. Relationships are not enough; ideas and facts are not enough; trust is not enough. Each person must make a personal commitment to Jesus Christ as his or her Saviour and Lord. Of course, you will want to urge this commitment carefully and lovingly and when the time is right, but it is a necessity.

Remember to share the whole message of salvation including the consequences of this decision. Often a young person will "accept Christ" to relieve pressure or to please a leader. This is not what it means to become a Christian. Let your young people know that commitment to Christ is serious and requires obedience to Him daily. Don't give the impression that all their problems will be over or that their lives will change instantly. In fact, difficult times will probably follow a decision for Christ.

These three basic steps may overlap each other and have no sharp beginning or end. Sometimes it will be difficult to differentiate the steps as a young person moves through them. The Gospel and the basics of the Christian life should be presented throughout your contact with young people, but only at the third step will they make a genuine response to the Holy Spirit. Until then, their response will tend to be superficial, most likely aimed at gaining your approval. Even their "prayers" before step three, while verbally addressed to God, will probably be emotionally related to you.

It is impossible to schedule these three steps. Total development will probably take several months—perhaps even years. The time span will vary for each person. For some, the first step might be taken in three days; it could take eighteen months for others to reach that point. The same is true of the other steps. Each troubled young person will develop at his or her own speed, depending on background, environment, peer pressure, and relationship with you.

The Bridge

This is a helpful and familiar illustration for communicating the Gospel. It is included *last* because it will only be effective as it is presented in the context of what we have outlined above. Draw the following diagram on an index card, a restaurant napkin, or any available piece of paper, explaining it as you draw.

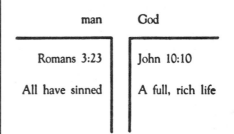

Begin by drawing a *chasm*. Explain that the gap between man and God is so wide that you cannot even see the other side. It's a chasm bigger than the Grand Canyon. Then explain that this gap exists because of the self-centeredness and rebellion of human beings (Romans 3:23). God *wants* us to have a rich, full life with Him, but we are hopelessly separated from Him (John 10:10).

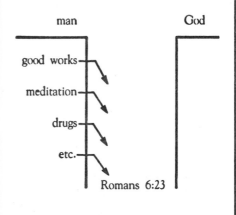

Next, explain how people try

many things to have a full, rich life; but all their attempts are futile, and they end up lost, in hell (Romans 6:23).

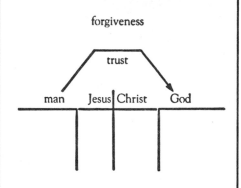

forgiveness

trust

man   Jesus│Christ   God

Finally, draw the cross in the middle of the chasm to illustrate how Christ has become our bridge to God (1 Timothy 2:5). Then explain how we can "cross the bridge" through personal commitment to Christ (John 1:12).

Prayer of Commitment

For *anyone* to become a Christian, he or she must profess personal faith (commitment) in Jesus Christ. This decision is made in the heart and expressed with the lips to God and to others (Romans 10:10). When leading a young person to Christ, explain that you will pray aloud for him or her. Then he or she should pray, preferably aloud, expressing the following to God:

● "I'm sorry for my sin and for living apart from You."

● "Thank You for sending Jesus to die on the cross for me and for making available forgiveness, eternal life, and a relationship with God."

● "Come in and take over as Lord of my life; I give my life to You."

Then you pray again, aloud, thank-ing God for what He is doing right now in this person's life.

Immediately following this prayer, be sure to give the young person two simple assignments:

● to read and think about a few Bible verses that you will assign,

● to tell another person who would really love to hear about what just happened in his or her life.

This is the heart and soul of our ministry with troubled young people—communicating the Gospel to them and leading them to a personal relationship with God. This process begins with a relationship, is smothered

What We Communicate Without Words

There are certain attitudes we are to have!

● Always be a beggar. Include yourself when you tell young people about sin and that Christ died for them.

● Keep it personal. Sharing your faith is sharing what Jesus did and is doing for you now—not just theory.

● Find out where the hurt is. The Gospel is like medicine. No one is interested in aspirin until they have a headache. No one will take penicillin until they have an infection they want cured.

"Christ loves you. He died for you and me." That is just a fact that hangs in space until kids see that it has something to do with their loneliness, their problems, their apathy, their inability to change themselves, their fears, etc.

Taken from *The Whole Person Survival Kit*, Youth for Christ, 1976, used by permission.

with love and prayer, continues with a careful and simple explanation of the Good News, and moves toward a personal decision for Christ.

7. Teaching the Bible to Troubled Youth

Cathy had accepted Christ as her Saviour a few weeks earlier. Now, fresh out of a drug rehabilitation center, she wanted to change. Her older friend, Lila, who had led her to Christ, told her that the Bible was a guidebook for living, and Cathy wanted to learn more about it. They met and began to read together, focusing on special verses scattered throughout the Bible. Lila thought that it would be helpful for Cathy to memorize Scripture, so she chose several about sin, one about God's love, and a couple about doubts. Lila was excited that Cathy was learning from the Bible and applying it to her life.

A few weeks later, Lila suggested that Cathy choose a verse to memorize. At their next meeting, Cathy was eager to share her selection, and she said that she had chosen one that reminded her of God's love. Then she proudly recited her verse: "If anyone conceives a child in my name, he conceives me."

After recovering from the shock of Cathy's fractured version of Matthew 18:5 and her interest in conceiving, Lila began to rethink her Bible teaching methods. She quickly realized that there is more to teaching biblical truth than memorizing verses.

Teaching the Bible to troubled youth can be hilarious and heartbreaking at the same time. In this chapter you will learn how to teach God's truths in a way that is both effective and exciting.

Before you can teach effectively, you must consider your audience. This is true in any teaching setting but especially with troubled young people. Lila, for example, made certain assumptions about Cathy (such as her ability to read and to understand what she was reading) which led her to give Cathy the counterproductive assignment. Though you will never know an individual completely, there are certain facts to consider which will affect how you teach the Bible.

HOW TROUBLED YOUTH LEARN

Deficiencies

A person's background directly affects how he or she learns; and the backgrounds of most troubled young people are woefully deficient. Each person is strongly influenced by heredity and environment, and how a troubled youth learns will be directly related to the quality of his or her home, neighborhood, school, friends, and personal history.

Assuming that you already know the general facts about the person, you should also be aware of specific and present influencing factors. For example, is the person ill or hungry? Is she struggling with a conflict at home? Does he carry guilt over an act in his past? Is pressure being exerted by her boyfriend? Because you have a friendship with this person, you should be able to sense any conflict or turmoil. It also will be helpful, however, to ask how things are going in his or her life. Besides providing valuable information, your question will demonstrate your concern for him or her as a person.

Differences

In general, all young people learn in the same way. That is, they process and organize information according to meaning. Research indicates that new information is stored in the brain in the categories formed from information used previously. In other words, the brain is like a house with different rooms and closets where information can be stored. When a new fact or concept comes in, it is placed in the room where the receiver believes it fits best. If it doesn't fit there, he opens a new "room" or forgets the information. For this new room to be opened, however, the new information must be understood. Some troubled youth need to open new rooms in their storehouse to retain what you are teaching them. This means that other information must be supplied to help the new data find a place and stay there. Knowing this, it is also important to realize the unique factors in how troubled youth learn.

● *They tend to process information more slowly.* This can be caused by neurological problems, poor reading skills, deficient background information, or a number of other factors. Regardless of its cause, this slower process means that there is a higher risk of losing new information because it cannot be classified (put in its room) with supportive facts (the

Becoming Familiar with the Bible

Teach familiarity with the Bible by giving one to your young friend, remembering the psychology of having something brand new. To give an urban youth an old, beat-up Bible only reinforces the feeling of getting a "hand-me-down." A new Bible stresses self-identity, self-worth, and new purpose in life. You should place your address and phone number on the front page along with a personal note. Choose a Bible that reads easily, such as *The Living Bible*. It is helpful for you to have the same version as your friend, so you can use page numbers to find your place along with book, chapter, and verse references. Be sure to go through the table of contents, identifying the Old and New Testaments and explaining them simply.

explanation process) quickly enough.

● *They tend to be late afternoon or evening learners*, as opposed to morning learners. It is ironic that most public school alternative learning programs for troubled young people are designed for a shorter school day—one that begins early and ends early. Many young people start to hit their learning peak each day right after school lets out.

● *They need a variety of learning modes and methods*. Effective teaching should utilize sight, touch, hearing, and movement. Lecturing is the least effective teaching method. Troubled youth need to see and do as well as be told.

Disabilities

Many troubled young people have learning disabilities, conditions which interfere with the learning process. Obviously, these will greatly affect the success of any teaching that you provide. Learning disabilities fall into two categories: *hard* and *soft*.

Hard disabilities have a physical or neurological cause and include sight and hearing problems as well as dyslexia and similar learning disorders. Though we should be aware of these problems, realizing that they will greatly affect a young person's ability to learn, we cannot help him or her overcome them without professional help. Instead we must turn to a specialist who can help the person adapt to or compensate for his or her disability.

Soft disabilities are caused by "controllable factors" and can be overcome. Soft disabilities include hyperactivity caused by diet, blocks resulting from emotional difficulties, poor reading skills, and others. Many of these root causes are addressed in the pages of Scripture (e.g., forgiveness, love, self-acceptance, etc.), and

---

Prayer

There should be a time for prayer when you meet with troubled youth. Remember that as you pray you are teaching them to pray. And when you pray, use terms and words the teenager can understand and also use.

Be aware of the "in" attitude regarding prayer. Many young people use prayer as a magic formula or a pious act. They feel that if they get on the right side of God, He will do anything they want, that God can be manipulated and bribed. When their prayers appear (by their standards) to be unanswered, they think God is angry with them or they feel that prayer does not work. Prayer is a good example of an abstract concept that is difficult to teach.

---

nonprofessionals can be of significant help. We must be aware of these and deal with them if we are to teach effectively.

HOW YOU SHOULD TEACH

Assuming that you know the troubled young people-how they learn, including their deficiencies, differences, and disabilities—understanding some basic teaching principles will help improve your communication skills.

Principle #1–Keep it simple

Remember that your audience is younger and less educated and sophisticated than you are, so don't expect them to catch the subtle nuances of a passage, a profound concept, or your deep theological insight. Instead, constantly relate the Bible to their levels of understanding. This can be done

Teaching Trust

A simple way to teach trust is a trust walk or a trust fall in which a blindfolded individual is required to trust someone whom he cannot see. It is important not just to talk about such a concept but to actually let young people experience it, then to discuss how it felt. Then it is easier to discuss the concept of faith in a God whom they also cannot see but who has made certain promises to them.

by:

● speaking in short sentences with understandable words and phrases

● using illustrations with which they can identify

● having one main point for each lesson

● making specific life applications

● moving slowly

● asking questions to see if they understand

● reading from a recent Bible translation (i.e., *The Living Bible*).

Biblical truths are simple and profound. Beware of complicating the message.

Principle #2–Start with the concrete

When learning a new concept, most young people need to move from concrete experiences to the abstract. What is real and understandable to them is what can be encountered by the five senses. This is very important to remember when teaching the Bible. Concepts such as "love," "salvation," "faith," "Christian growth," and "sin" must be taught in terms that they can understand.

"Trust," for example, could be taught by referring to an experience in their lives, by using an object lesson, or by structuring an opportunity for them to trust you or others. Then the parallel between the concrete and the biblical concept can be drawn.

Scriptural truths must be made real to be understood.

Principle #3–*Keep it interesting*

Too frequently the Gospel is presented in a matter-of-fact, uncreative manner which neither captures nor maintains the young person's interest or imagination. It will take preparation, but you can teach the Bible creatively using a variety of approaches and techniques such as these:

● *Felt needs*–Begin by discussing something that they feel deeply or with which they are struggling (sexual temptation, loneliness, hate, etc.), and then apply scriptural teachings.

● *Stories*–Young people enjoy listening to good stories. You can draw these from the Bible or from life, but in either case, be sure the story is told well with the lesson or moral clearly depicted.

● *Case studies*–A case study is a story about a person who is confronted with a moral dilemma and who must decide among two or more options. The dilemma is not resolved in the story. Instead, the listeners must make the moral decision. ("If you were Sharon, what would you do?") The various choices can be discussed in the light of biblical principles.

● *Values clarification exercises*– These group and individual exercises help people think through their values. Usually a situation is set up where priorities must be determined and choices made. (e.g., "Ten people are in a lifeboat. . . .But the boat only holds five. Who should be allowed to stay in the boat and live?") Again, the values expressed can be compared to biblical priorities and values.

● *Simulation games*—These group activities give everyone the opportunity to experience a specific situation. For example, a small group could be given a six-foot board and the instruction to get everyone over a rope which is five feet off the ground, stretched between two trees. The rope is an "electric fence," so no one is allowed to touch it or go under it. To accomplish this, the group members must solve the problem and work together.

● *Starters*—These short "games" are fun and set the stage for the lesson. An example of this would be an "indoor scavenger hunt" where group members must produce a list of items as you ask for them. As the leader, you know that each one relates to "love" (or another topic). After determining the winner, you could ask about the specific items, how they chose them, etc., and then move into a discussion of 1 Corinthians 13.

● *Art and drama*—Tap the creativity of your young people and use their talents as vehicles for interacting with biblical content. Act out a Bible story together. Then you could discuss the characters, their faith in God, and how God helped them in the situation.

Regardless of the methods used, you must have a communication strategy. That is, you must know where you are going. After assessing the group's (or individual's) knowledge and understanding of biblical truth, you should ask yourself, "What do they need to know to have a fuller comprehension of God's love and forgiveness and of commitment to Christ?" Then develop a communication approach which begins where they are and successively adds to their knowledge and understanding. Always remember to translate the

Seeing Themselves in Scripture

In teaching the Bible to troubled youth, it is important that they see themselves in the Scriptures. The Word cannot be some abstract book with little or no relation to who they are. Bible study should be used to help reinforce values, moral decisions and other life choices.

Bible into their "language."

Principle #4—Begin where they are.

Do not assume that any young person has attained a specific level of biblical understanding. Words and phrases whose meanings are obvious to you may be totally incomprehensible to a troubled youth. Carefully explain your clichés and avoid

Program Ingredients for Effective Correctional Education

1. Understanding teacher

2. Individualized diagnosis

3. Specific learning goal

4. Individualized program

5. Basic academic skills

6. Multisensory teaching

7. High-interest material

8. Sequential material

9. Rewarding attention and persistence initially

10. Differential reinforcement of learning performance

Taken from Dennis A. Romig, *Justice for Our Children*, D.C. Heath and Company, Lexington Books, 1978.

Teaching Commitment

As you teach youths with backgrounds of disappointment and rejection, it is important to present the complete message of Scripture. They will eagerly accept anything they feel will take away their problems. But if they begin to think what they hear is not working, they will quit. Therefore we must stress their *commitment* to God, not merely an escape from sin and life's problems. Yet, they may not understand the meaning of commitment. Often their parents have broken their commitments to each other. Your example of commitment to God and to them may be their first model of true commitment. Show them by your example your invincible commitment to God and your unconditional love for them. You are the most vivid communication of the Scripture most of them will ever see.

"ecclesiastical" terminology whenever possible. And be patient. It will take some time for troubled youth to gain enough Bible background and information to understand what you have

been trying to teach them. This means that you will have to lay a foundation which is relevant to their needs and then build on that foundation by communicating, over a period of time, essential biblical truths. Some truths which relate directly to their needs are:

● God accepts us and wants to forgive us even though we don't deserve it.

● God sincerely loves us and wants us to respond to Him.

● God and human beings may differ on what judgment is.

● People are valuable to God, and they can change through His power.

● God knows us thoroughly, as we are . . . honest and dishonest, trustworthy and untrustworthy.

● It is not enough to know what God wants us to do; we have the freedom and responsibility to decide to obey Him.

● The Bible is God's way of telling us His plans and purposes.

In addition, as we discussed in Chapter 6, troubled young people often harbor serious misconceptions about God. For example they may think:

● God is capricious (changes abruptly, for no good reason).

● God enjoys punishing people.

● God only cares about people who are good and who keep the law.

● God is the One who has kept certain people "down," trapped by their environment or past experiences.

● The Bible is irrelevant to their lives.

● God cannot be trusted.

● God is not fair.

These misconceptions may have come from their experiences with eccentric religious people, "folk religion," or adults who use "the fear of God" to intimidate and punish. Or they may have arisen from observations about life—the fact that some people seem to get away with wrong actions, etc. The only way to begin to dispel these misconceptions and to build a true understanding of God is to build a relationship with the person and to be an example of a real Christian. Then you can show and tell them what the Bible says about God.

One of the most effective teaching

methods is to be a living illustration of a biblical truth. Young people who feel rejected and inadequate need to know that God loves and accepts them, "no matter what." They will believe that this is possible as you love and accept them. Troubled youth must know that God's forgiveness cannot be earned but is offered freely to those who confess and repent. They will begin to believe in God's forgiveness as they experience yours and the healing of a relationship. Troubled young people need to know that God can be trusted and that He will never leave them. They will begin to believe in His faithfulness when they see you persist in your attempt to be their friend and to bring them to Christ.

Effective teaching of the Bible must begin where the young person is in his or her understanding of God and His Word.

SEVEN KEY STEPS

The following seven steps for effective teaching apply to teaching anything to anyone, and they are most appropriate when applied to the difficult task of teaching troubled youth. These steps have been gleaned from a review by Dr. Madeline Hunter and her colleagues of 20,000 research studies of the educational process. By following these steps, you can build your ability to teach the Bible to young people.

1. Focus–Why do the learners need to learn this? The focus gets students ready to learn. This can be accomplished by explaining why the material is important, presenting the advantages of learning this, and relating the material to their life experiences at school, home, neighborhood, or church.

2. Objective–What do you want the learner to learn? Simply tell them what you are going to teach them. State what you would like to see happen as a result of this time together.

3. Input–What content do you want them to learn? How will you teach this content? In this step, select the material to be taught and the appropriate teaching methods. Teach to your objective by using creative teaching methods.

4. Example–How can you show them what you mean? Don't just talk about

Teaching Methods

1. Brainstorming
2. Buzz groups
3. Case histories
4. Chalkboard
5. Charts
6. Conversation
7. Choral reading
8. Debate
9. Direct Bible study
10. Discussion
11. Field trips
12. Filmstrips and slides
13. Flannelgraph
14. Interview
15. Lecture
16. Maps
17. Memorization
18. Motion pictures
19. Models
20. Objects and object lessons
21. Panels
22. Picture studies
23. Problem-solving
24. Projects
25. Quiz
26. Question and answer
27. Reports
28. Review
29. Role playing
30. Skits
31. Storytelling
32. Symposiums and forums
33. Testimonies

it, give them a concrete example. Anyone can demonstrate the concept or skill that you are trying to get across, including another volunteer, a film, a young person, or yourself.

5. Check–Do they understand the material? Check to make sure the content and process are at the correct level of difficulty. Use a variety of monitoring devices such as raised hand, discussion, sharing with a neighbor, or comment cards. Monitor throughout the teaching session.

6. Practice–How can you let them try it? Learning plus practice equals retention. Give them an opportunity to practice with immediate feedback and reinforcements.

7. Assignment–How can you help them apply this to their lives? The assignment provides an opportunity for independent practice. Summarize the lesson, ask for questions and comments, and then give the assignment. Have young people report back to someone during the week or at the beginning of your next meeting. The assignment is not complete until they report back.

Whether teaching on an individual level or with a group, it is important to follow these steps. Usually, *teaching* stops after the *input*. But lasting lessons are taught in the *example, check, practice,* and *assignment* stages.

Sample Lesson

See how the sample lesson begining on page 133 adheres closely to the "seven steps for effective learning," providing an excellent example of the principles discussed in this chapter. It is taken from a Youth for Christ workbook entitled, *Breaking Free: How to Get Going and Keep Growing as a Christian.*

This is lesson seven on prayer and it is reprinted by permission of Youth for Christ/USA.

IN SUMMARY

Teaching the Bible to troubled young people does not have to be difficult—but it must be intentional. In other words, you must understand how troubled youth learn; and then, using sound teaching principles and following the effective teaching steps, you can prayerfully, carefully, and creatively teach them His truth, helping them understand and apply God's Word to their lives.

I Need to Pray

(Focus)

(Objective)

When you were very young, you learned how to talk. Learning how to talk was very important because you can now tell others how you feel and what you need. In the same way, learning how to talk with God is important. This lesson will teach you how to talk with God so you can tell Him what you feel and what you need.

(Input)

If you were visiting Washington, D.C., and wanted to talk to the President of the United States, do you think you could walk into the White House and begin talking with him? Probably not. The President is a very busy person with a lot of people to talk to. It's a great honor to talk to the President. He is a very powerful man.

God is much greater than the President. You might think He would never want to talk with us. However, strange as it may seem, God wants us to come to talk with Him. Wouldn't it be exciting to visit with the Person who made you? Don't you want to talk with the Person who could tell you everything you need to know and who is always willing to help? God is never too busy. He wants to talk with you. Talking with God is called prayer.

(Check)

Read Philippians 4:6-7

What is the wrong way to handle problems?
To w__ __ __ __.
What should we do?
P__ __ __ about everything.
T__ __ __ God about our needs.
T__ __ __ __ Him for His answers.
What does God promise to give us?

(Input)

How would you feel if you knew what your friends needed and could help them, but they wouldn't talk with you? In the same way, God feels sad when you won't talk with Him. Prayer is simply talking to God as you would a close, trusted friend and telling Him what you feel and what you need.

Because God is perfect and knows everything you need, how do you think He would answer a prayer if you asked for something that He knows would not be good for you? That's right. He wouldn't give it to you. Because God knows everything, He can decide what's best for us. We can trust God; God won't make a mistake. Prayer is not trying to persuade God to give us what we want. Prayer was made to help us discover what God wants us to do.

(Example)

Sometimes we feel that God doesn't hear us, or that He refuses to answer our prayer. But God always answers our prayers. Sometimes He answers, "Yes, it's best for you." Sometimes, "No, it's not best for you," or "Wait, I have a better time."

Mark the one best answer.

Suppose you pray and nothing happens, then:
( ) this proves that God isn't listening.
( ) this might be the wrong time and God wants you to wait.
( ) this prayer is a waste of time.
( ) this proves that God is mean and trying to make you unhappy.

(Check)

Mark what is true for you.

When I pray . . .
( ) I feel good.
( ) I don't feel anything, but I think God is listening.
( ) I never pray.
( ) I don't feel anything, so I'm not sure God is listening.
( ) I feel silly.
( ) I feel _____.

(Objective repeated)

Remember: Prayer is talking with God. God is always ready to listen and help us. God knows what is best for us.

Read Matthew 6:9-13 and do the matching quiz below.

The model prayer of Jesus contains guidelines we should follow as we pray. These guidelines are listed in the left column. In the right column is the Bible verse for each particular guideline. Match the verses to the guidelines. One verse may contain more than one guideline.

(Creative teaching method)

A. Pray for God's will to be done on earth as in heaven. ——Matthew 6:9
B. Pray that God's name may be honored. ——Matthew 6:10
C. Pray to God as "Our Father."
D. Pray for forgiveness of sins. ——Matthew 6:11
E. Pray for deliverance from temptation and evil. ——Matthew 6:12
F. Pray for daily bread.
G. Pray that God's kingdom may come on earth. ——Matthew 6:13

(Creative
teaching
method)

Memory verse: Philippians 4:6—Tell God your needs
"Don't worry about anything; instead, pray
about everything; tell God your needs and
don't forget to thank Him for His answers"
(*The Living Bible*).

(Practice)

Stop right now and talk to God. Silently tell Him just
how you feel about what we have talked about.

(Assign-
ment)

Now, think about something you really need. Read
Philippians 4:6. Pray to God about it every day this
week.

8. Teaching Pro-Social Skills

Graeme is in the process of discipling a young man who has come to know Jesus Christ as Saviour in the last several months. Graeme has known Bob for more than a year. A year ago Bob showed up at the high school wrestling match drunk and "wanting to take on the world." Graeme, as the college intern coach, was asked to usher Bob out. Now seventeen, Bob is every bit as big physically as Graeme and can certainly hold his own in the weight room where they spend time together at least twice a week. Graeme is ambitious about teaching him the basic truths of Scripture but realizes all too well that it is going to take a lot of hands-on help.

Graeme has also talked to school officials in Bob's behalf. A year ago Bob was expelled for poor attendance and "non-compliance" —he spent too many noon hours smoking and fighting on school property. Now school officials are not very optimistic about his re-enrolling.

Recently Bob has started to listen to his friend Graeme, who is almost like an older brother. Bob says he really wants to try and be an example to some of his peers. One afternoon in the weight room Graeme confronts Bob about stopping his smoking and partying with old friends who are still getting into trouble.

Bob replies, "What's wrong with that? What does it hurt? When I don't get up until noon anyway, why not stay out late? I get plenty of sleep."

"You think that's what God wants you to do?"

"Umm, I don't know. . . . but I'm not going to stay home and listen to my old man bitch at me about getting a job and making something of myself."

Graeme has met Bob's dad and is aware that he is often drunk if not abusive, and only avoids hitting his son because Bob is very capable of defending himself.

"Why not get a job, Bob?" Graeme continues.

"Man, I tried. Two times. They never called me."

"Where did you go?"

"Paint store," Bob answers. "There was a sign that said they wanted part-time help."

"Have you tried any place else?

"Where? . . . I don't know . . . I don't like talking to those guys."

"Bob, how are you going to get a job if you don't go try?"

Then it hit Graeme. How could Bob ever get a job? He doesn't read well. He can't write so you can read it, and he just plain can't spell. Furthermore, Bob hasn't learned to communicate with adults at all, let alone make a favorable enough impression to get a job. Even if Bob were to get a job, could he work? Could he get along with other employees without becoming aggressive? And then there's the drinking problem.

Teaching kids biblical concepts such as prayer is just the beginning of a much longer discipleship process of teaching them how to do what the Bible says. The real challenge comes when the biblical concepts have been taught but the youth's behavior hasn't seemed to change all that much.

Behaviors that many find easy and commonplace in middle class America (carrying on a conversation, interviewing for a job, etc.) can present major hurdles for a young person who has not developed the necessary skills and whose deficiencies are compounded by emotional, behavioral and social issues. In addition, troubled youth who are capable of demonstrating appropriate social skills still may have a difficult time recognizing when, where, and with whom to use a particular skill. To complicate matters further, successful interactions depend, to a large part, on the ability to perceive and correctly interpret the nonverbal behaviors of others and to demonstrate sensitivity to their points of view.

Troubled youth are often individuals who develop a variety of aggressive, acting-out behaviors in combination with a considerable lack in alternative, pro-social behaviors. They may be skilled at fighting, insulting, bullying, intimidating, or manipulating others but quite inadequate when it comes to more desirable behaviors such as negotiating differences, dealing appropriately with accusations, responding independently to peer pressures, or understanding their own or someone else's feelings.

Over the last few years there has been an increased interest in developing and implementing alternative education programs that teach these pro-social skills. As the secular "alternative school" movement continues to grow (for both educational and political reasons) the lessons learned will help to broaden our understanding of how best to teach troubled youth to do what the Bible says.

START WITH THE BASICS

Graeme is a good example of someone faced with the difficulty of teaching social skills to a troubled young person. These kids typically lack so many skills that it's difficult to see the forest for the trees and come up with an approach to teaching that gets the job done. With so many skill deficiencies it may seem difficult to even know where to start.

Believe it or not, teaching life skills is, in practice, just helping kids learn how to do what the Bible says as they live, day to day, in the real world. Principles to follow in this teaching are similar to the ones you learned in the previous chapter. And the place to start is identifying the skills the young person needs to learn.

This may seem like a major hurdle, but, in reality, most deficiencies are pretty easy to spot. The best place to start is usually with the most basic skill needed. Here is an example.

When I was a much younger parent my wife was working the evening shift and delegated to me the responsibility for toilet training our son. For reasons all parents of sons will understand, the first skill I taught him was how to distinguish between the bathroom and other rooms in the house. Next, I taught him the skill of removing his pants. Then I helped him learn how to sit on the toilet seat. After that everything else kind of fell into place (excuse the attempt at humor). The point is, if I had

As human beings, we live in social groups. Most of us learn early in life that there are consequences, both positive and negative, attached to how we interact with the people and things around us. This process of "socialization" that began in the earliest interaction between us and our parents, prepares us for more complex situations as we grow and mature. Ideally, lessons learned in each stage of our life become the tools that are used to successfully meet the demands of subsequent stages of life.

Today, however, adolescents are confronted by an increasingly difficult world. Family problems, substance abuse, economic pressures, and the lure of gangs and "trouble" threaten kids physically, emotionally, and spiritually. The tools required to successfully cope with these internal and external pressures include the ability to interact with others in socially acceptable ways and to make appropriate choices in life.

The simple truth is that teaching a troubled young person even the most basic social skills is complex and difficult—many youth will not develop these skills without active interaction and encouragement from caring adults. Consequently, it is up to those of us who are called to minister to troubled youth to accept the fact that teaching pro-social skills is an integral part of the discipleship process. Remember, teaching a troubled youth that God can help him cope with his "day to day" problems as well as his spiritual shortcomings is one of the most important contributions you can make.

started him off on the seat without teaching the other skills, the two of us could have had some real relational problems. But I started with the most basic skill.

Using the illustration of Graeme and Bob, we can see how this principle of starting with the most basic skill applies to teaching troubled youth. Bob has considerable deficiency in a number of skill areas. He needs to learn how to read, write, spell, communicate, apply for a job, stop drinking, and control his aggressive behavior. So, where does Graeme start? Teaching Bob the basics of how to communicate. When Bob learns how to ask for help, express his feelings and carry on a conversation, Graeme and others will be able to teach him how to get a job, complete his G.E.D., and control his impulsive behavior.

Following is an inventory of some of the most basic skill deficiencies typically identified with troubled youth. This is not an exhaustive list but will be helpful as you evaluate where to begin with your young person.

For each young person, rate his or her use of each skill based upon his or her behavior in various situations.

Circle 1 if he/she is NEVER good at using the skill.

Circle 2 if he/she is SELDOM good at using the skill.

Circle 3 if he/she is SOMETIMES good at using the skill.

Circle 4 if he/she is OFTEN good at using the skill.

Circle 5 if he/she is ALWAYS good at using the skill.

SKILL

Listening	1 2 3 4 5

SKILL *continued*

Communicating honestly	1 2 3 4 5
Getting another person's attention	1 2 3 4 5
Asking for help	1 2 3 4 5
Following directions	1 2 3 4 5
Avoiding trouble with others	1 2 3 4 5
Using self-control	1 2 3 4 5
Saying "no" correctly	1 2 3 4 5
Understanding the feelings of others	1 2 3 4 5
Helping others	1 2 3 4 5
Making good decisions	1 2 3 4 5
Dealing with failure and rejection	1 2 3 4 5
Being neat and clean	1 2 3 4 5
Using good eating habits	1 2 3 4 5
Using good sleep habits	1 2 3 4 5
Using good exercise habits	1 2 3 4 5
Using leisure time wisely	1 2 3 4 5
Dealing with school	1 2 3 4 5
Having appropriate relationships with the opposite sex	1 2 3 4 5
Learning to wait	1 2 3 4 5

CUT IT INTO PARTS

Even the most basic, every-day skill can be overwhelming to some young people. That is why, once you have selected a skill to teach, it is up to you to cut it into easy, digestible pieces. Let's go back to Graeme's challenge with Bob.

Graeme has decided that he needs to start by helping Bob learn how to communicate his need for help. The problem is that Graeme can't simply tell Bob he has to open up and start asking for help. It won't help because Bob has never learned how to get started. So Graeme has to simplify the skill of asking for help by breaking it down into easy steps.

Here is how the skill of asking for help could be cut up and simplified:

1. Decide what you need to ask

2. Decide whom you will ask

3. Choose a good time and place

4. Get the other person's attention

5. Make eye contact and speak clearly

6. Ask your question

7. Check to make sure the person understands

Each skill you decide to teach can be broken down into easier-to-understand and easier-to-do steps. Here is another example.

Bob has a problem with getting into fights. Needless to say, this way of dealing with problems won't work for him in the workplace. Here is how Graeme could teach Bob to stop fighting:

1. Stop and count to ten

2. Think about the consequences

3. Think about your choices

    a. walk away

    b. talk to the person in a respectful manner

    c. ask someone for help in solving the problem

4. Do what you think is best

There is no real trick. Just think about the individual steps you would go through if you were assigned to teach yourself the skill. Then individualize the steps so they make sense to the young man or woman you are trying to help.

CHOOSE THE BEST METHOD

Now that you have assessed where your troubled youth stands, chosen the deficient skill with which to begin, and simplified it into easy-to-follow steps, it is time to choose the best method or procedure to teach it. Here it may be helpful for you to review the "How You Should Teach" section in Chapter 7.

One of the more practical works along this line is a book entitled, *Skillstreaming the Adolescent.* (Goldstein, A.P., Sprafklin, R.P., Gershaw, N.J., & Klien, P., Champaign, Ill.: Research Press, 1980.) In it the authors outline a skills-training approach designed to teach a curriculum of fifty or so pro-social skills. To teach this skills curriculum effectively, they suggest using a sequence of four separate procedures: modeling, role-playing, performance feedback, and transfer training. I have found these procedures to be extremely helpful methods of getting the particular skill I'm teaching across.

Back to our case study—let's see how Graeme could make these methods work while teaching Bob.

First, Graeme could start out by showing Bob the seven steps of asking a question. He would become Bob's example of expert behavior in this skill. (Modeling)

Next, he could give Bob several guided opportunities to practice these component steps. Here even a less serious atmosphere will work because it will help Bob to feel more at ease to try and inevitably make mistakes. (Role-Playing)

Then, as Bob practices asking for help, Graeme can encourage, re-instruct, answer questions, and give feedback regarding how well he is

Like most facets of learning and behavior, defining skill areas can be as simple or complex as one wants. One of the most notable approaches termed "structured learning" packages fifty different skills into a curriculum consisting of six different skill families:

● Beginning social skills—for example, starting a conversation, introducing yourself, listening

● Advanced social skills—for example, asking for help, apologizing, giving instructions

● Skills for dealing with feelings—for example, dealing with someone's anger, expressing affection, dealing with fear

● Skill alternatives to aggression—for example, responding to teasing, negotiating, helping others

● Skills for dealing with stress—for example, dealing with being left out, dealing with an accusation, preparing for a stressful conversation

● Planning skills—for example, goal setting, decision making, setting priorities

(Goldstein, Sprafkin, Gershaw, and Klien, 1980)

Another recent work (*Dowd and Tierney at Boys Town*) in developing a curriculum for child-care providers, packages skill areas by curriculum (beginning skills, intermediate skills, etc.) and by behavioral problems (aggressive/antisocial, depression/withdrawal sexual behavior, etc.), and grouped by situations (interactions with parents and families, classroom/academic, etc.). The complete work is very extensive,
Continued

with almost two hundred individual skills, yet it is practical.

(*Teaching Social Skills to Youth*, Tom Dowd, Jeff Tierney; The Boys Town Press, 1992)

Both of these works, as well as others you can find in your public library, will help you develop an understanding of the pro-social skills the young person you are working with may need.

doing. At this point it isn't important that Bob expertly follow his example or even the skill steps. The bottom line is: Will Bob's performance of the skill work in the real world? (Performance feedback)

Finally Graeme is ready to encourage Bob to use the skill of asking for help when he needs it in the real world. (Training transfer)

GETTING HIM TO USE THE SKILL WHEN IT COUNTS

As in our case study above, with patient encouragement from you there is a every likelihood that the young person you are working with will acquire the skill you have taught. With practice, he or she will know how to do the skill. But will he use the skill when and where it counts?

As appears to be true following intervention with troubled youth in general, upon return to a facility, home, or peer group, newly-learned skills tend to disappear in the face of anti-social peer pressure, non-supportive parents, teachers or employers. The fact is, even the best, most experienced professionals can't assure that this transfer of behavior will take place. Even great parents with average kids aren't successful all the time.

But there are some practical steps you can take to diminish the chances of failure in this transfer to the real world. Go easy on yourself and try the following:

● Practice the skill in the real world as much as possible.

● Help your young person identify triggers or cues that will let him know when he is about to need the skill he has just learned. For instance, Graeme could help Bob think about when he has feelings of frustration or anger.

● Use reminders, i.e., self-statements such as "stay calm," "count to ten," "ask for help."

● Take it one step at a time. Make sure the first skill has transferred before going on to the next. Too much "new" will overload the kid and cause him to feel like he has failed.

● Use incentives. Verbal rewards, a trip to McDonalds, an activity, helping him get a job—just about anything done right will encourage him to keep trying.

● Create a helping environment. Chances are you are not the only caring adult who could help transfer this skill. Parents, teachers, other adults in your church—make them aware of the skills you are trying to teach your young person and let them know how they can help.

But most importantly, stick with him. Remember that someone early in your life helped you learn how to walk. You didn't master the skill after the first effort, or the second, or probably even the third, but today you can stand on your own two feet. Teaching pro-social skills to troubled kids so they can do what the Bible says, on their own, will take the same kind of parental encouragement.

SAMPLE LESSON

In Chapter 7 you learned seven steps for effective learning. The sample lesson at the end of the chapter used these seven principles:

1. Focus—Why do the learners need to learn this?

2. Objective—What do you want the learner to learn?

3. Input—What content do you want them to learn? How will you teach this content?

4. Example—How can you show them what you mean?

5. Check—Do they understand the material?

6. Practice—How can you let them try it?

7. Assignment—How can you help them apply this to their lives?

Here is another lesson plan, "How to Get Others to Pay Attention," which uses the same seven steps. You will find that these seven principles will help you form a lesson plan for any pro-social skill you wish to teach.

HOW TO GET OTHERS TO PAY ATTENTION

Focus

Joe can't wait until his mom gets home. He wants to go with his friends but he needs some money. He can't figure out what is taking her so long to get home. Finally he remembers his mom was going to go shopping after work. When he hears the car pull into the garage and the door slam, he rushes to the back door. He sees his mother unloading the groceries. Just then the phone rings and he runs over to answer it.

His mom walks through the door and he tells her she is wanted on the phone. She starts to talk and Joe asks her for some money. She shakes her head and puts her hand over her ear so she can hear the person on the phone. Joe immediately gets mad. He thinks his mother doesn't want to listen to him. As soon as she hangs up the phone, Joe's little brother comes running into the kitchen. He's yelling at the top of his lungs and is covered with mud. Mom starts to talk to Joe's little brother and that's when Joe starts to ask for money to go to the show. His mother still can't answer him. Joe keeps bugging, hoping his mother will say yes. That's when she yells, "Not now! Not tonight!" Joe gets mad and slams out of the kitchen. Joe didn't get what he wanted. His mother was so busy she couldn't pay attention to Joe. Joe didn't know how to get through to his mother.

Objective

This lesson will help you learn how to get others to pay attention to you.

Input

There are two steps you must take in order to get through to others. Doing these will help you make a connection with the person you want to talk to. Step one: go the the person you want to talk with. As you look at this person ask yourself, "What is he doing? Is he doing something I should interrupt? Is he talking to someone else? Can he look at me and really listen to what I want to say?"

Now listen to what he is saying. As you tune in, ask yourself, "What is this person saying? How does this person feel? Is he happy or sad or angry?" By looking and listening before you speak, you can decide how a person feels and know about what is going on. When you first go to a person, look and listen. It will help you decide whether or not it is the best time to make connections. By waiting to see what another person is doing before you talk, you show him that you care about him. When you show that you care, you begin a relationship that will help the other person want to give you what you ask for. When your friends and adults are busy doing other things and you don't wait until they can listen, they won't hear or understand what you are asking for. If you wait, you stand a better chance of others being open to what you are asking for. Waiting means standing still, out of the way, and keeping your mouth shut. Waiting helps you to learn about another person through what you see. Waiting will help you pick the right time and place to ask your question.

Sometimes peple don't want to listen. They may talk right when you start talking or ignore you. Try your best to wait until they are ready to listen, and then start your request again.

Check

Going to the person means (check one):

( ) Looking at what the other person is doing.

( ) Listening to what the other person is saying.

( ) Thinking about how the other person feels.

( ) All of the above.

Input

Once you have waited your turn and there is a pause in what the other person is doing, you are ready to go on to step two—get the person's attention. Make eye contact witht the other person. Regardless of what the other person has been doing, you can help him listen to you by standing straight in front of him, looking directly at him, and talking to him. It's important for you to get his attention so you can tell him what you want. Getting someone's attention is important every time you want to ask something. Suppose you are driving in the car and want directions. It's important to get someone's attention. You could go up to the person and say, "Excuse me, I'm looking for . . ." or, "Pardon me, do you know where. . ." Taking time to ask for someone's attention will make sure that they are ready to listen.

Check

You can get someone's attention by (check one):

( ) Yelling at the tope of your voice.

( ) Sending a friend to talk in your place.

( ) Writing it down on paper.

( ) Making eye contact and talking directly to the person.

Input

Learning how to get through to others is very important. In any relationship, with our friends, our parents, or other adults, there can be problems getting through. If you have lied to your parents or friends recently, you'll have a difficult time talking to them. If you have just had a fight with you boyfriend or girlfriend you probably won't be talking at all.

We don't have to pray a certain way or do certain things in order to get God to listen to us. God is always ready to listen to us, but sometimes we break his commandments when

we sin. And when we feel guilty, we are afraid to talk to God, or we think he won't pay attention. At those times, we need to clear the air by confessing our sins and trying to obey him.

Check

Before you can pray to God, you must (check one):

( ) Fold your hands.

( ) Kneel.

( ) Think religious thoughts.

( ) Go to a church.

( ) None of the above, you only have to trust God.

Remember

Learning how to get someone to pay attention means going to the person, looking and listening, making eye contact, and talking. We can always talk to God any time, anywhere because he is always paying attention to us.

Memory Verse

"And we are sure of this, that He will listen to use whever we ask Him for anything in line with His will. And if we really know He is listening when we talk to Him and make our requests, then we can be sure that He will answer us (1 John 5:14-15).

Your move

This week practice getting people's attention before you talk. Go to someone, practice not interrupting, make eye contact, and get his attention.

Sample lesson taken from *How to Get What You Need* (Denver: Youth for Christ, 1987), pp. 16-20.

9. Getting Troubled Youth into the Church

The sharp ringing of the phone woke Greg out of his 1 A.M. dreamland. In his best gravel voice he answered. First there was only silence . . . then a voice said, "You probably don't remember me. . . ."

Greg tried to place the voice, but sleepiness and the lack of other clues made it impossible. And with a click, the voice was gone. Greg prayed for the mystery person and for a return call, and he waited. Moments later the phone rang again. This time, the voice had a name: Mike. Greg remembered now. Mike was a boy whom he had known quite well a few years before and with whom he had shared the Gospel on a camping trip. Mike had said yes, committing his life to Christ. A few weeks later, he had moved cross-country to live with his father. And now it was 1:15 in the morning. What did he want?

"Greg, have you ever heard of Moody Church? I like it, but I wanted to make sure it was an OK church—one that believes what you and I talked about on that trip we took. And Greg, I need help bad. I really want to be closer to God 'cause I'm in trouble, and I think only He can help me out."

Mike and Greg spoke for awhile, but Mike wouldn't tell Greg how to reach him. It looked like Greg would have to trust the church to make an impact in Mike's life. After urging Mike to call and share his needs with the pastor, Greg made a mental note to pray for Mike and to call the pastor himself the next day. He wished he had gotten Mike involved in church much sooner.

Greg's experience and feelings are not that uncommon. Young people grow, change, and move quickly in and out of our lives. We cannot always be there when we are needed, and when a problem arises, we feel almost helpless. Ministering to troubled youth must be a team effort in the body of Christ. But, as someone has said, "How can you get them in the front door once they've seen the cross?"

The local church should be an indispensable partner in the discipleship process, and there are several ways you can help a troubled young person become involved in church.

THE NECESSITY OF CHURCH

The main reason every Christian should be involved in church is that it is a part of God's plan. A local assembly of believers is a microcosm of the *church*, the worldwide fellowship of God's family. Christ started the church (Matthew 16:18; Ephesians 2:20), and Peter, Paul, and the other apostles and first-century disciples established churches for worship, fellowship, encouragement, and teaching

(Acts 2:41-46). Followers of Christ are expected to meet together regularly (Hebrews 10:25); therefore, the Christian young person, like all other believers, should become involved in a church as an act of obedience to Christ.

Advantages and Opportunities

A second reason for church involvement hinges on what church has to offer. Just as the early Christians needed to gather for mutual support, today's believers need fellowship and encouragement in the faith. It is not easy to live for Christ in a world of anti-Christ sentiment and upside-down values. God's people need to gather together for strength and for preparation to go back into the "battle." And there is a certain dynamic in fellowship and friendship with Christians of all ages. Without consistent support and feedback, the young person from a troubled background will face almost impossible pressures and problems.

Church also offers worship, an atmosphere for reverencing and praising God and for quiet meditation. Integral parts of worship are the sacraments (ordinances). The new Christian needs to learn how to actively worship God "in spirit and in truth" (John 4:23).

The church gives consistent spiritual input—biblical content applied to life through solid preaching, teaching, and interaction. Trained pastors and mature and experienced older Christians build up younger and newer believers, and Christians of all ages and levels of maturity stimulate each other to grow spiritually. Church is the place where the young person can learn.

The church also provides a place to serve. Because of the human interaction within the membership and because of its unique place in the

---

When someone says, "Church is boring."

Perhaps there is some truth to this, especially in some churches, but I've found that most of the boredom lies in the fact that we don't understand what's going on. If you took a person from Zimbabwe with you to the high school championship football game, or even to the Super Bowl, he would probably be bored. Why? Because he wouldn't understand American football and, what's more, he wouldn't know the players involved. Often we don't understand church, nor do we know the people involved, so we become bored.

world, the local church offers countless opportunities to reach out to others. *All* Christians are called to minister to others, and in the local assembly, even the newest and youngest child of God can find a place to serve.

Teamwork

There is an ebb and flow to relationships. Young people mature, marry, and move; and your own life changes as well. The truth is that you will not always be there to listen, counsel, teach, and encourage a young person. And who will continue the ministry when you're gone? The church provides this needed continuity. As the young person meets and establishes friendships with other Christians, a strong, supportive network of believers is formed which can withstand your departure. If your young people have learned the necessity of church involvement and how to relate to other believers, when they move to another city, they will find a church body who will embrace them and nurture them. The discipleship process involves teamwork . . . sowing, watering, harvesting (1 Corinthians 3:5-9), and building up one another in love (1 Corinthians 12-13).

The church can also provide peer support, adult models, a family feel, a place to grow in relationships in a forgiving setting, and a network for jobs, spouses, and friends. So no matter how much you as an individual do for a troubled young person, there is no substitute for involvement in a local church.

Since the church has so much to offer, troubled youth must be breaking down church doors to get in, right? Wrong! There are many barriers which stand in the way of their involvement, not the least of which is the label "troubled" and all that we have seen that it implies. Our next consideration, therefore, is *how* to

When someone says, "Church is irrelevant."

We tend to ask, what difference does what the minister is talking about on Sunday morning make in my life? It doesn't make my break-up with my boyfriend/girlfriend any easier, pass my English exam for me, or get rid of my pimples. So why listen? Perhaps those are better questions than many of us involved in church would care to answer, but still I'd now maintain that the reason I didn't get any help out of most of my minister's messages is that I didn't listen. He had some good things to say. I just never took the time to figure out how they applied to me. When I started listening, even taking notes, I soon discovered that the principles about which he was talking did apply to practical, everyday circumstances. (My pimples didn't go away, but I could handle other situations better.)

interest and involve the troubled young person in church.

PREPARING THE PERSON

Motivation

The first step in preparing troubled young people for church is to help them understand *why* we go to church. Essentially, this will involve communicating the information just covered above, but in terms which they can understand. It would be helpful to read together Acts 2:42-47 which tells of the beginning of the church in Jerusalem. Describe the cultural and sociological climate of that day, the kinds of pressures to which new believers in Christ were sub-

When someone says, "Church people are hypocrites!"

Yes, some are, but so are unchurched people. The church doesn't have a monopoly on hypocrisy. All people have a nagging tendency to act differently than they preach. That's not to excuse hypocrisy in the church, but simply to say, Don't think of church people as the only hypocrites. The church is founded on Jesus Christ, and you will find no hypocrisy in Him. You will eventually discover that there are fewer hypocrites in the church than you first thought.

jected, and what it cost to be a Christian. Then explain how the climate today is very similar. This will help young people see that church is necessary for support and spiritual preparation. Outline together, from the text, what those early church meetings included . . . and why. It is also important to emphasize the necessity of regular Bible teaching for Christian growth and that churches offer many learning opportunities.

Undoubtedly a young person will already have an idea of what church is like. Perhaps she had a bad experience with a church program or person. Or maybe she simply assumes that what she has heard from her peers and the media is true—that churches are for old people and are out of touch with the real world. Be alert for these misconceptions and be ready to correct them.

Also be aware of the fear factor. Though the young person usually will not admit to being afraid, put yourself in his or her shoes. How would you feel about going into a strange-looking building filled with mostly older and "better" strangers and having to sit through a strange program. Meet these fears head on by saying something like, "I don't know how you feel, but I would be afraid of going to church. After all, it's pretty unknown. Anyway, here's what we'll do . . ." Then assure the youth that you will go with him and help him fit in. You may even want to make it a kind of challenge or "game" so that the experience won't seem so threatening.

Expectation

To be adequately prepared, the young person needs to know what to expect in a church, especially in a specific service or program. If you will be attending a worship service together, get an order of service from the previous Sunday and talk it through. (It would be better if you had one from the service which you will be attending.) Also, bring a hymnal and a Bible. Look up the songs and the verses in advance so that you both will know what to expect. It will help to explain *why* the various parts of the service are included. And tell him to watch you if he is ever unsure when to sit or stand. If possible, try to have his *first* church service a relatively simple one (i.e., without communion, baptism, etc.). Follow the same procedure for Sunday School, youth group, or any other service or program. The more the person knows about what to expect, the better prepared he or she will be.

Another important aspect of *expectation* involves the way people act and dress in church. Think through the possible social and/or economic gaps between the young person and most church members. Then explain how others will be dressing (clean, modest, etc.), why people "dress up" for church, and what kind of attitudes the young person could encounter (welcome, surprise, ignoring, etc.). Again, this will eliminate the unknown, and thus fear, and the only surprises will be good ones.

Presentation

You may find it necessary to work on the young person's appearance, avoiding a potential barrier by making him or her "presentable." Usually a wide cultural gap exists between the typical troubled young person and the typical church. What is acceptable dress and grooming on the street is unacceptable in most churches. Though you may disagree with many religious and cultural mores, this is not the place to take a stand, using the young person to make a point. Remember, you are trying to help this adolescent, a new believer, find a church home—not change church traditions. By removing the barrier caused by appearance, you will help the young person and the church members feel more comfortable with each other. But this is easier said than done.

Bobby's entire wardrobe seemed to consist of two pairs of dirty jeans, some T-shirts, a hand-decorated denim jacket, and an Ozzy Osbourne tour jacket. His adult friend, Joe, had only two alternatives. He could call everyone in the church and tell them not to stare, or he could do some straight talking to Bobby. Straight talking won out. Joe sensed that Bobby wasn't hostile to cleaning up his act a little; he was just unaware of the need. So Joe explained worship, reverence for God, and why people "dressed up" for church. Joe helped Bobby choose the clothes to wear (even in his limited wardrobe they found a good combination), and he suggested that a shower on Saturday night (with soap) would help Bobby look really sharp.

In Bobby's case, Joe didn't have to supply a whole new set of clothes; at times, however, that will be necessary to help a young person who otherwise would be uncomfortably out of place. Style is usually not the consideration, but rather the modesty of the clothing and its condition. Remember not to offend the young person or his parents. A well-timed "birthday" gift of new jeans or a dress can help a young person have an initial good experience at church.

PREPARING THE CHURCH

It is also important to inform the church about your upcoming visit. Assuming that you already know the church well because of your involvement there, this will not be too difficult. If, however, you are introducing the young person to a church which is new to you both, you will have to do reconnaissance to determine the key individuals to inform. Preparing the church involves the pastor, selected adults, and other young people.

The Pastor

Most pastors will be happy to learn

When someone says, "I don't get anything out of church."

The answer to this question is, How much do you put into it? Church has become far too give-me oriented. This just means that we all go to church expecting to be entertained. But worship should be *active*, not passive. Worship is us appreciating God and His Word, and thanking Him for all He's done for us. Sure, we get encouraged and fed at church, but church is primarily God's people coming together to worship Him. In the process, we are the beneficiaries.

When someone says, "Church is just too spiritual."

This may be true but not what it implies. Yes, too many churches speak a confusing language of thees and thous, and I can't see-mest to understandeth them. But it is wrong to think that God is only interested in spiritual matters. Or that when we pray, sing hymns, or go to church, it is only then that He is interested in us. That is simply untrue! God is the One who created life, every aspect of it—physical, spiritual, mental, and social. He is just as interested in you when you're at a party or on a date as when you're at church.

that you will be bringing a new Christian to church, and they will be very willing to help make his or her visit comfortable, meaningful, and enjoyable. Besides giving you the outline of the service (and perhaps even the message) and greeting both of you at the door, there is not a lot that he can do *during the service*. He can, however, provide valuable counsel about potential problems and key people to involve in the process. He will also be able to help defuse any potential problems and answer questions from other members. Tell him about your ministry and about the young person, ask for his advice and help, and pray together.

Other staff members, especially the youth pastor(s), should also be informed. Ask for suggestions on how to fold your friend into Sunday School and the youth group.

Key Adults

Because one of the most threatening aspects of church for a young person is the "generation gap," it is very important to build relational bridges to other adults. This does not mean that these people will necessarily become close friends with the young person, but they should approach him or her in a friendly, accepting manner. These adults could be leaders in the church, but that is not the main qualification. Instead, think of those who are personable and who can build bridges to other adults. Youth sponsors, Sunday School teachers, and parents of other young people of the same age would also be helpful. Remember, the more adults who are praying for you and who know your young friend as a person (and not a rough-looking, threatening, juvenile delinquent who could be a bad influence on their kids), the better his or her church experience will be.

A small group or teaching setting like Sunday School or the youth group can be quite threatening to any newcomer, let alone someone with added social and intellectual limitations. Youth leaders and Sunday School teachers should be alerted to the troubled young person so they can make sure he or she is not isolated or threatened. Bobby, for example, was a poor reader. Imagine how he would feel if he were asked to read a passage, or answer a question from the Bible, or pray aloud. The leader or teacher can make sure that the new group member feels comfortable and welcome.

Young People

What about other young people in the church? The fact that the troubled young person already knows young people who attend the church can be good or bad. A member of the youth group may be someone whom he dislikes greatly, or he himself may have a reputation as a real troublemaker. These problems will have to be dealt with on an individual and specific basis when they arise.

It is important, however, that the young person establish relationships with his or her peers in the church as soon as possible. According to church growth research, if an adult knows seven people at church, he or she will not leave. This is known as "closing the back door." The same principle holds true with young people. They will want to come back, if they know and like other people who attend. With the youth pastor and sponsors, identify specific young people who will be willing and able to reach out to your friend. Then meet with them and give them a little background on the person and what you expect of them (to welcome her, to be friendly, to encourage her during the week, etc.), and *pray* together for them and their loving efforts. If the worship service is the first church program which the troubled young person will attend, encourage these peers to invite him or her to the youth group or an upcoming social event. Christian peers can play a vital role in helping the troubled young person become involved in church.

THE FIRST VISIT

We now come to the critical moment. The actual time when you and your young friend go to church together. Assuming that you are convinced of the necessity of church and that you have prepared the young person and the congregation, the rest should be easy, right? Ideally, yes, but here are a few other factors to consider.

● *Early mornings*—Many people have trouble waking up early, especially on a weekend, and most non-churched young people are used to sleeping in on Sunday. Call your friend to make sure he or she is up and getting ready. Also, remember that most troubled young people are

Why I Go to Church

First, I go to church because I believe it is the best way to organize God's people together to be taught (how to handle life's everyday problems), to be encouraged (by each other), to praise God (collectively as well as individually), and to help and be helped. God knew we couldn't make it on our own, so, as our Father, He provided for us a family with whom we can laugh, cry, love, and be loved. A church has the innocence of children, the leadership of adults, and the wisdom of the aged. I go to church because it's the only organization on earth that provides the wide spectrum of a family in which God is the Father.

Second, I go to church on a regular basis because God wants me to. As a log will not burn long apart from the fire, so I, as a Christian, will begin to smolder without the encouragement of others.

Third, I go to church because that's where I get fed. God's Word is to our souls what food is to our bodies. Sure, I can eat at home, but there's nothing much better than a message that has been prepared for twenty hours before it is delivered. My soul gobbles that up and says, "That's good stuff. Let's come back for more."

late-afternoon learners, so sitting and listening in the morning may prove to be boring to them.

● *Transportation*—At first, don't expect the young person to get to the church on his or her own. Remember, there are fears and other barriers to his attendance, and it is quite

A Case Study

Sharon was concerned about taking Ruth to church because Ruth didn't know anyone else there, so she decided to invite the youth pastor (who taught the high school Sunday School class) over for dinner on Thursday night. When she called the pastor and explained the situation, the pastor suggested that he bring a guy and a girl from the youth group also. So, on Thursday night, Sharon and Ruth had dinner with the youth pastor and two understanding members of the youth group.

Sharon also called a family who usually sat in the same general area of the sanctuary as she did and told them about Ruth. When Sunday arrived, Ruth had Sharon, the youth pastor, two young people, and a family as friendly welcomers to the service.

natural to avoid, subconsciously, something which is unpleasant. Even if he agrees that church is important and says he wants to come, he will easily find excuses for not getting there. Set a time and pick him up. On other occasions, other adults or youth group members can be enlisted to provide rides. Eventually, he will want to get there, even if he has to arrange his own transportation.

● *Timing*—Your arrival time at the service or meeting is very important, especially at the first visit. Getting there too early, when you are the only ones, will feel awkward, as though you made a mistake and are in the wrong place or as though everyone else who enters the room is looking at you. Arriving late is also a problem. As you make your way to a seat, it feels as though every head is turning and all the eyes are on you. Try to arrive about five to ten minutes early. This will give you enough time to feel comfortable with the building, to greet people, and to be seated.

● *Relationship*—Throughout this book we have stressed the importance of building a solid relationship with the young person. This friendship is the vehicle by which you gain a hearing, solve problems, communicate the Gospel, and teach the Bible. It is also the main reason that this

specific young person will attend church. It is important, therefore, to keep as close as possible to your young friend during this entry and establishment process. Don't bring him in and drop him off with strangers. Instead, go with him and stay with him in those initial encounters. And add others to the relational process—adults and young people with whom he can build new friendships.

● *The Beginning*—The first visit is critical, but it is only the beginning. If you are successful at getting your troubled young person to attend a service or youth meeting, that will be a major victory, but it is only the first step in getting him or her involved in church. What happens once he or she gets in the door will make the difference in future attendance. Remember that the goal is to keep him or her coming back, week after week, for a lifetime.

SPECIAL PROGRAMS

We hope our new Christian young people will become active members of loving, supportive local churches. But our churches should be asking what they can do to better reach out to troubled youth. Here are some ideas for you and your church to consider which will help reach and keep troubled young people.

● *Seminar on understanding troubled youth*—Youth for Christ, Young Life, Teen Challenge, Prison Fellowship, and many other specialized ministries offer expertise in dealing with troubled youth. They would be delighted to come to the church and help key leaders understand what it takes to communicate with and draw in these hurting young people. These seminars will raise the awareness of the whole congregation of the need, provide practical guidelines and training for ministry to these children and their families, and give ministry opportunities for caring Christians.

● *Big Brother/Big Sister outreach plan*—One building block that is indispensable in getting troubled young people into the church is the one-to-one relationship. Working with the Christian agencies mentioned above, the YMCA, the court system, or Big Brothers/Big Sisters of America, you could have a core of 2 to 200 volunteers touching one life at a time in your community.

● *Alternative sermon*—This is another adaptation which a church can make to better communicate to the troubled young person, especially if a small group of them attend. A pastor, elder, or teacher could meet with them before the service or afterward to give a condensed, practical, and simple sermon based on the text of the morning. This will help the young person get the message, feel better about understanding the sermon, and enjoy the worship service. It will also help prevent the toe-tapping and whispering that happens when a bored teenager has to sit through a sermon which is over his or her head.

● *Special class*—One of the most important things that you can do for a young person is to give him or her a relevant Sunday School experience. This, like the sermon above, is a class that is designed specifically for troubled young people. The teacher is trained in how to communicate with this type of person, and the material is simple and very practical. The benefits of this class are that the teaching will be geared to the needs of the students and the young people will have a place where they fit in and belong.

Troubled Youth and the Church

There is an ever-widening gap between our youth and the institutional church. This is especially true for those young people who are nonschool-oriented and whose behavior is antisocial. These are frequently the same young people who become involved with the juvenile courts. Their behavior expresses their deep need for acceptance, but often is viewed as a threat rather than a plea. There is no needier segment of the teenage society, yet no element receives less acceptance from the Christian world than does the young person in trouble.

The church is often fearful of a problem kid who receives Christ and becomes active because this creates tension and uneasiness within the congregation. The true church, however, holds the power of divine love. The problem lies in how to effectively transmit that love to those who are intimidated by "stained-glass windows." The church building itself has come to represent to many youth a distant and nonfunctional religious identity.

In all of these special programs, you run the risk of segregating troubled young people from the mainstream life of the church and thus doing more harm than good. It is important to realize that the "alternative sermon" and "special class" should be short term, until the young person has the skills which will enable him or her to feel comfortable in the church as a whole.

Involving young people in the church is a difficult but necessary challenge. This is true for *all* young people and especially those from deprived and chaotic backgrounds. But the church is Christ's body on earth, and local churches are important gatherings of that body. Through your relationship with the young person, careful teaching, and adequate preparation, you can help him or her begin a lifetime of involvement . . . for worship, fellowship, teaching, encouragement, correction, and service.

Possible Seminar Format			
8:30-9:00	Registration		
9:00-9:45	General Session: (Keynote)		
10:00-10:45	The World of Troubled Youth (general)	Youth and Family Conflict	Drugs and Alcohol Abuse	Troubled Youth and the Church
11:00-11:45	Dealing with Family Crisis	Discipline	Teaching the Bible to Troubled Youth	Counseling Major Youth Problems
12:00	LUNCH BREAK		
1:00-1:45	Evangelism and Troubled Youth	Pregnancy and Sexuality	Understanding Adolescent Crisis	Troubled Youth and the Church
2:00-3:00	General Session (Challenge)		

Resources

Youth for Christ
P.O. Box 419
Wheaton, IL 60189
312/668-6600

Young Life
Box 520
Colorado Springs, CO 80907

Prison Fellowship
P.O. Box 17434
Washington, D.C. 20041
703/959-4521

Teen Challenge
Division of Home Missions
1445 Boonville Avenue
Springfield, MO 65802
517/862-2781 ext. 1367

10. Working with the Parents of Troubled Youth

The fast food restaurant rang with laughter and animated discussion as youth group members gulped down the hamburgers and shakes. Debbie, however, seemed glum and uninterested, quite apart from the enthusiasm and easy humor of everyone else.

Steve and Karen Wilson, the volunteer sponsors, sensed Debbie's mood and decided to talk with her on the way home. It was easy to arrange to drop her off last. During the drive, Karen mentioned tactfully that they noticed it hadn't been a real great evening for Debbie and asked if she wanted to talk about it.

With a little coaxing Debbie did talk, explaining that things weren't going too well at home. Mom and Dad hadn't let her spend the night at her best friend's house last Friday, and they were always griping about her hours, grades, and friends, especially Mark who was her steady and whom they seemed to detest.

"My parents are just so unfair. My older brother and sister can do anything they want, but I'm still treated like a little kid. Well, I'm not a baby. I'm in the tenth grade, and it seems about time that they quit picking on me and my friends," she concluded with a mixture of defiance and tears in her voice.

As they pulled up to the house, Steve replied that it was getting late and she better go in now, but they would talk with her in a few days about the problems she had presented.

After listening to Debbie, Steve and Karen realized that they had to proceed with caution. Debbie's parents weren't in their church, and they had been less than enthusiastic about their younger daughter's involvement in the youth group. Handled carefully, Debbie's problems could be a way to open the door to the whole family, but mishandling could make the small door of acceptance quickly slam shut.

A few days later, Karen saw Debbie and suggested that she and Steve stop by to visit with her parents and talk over what was happening at home. Debbie was firmly against the idea, considering her parents to be belligerent and not open to talking with anyone. But Karen persisted, explaining that they really wanted to help and that the only way to do that was to talk with everyone involved, not just Debbie. Karen also stressed that she and Steve cared for her and had her best interests at heart, which Debbie knew.

Later, they called Debbie's house and made an appointment to visit and meet with her mother and father. They received a cordial welcome, and Debbie's parents seemed interested in learning more about this group which had appealed to their daughter.

During the conversation, Steve carefully mentioned Debbie's recent unhappiness and asked if there was a way that they could help the family. Then the Wilsons learned that there was another side to the story.

Yes, Debbie's parents had clamped down on her time out, her television viewing, and her time with the boyfriend; but their motive was concern about her declining grades at school and her responsibilities around the house which had been poorly handled.

Debbie's mother and father were not terrible despots, insensitive to their daughter. They were caring people who wanted what was best for Debbie and didn't know how to achieve it. They were open to any help offered, and the Wilsons were ready to give it.

The Wilsons had a chance to minister more effectively to Debbie and to broaden their ministry to her family because they recognized the importance of parents in the lives of young people. You cannot fully minister to any young person without understanding his or her family and relating to it.

Part of a family

Every young person is related in some way to a family. In extreme cases, the state has intervened and now acts as or appoints others to act as the parents. Whatever the case, there are adults who are legally responsible for the welfare of children. We must never assume, therefore, that these adolescents are just like adults, independent and mature members of society. We know that parents run the gamut—from those who are caring and responsible to those who hate and abuse their children. But until authorities say otherwise, parents are in charge and we must communicate with them

YOUR RESPONSIBILITY

Communication with parents usually includes *information* (what we will be doing and when), *approval* (asking for their permission), and *assurance* (that the program and/or activity is safe). Because each child is part of a family, we must take the time and effort to involve the parents.

Part of the ministry

We must also relate to the family because it is an integral part of the ministry. As we have stated so often in previous chapters, children are to a great extent shaped by their environments. To adequately understand a young person, therefore, we should know the forces and influences which have affected his or her life to this point. Parents are undoubtedly the greatest influencing factor in a child's life. Learning that Susie lives with her mom and three younger siblings in a one-bedroom apartment (her father left four years ago) will give insight into her attitudes and

A Memo from Child to Parent

1. Don't spoil me. I know quite well that I ought not to have all I ask for. I'm only testing you.
2. Don't let me form bad habits. I have to rely on you to detect them in the early stages.
3. Don't be afraid to be firm with me. I prefer it. It makes me feel more secure.
4. Don't make me feel smaller than I am. It only makes me act big.
5. Don't correct me in front of people if you can help it. I'll take more notice if you talk quietly with me in private.
6. Don't make me feel that my mistakes are sins. It upsets my sense of values.
7. Don't be too upset when I say I hate you. It isn't you I hate, but your power to thwart me.
8. Don't protect me from consequences. I need to learn the painful way sometimes.
9. Don't take too much notice of my small ailments. Sometimes they get me the attention I need.
10. Don't nag. If you do, I protect myself by being stubborn.
11. Don't make rash promises. Remember that I feel badly let down when promises are broken.
12. Don't forget that I cannot explain myself as well as I would like. That is why I am not always very accurate.
13. Don't tax my honesty too much. I am easily frightened into telling lies.
14. Don't be inconsistent. That completely confuses me and makes me lose faith in you.
15. Don't put me off when I ask questions. If you do, you will find that I stop asking and seek information elsewhere.
16. Don't tell me my fears are silly. They are terribly real and you can do much to reassure me if you try to understand.
17. Don't ever suggest that you are perfect or infallible. It gives me too great a shock when I discover that you are neither.
18. Don't ever think that it is beneath your dignity to apologize to me. An honest apology makes me feel surprisingly warm toward you.

Are Parents Enemies?

When we think of how many of our youth have problems which stem from inadequate home situations, it is easy for us to assume that our enemy is the parents. If we fall into this trap, we will be seriously handicapped in seeing any real, lasting change come about in our youth. The parent should not be viewed as the enemy, but rather the ally. We must recognize one simple truth: a parent is unable to meet the needs of his child that are yet unmet in himself. An abusive parent was quite possibly an abused child. If this cycle is to be stopped, we must be committed to minister not only to the child, but also to the parent.

actions. Knowing that Gary was abused as a baby by his father will reveal his emotional baggage. And discovering that Beth is virtually in charge of the house because Dad works nights and Mom is an alcoholic will make it easier to cope with her defiant outbursts and periods of depression.

In addition to providing knowledge and understanding, getting to know the family will help you help the young person you care about. If the parents are part of the problem, you can ease tensions and resolve conflicts. And if the parents, like Debbie's, are caring and well-intentioned, you can work with them to build up their child.

If conflict seems an inevitable part of a teenager's growing up, it also affects the family as a whole. A good counselor will never work with a young person as an isolated unit but will always see that youth as part of a family unit, however fractured and poorly functioning it may be.

Working with parents is a necessity for responsible ministry to troubled young people.

YOUR RESOURCES

At times you may question your level of expertise, wondering what you can possibly do to help the families of troubled youth. But as a caring adult, you have special resources which can provide immeasurable assistance.

Openness

The very fact that you accept each young person and his or her parents and are willing to listen and to get involved, speaks volumes to everyone concerned. Many parents will be impressed that you want to get to know them and help their son or daughter, with no "ax to grind" or product to sell. Agape, unselfish love, is powerful.

Objectivity

When you work with other people's children, you are an outsider in the best sense of the word. You have nothing to defend or protect in the family. Instead, you bring an honest, objective perspective. Your insight can be like a fresh, cool wind to a burned-out relationship.

Experience

You can bring your experience-forged expertise from childhood (and possibly as a parent) to family situations. You may have learned much about raising children, relating to parents, and building relationships with teenagers from your own parents and families. These "life-lessons" can be invaluable in helping others.

Relationship to God

Our deepest motive for reaching out

to troubled young people is the love of Christ; therefore, God gives us the strength to continue to minister to them during the most difficult and painful times. He also gives us power through prayer—the direct link to God. As you meet parents and learn about their pressures, conflicts, and dreams, you can pray fervently and continually for them (James 5:16). Your prayers will make a difference in lives.

YOUR RESPONSE

Knowing that you have a responsibility to parents and that you bring special resources to the situation, you are now ready to act. Here is what you can do.

Be Sensitive

This means watching for clues and listening carefully to what is being said behind the words.

When Tina told Gary, her youth minister, about the heavy drinking in her house and the rages her stepfather often had when he had been drinking too much (which was several times a week), he knew that the situation would not be easy to handle.

While the man rarely struck Tina, her younger brother was less fortunate and usually received the brunt of his stepfather's anger. Tina was surprised that her brother's teachers hadn't noticed his bruises and cuts. She hoped that the teachers or a school nurse would discover the root of the problem and seek intervention.

Tina's abuse wasn't physical as much as it was mental. When drunk, her stepfather would call her the most insulting and degrading names— a slut and a tramp among others— and her friends were afraid to come near the house when he was on one of his rampages.

Family Systems

To learn about a family system, ask questions such as, "Who talks to whom about what? What is taboo? Who relates to whom? How are decisions made?"

By studying specific roles you can discover how a family functions. Who is the leader, the mediator, the authority, the judge, the placater, the antagonist, the victim, the scapegoat? In the healing process, the counselor's job is to help the family work through the changes and emotions that bubble up unexpectedly when traditional roles are altered. The counselor helps individuals discover new ways of relating to each other and new ways of approaching old problems.

An unhealthy family is one that is not open to new ideas, with role systems that are closed and rigid. Often such families place the children first, above the adults and their relationships. In a healthy family the two adults put themselves first, their mutual relationship second, and their children third.

Excerpted from *Youth Guidance Operations Manual*, Youth for Christ/USA

Tina was usually quiet and withdrawn, burying her problems inside an emotional shell which she kept closed to the outside world. In church activities, she always seemed to be on the fringe of the group, never fully taking part or really enjoying what was so much fun to the others. If anyone asked what was wrong, she usually replied, "Nothing," and the door to an anxious, unhappy life remained firmly shut.

Eventually Gary gained Tina's confidence, first by just being friendly with her and taking a little extra time to ask how school was going and about her love for music.

One day Gary tactfully asked about her family, and Tina said just enough to encourage him to call on her parents. When he stopped by, everyone was all smiles, and they expressed their gratitude for his work and for the fact that Tina was in church. They didn't seem the least bit concerned about their own lack of involvement, nor did they seem to feel any need to participate.

"How is Tina doing at home?" asked the pastor. "Just fine," was the direct response, and it was said in a tone that left no doubt that the subject was closed. Whatever problems there may have been weren't about to be revealed. The visit ended quickly with Gary leaving his card in case anyone wanted to contact him.

A few days later, Tina's mother phoned and said she appreciated the visit, but her husband didn't like "any outsiders meddling." And, she admitted, there were problems with her husband's drinking and times that she herself was afraid of what might happen.

Gary invited the mother to an informal women's Bible study in the home of one of the church members, and she came. In fact, she became a regular attender and soon shared with the other women some of her concerns. She also went to school to talk about what was happening with her young son and was able to get the father into a counseling program.

Tina's youth pastor—and Debbie's youth sponsors—were sensitive to the deeper, home issues which were involved, and they were able to help.

Sometimes the clues will be obvious: loud complaints or whispered discussions of problems on the home front. But there are also times when you must probe gently, asking about a person's family, giving him or her the opportunity to open up to you.

Be Neutral

Remember that there are two sides to every story. This is true no matter how convincing the side you have just heard may be. Consider Debbie again. The Wilsons helped bring a family together by being good listeners and by not taking sides in the family dispute until they had heard the whole story. Even then, they understood their roles as healers and helpers, not partisan advocates for one side or the other. While being sympathetic to Debbie, the Wilsons understood the role and responsibility of her parents, imperfect though they were, and they did not allow themselves to be pushed into a position of conflict with Debbie's mother and father. Thus they could help bring both sides to hear what the other was saying, and they could work out guidelines together which greatly improved the home atmosphere.

Be Quiet

The first step in practicing sensitivity and neutrality is *listening*. Look for clues, and get all the facts before you respond or act. Listening is also important, however, in the whole counseling process, as we have discussed thoroughly in chapter 3.

When you meet parents, then, be careful to listen to their verbal and nonverbal communication. Some parents know that they need help, but they don't know where to turn or how to ask for it. Here is where it is important to listen not only to what is being said, but also to the hurt behind the words. As in Tina's case, a "no" is not always a final answer, and an undesirable response should not be taken as a personal insult as much

One half of all children born in the United States will, at some time, live with only one parent. The primary reason, of course, is the escalating divorce rate. Fathers are walking away from their wives and children; women are leaving home to find themselves with new husbands or careers. Single parenthood has become an accepted social phenomenon.

When parents divorce, almost all children entertain the secret hope that their parents will be united again. Usually, the death of a parent is not as traumatic as a divorce. If the child feels he was loved by the deceased parent, he can accept the death. But if he feels rejected or responsible for the divorce, his emotional scars run deep.

Parents should never use children as weapons in marital disputes. Regardless of who is at fault, a child should be taught to respect both parents. Parents who speak well of one another—no matter what happens—teach their children love and respect, rather than hate and disrespect.

The foundation for a solid marriage is built in childhood. If biblical values are not taught in the home, seeds are sown for the disintegration of another family in the next generation. A fractured family produces fractured children who tend to perpetuate the disobedience of their parents. Although God's grace can reverse the trend and break the cycle, statistics do confirm the cause-effect relationship.

Marriage partners can be rightly related to each other when they are rightly related to God. The strongest marriages cannot survive unless the partners have learned the painful lesson of forgiveness. The best marriages are those that form a triangle between God, the husband, and the wife. Christ holds a home together, making it a rich and pleasant oasis.

Taken from *If I Could Change My Mom and Dad*, by Bill Orr and Erwin Lutzer, Chicago, Moody Press, pp. 114–115.

as the frustrated self-anger it often is. For the sake of the boy or girl who needs you even more when the home is in turmoil, you shouldn't give up caring or reaching out to the family in need.

Of course not every problem that a young person brings to you will be as "simple" as Debbie's, or the parents as cooperative and easy to understand. These days, even a volunteer finds himself or herself confronting difficult issues: home break-up and divorce, sexual abuse, alcoholism and misuse of other chemicals, intense conflicts with siblings. Opening yourself up to be a friend of youth, even those in the supposedly peaceful suburbs, rural areas, or small towns,

often means being an eyewitness to all kinds of despair and personal tragedy. This takes all the patience, kindness, and wisdom that God can give. Fortunately James 1:5 reminds us that God's wisdom is available to those who ask, and He promises to provide it without making us feel foolish or guilty.

Being quiet also means keeping "secrets." Sometimes young people will trust you enough to share special, private information. These confidences must always be respected. Everyone has felt the disappointment and frustration when secrets trusted to a friend are whispered and spread by others. When this happens, trust is destroyed and relationships wounded. We must, therefore,

Projecting the Right Attitude

Try to have a good attitude when approaching parents. Do not let them think that you are out to do their job, but show that you want to be available to assist them in their difficult responsibility of raising children. Never give the impression that you are only interested in their children but rather that you are genuinely interested in them as well. Visit in the home, and talk to all the family members, not just the young person in your small group or club. Work at building a friendship with parents.

discipline ourselves to be tight-lipped, even when the information we possess is juicy gossip or sensational in nature. This includes telling a young person's story in a letter or at a prayer meeting, and it is especially important when communicating with both parents and children. We must not reveal what Mom and Dad said about John or how John feels about his parents unless we have permission. Anonymity, trust, and confidence must be valued and respected.

In keeping confidences, be sure to avoid the trap that occurs when a young person says that he or she is going to tell you something on the condition that you don't tell anyone else. Never make that promise. You may have to break it to save that person's life or someone else's, or to truly be of help. The best response is, "If you are going to tell me something, you must trust me to do with that information whatever is right and in your best interest. If you can't trust my judgment, then you shouldn't tell me what it is you were going to say." Rarely will a young person reject that arrangement, and, if one does, you

may be better off not knowing that particular secret. When a girl expresses her thoughts of suicide, or a boy tells you about violence in his home, or someone shares information about a soon-to-be-committed crime, your responsibility moves beyond "keeping a secret." You will have to pass the information to others who, with you, can help and protect.

Be Intentional

Don't assume that young people and/or their parents will come to you with their concerns and problems. Often you will have to take the initiative, asking the right questions and visiting their homes.

There are parents who know about their children's problems, but resent any outside involvement. Others don't know what is happening and really don't want to know. A few even encourage the antisocial activities of their young, as when an inner-city youth is involved in the same street gang as his older brother, father, uncle, and perhaps even grandfather before him. If you contact young people under these conditions, you may have to confine your ministry to the youth directly, knowing that the foundation on which you are building may be very weak in terms of moral integrity and support at home. At best you may encounter indifference; at worst, hostility to your efforts.

On the other hand, try not to assume the worst from what you hear in the community, or even from what you are told by counselors, probation officers, teachers, neighbors, and other reliable sources.

José came from a tough neighborhood in the inner city, and his family had a reputation to match. His father, older brother, and uncles were all affiliated with and active in street gangs. For José to grow up around guns and violence was as normal in his community as a suburban child growing up with a Little League baseball team.

José started his gang activity when he was only seven, running errands for the older boys and carrying the weapons for their street wars. No one ever thought that such a nice little boy was carrying a gun, so he was never searched, even by experienced police officers who were quick to challenge his older partners.

By age eleven, José was using the guns himself, and at thirteen was an accomplished gun fighter and hit man, as well as a drug dealer (drugs are the main revenue source for street young people).

After a shooting incident, José was sent to a juvenile institution, and there he looked for ways to learn more about crime and to enhance his "tough" image. But after he had been there a few months, one of the other boys whom he had known from the streets invited him to a Youth for Christ Bible study meeting. More out of curiosity than anything else, he came. There, contact was made with Gordon, a Y.F.C. staff person. They got along well because Gordon knew many of José's friends back home in the city. Much to their amazement, José became interested in the group discussions and began to come every week.

Soon after, following one of the meetings, José and a friend spoke seriously with Gordon about opening their lives to the Lord and the very real changes it would make. If José was to become "a new creature in Christ," he couldn't return to his old lifestyle and habits. José understood, and he gave his life to Christ. This commitment was a sincere and genuine turning point in his life. As he

---

Variety

In your contact with parents, you will meet some who are very rich and some who are very poor. They may be very religious, or out of work, or alcoholic, or mentally ill, or domineering, or apathetic, or transient, or sociable. They may even be wonderful people! But you never know for sure until you meet them.

Excerpted from Campus Life Operations Manual, Youth for Christ/USA

---

was to be released, however, parole counselors told Gordon that José's family would pose a serious problem and would be no help if he wanted to get José into neighborhood Christian activities and church.

Surprisingly, that was not the case. When Gordon met José's family, he was received warmly and told how glad they were that the young man was straightening out his life and that they would be happy to help any way they could to encourage him. And they did exactly that, giving support, seeing that José was ready to go to at church time, making sure he got to camp, and even encouraging his Bible reading. There was no evidence that the other family members were going to be anything but what they had been all along, but there was no resistance to José changing his life. As a result, he is doing well today and has not reverted to a criminal lifestyle.

Not all contacts with such families work out that well.

Charlie was a bright young man in juvenile detention. He had been caught breaking into a school and both his mother and older brother had come to the juvenile court

Watch Out for the Messiah Complex

When working with parents and children, remember you are the tool being used to minister to these hurting people. It is your responsibility to do what you can with the skills that God has given you; it is God's responsibility to work in the hearts and minds of these individuals. It doesn't all depend on you!

hearing with him. Gordon was there and was very impressed as he heard Charlie's mother tell of her concern that Charlie stay out of trouble. And the older brother testified that he had heard about the school break-in and had rushed over to the building to get Charlie out, but the police had already arrived. The judge postponed his decision to another date.

Afterward, Gordon talked to Charlie in detention, telling him he was impressed by how Charlie's family supported him at court and wanted to help him. Gordon said Charlie ought to be ashamed of himself and try to straighten out.

Charlie smiled and laughed. Then he said, "Let me tell you about my wonderful, caring family in court. Everything I steal goes home to my mother, and she either keeps it or fences it through a local contact. And there's real trouble if I don't bring home enough stuff from a burglary. As for my older brother, he was acting as a lookout. He's been in trouble and couldn't afford another charge or he'd go to prison, so he waited outside to warn me and my partner if the cops showed up. They came too fast, and he couldn't get to us inside, so he took on the role of the caring brother who came to get little brother out of trouble. Pretty good

actors, aren't they?"

Gordon had to admit that they were.

Because Charlie was going to be locked up for awhile and because he had been so honest and frank, Gordon thought there was a chance to challenge him to turn his life around before it was too late. It took some time, but Charlie agreed. When it came time for Charlie's release, there was no way Gordon could recommend that he return to his family. Fortunately, Charlie had relatives in another city who were more law abiding than his mother and brother, and he could stay with them. For Gordon it was another lesson that things are not always as they appear.

Being Patient

You won't run into many families like Charlie's. More often, you will find people who are hurting, don't know how to ask for help, want help, and, if you can be patient with them, will appreciate and respond to your efforts.

Getting to know the parents of the young people with whom you are working will not always be easy, but patience and persistence will usually bring about good results.

Setting the Climate

Let your young people know that you want to get acquainted with their parents. Of course this will be imperative when you discuss specific problems with troubled teenagers which involve relationships at home. It is important, however, that young people do not feel threatened by that contact and see it as a loss of friendship with you or that you are siding with the "enemy."

Whenever possible, the young person should be present when you meet his mom and dad. In fact, it would be most helpful for him to arrange the appointment or at least pave the way for it. Only when the home is in complete disarray should you skirt the young person and call the parents without him being fully aware of the call. Ideally, you should try to meet with father and mother together if both are present in the family structure.

Such a contact may be threatening to a family which is having problems and in which the parents know their child has discussed the situation with you. So a relaxed, friendly beginning is important to ease tensions. You can explain that you have appreciated the privilege of knowing their son or daughter and that you wanted to meet them to let them know about the program, activities, and goals and their child's participation.

Using Tact

It is important to speak carefully and lovingly to both children and their parents. You don't want to erect barriers through misinformation or judgmental statements.

After beginning the conversation, you will need to be sensitive on how to proceed. At first you may not get beyond the initial getting-acquainted stage. If you sense a warm response, however, you might discuss the concerns which the child has expressed or your tentative conclusions from personal observations and other sources of information. Your goal should be to build a trusting relationship with the parents which will encourage them to be open with you and to become part of the solution to their child's problems.

Offering Help

At this point you need to express your desire to help in any way you can, offering your services and the

Status Offenders

There are times when parents seek to have a child confined for being disobedient, not attending school, or being beyond parental control. Such a complaint is called a status offense, a violation that is only committed by a minor under a certain age and is not an offense for an adult. While the laws vary in different jurisdictions, the trend in the last few years has been to keep such minors out of jails and lockups, treating their problems as ones that require counseling. Generally it is not possible for police even to detain such an offender until the parents come. Currently, efforts are being made to change this situation and again give juvenile authorities some power to deal with rebellious young people.

Few communities have facilities for status offenders, and confining them in juvenile detention centers with law breakers, or in jails with adults who have committed a wide range of crimes, hardly seems the best way to teach an already disturbed, angry youth a lesson in respect and obedience. It is a route which parents should not be encouraged to take. Too often sexual assault and other tragedies have occurred from locking up young people while building their rebellion, mistrust, and even hatred.

When a child gets beyond control, two parties have a problem: the parent and the child. Locking up one of them won't solve the problem. Perhaps getting both of them into the hands of a knowledgeable, competent professional counselor may help, and that should be the direction we encourage.

Resources

When a young person tells you of alcohol and other drug problems in the home, you will want to offer all the encouragement you can, emphasizing that the youth should not feel guilty or responsible for the weaknesses of the adults in his life. The resources of Alateen, an organization designed to help children of alcohol abusers, can often be a real help. In other situations, a family counselor, school counselor, family physician or attorney, and church pastor may be able to lend knowledge and guidance to understanding a family's needs and providing assistance.

resources of the church or any other agencies or professionals who can be of assistance. An invitation to attend a parents' meeting or group or the church itself is in order. Above all, try

Parental Conduct

When Alex's parents were concerned about the group of boys with whom he ran around, Peter, Alex's adult counselor, suggested that they open their home to his friends to get to know them. But Mom and Dad considered the whole crowd a bad influence, and they refused. Alex thought this was unfair because he wanted his friends to come to his house to enjoy his pool table, tapes, and other recreation. There was no way that his parents would permit it, and all they succeeded in doing was pushing their son farther away from home and closer to his friends. By rejecting these friends, they relinquished any opportunity to influence them, and their conduct resulted in further alienation from their son.

to be respectful and avoid sounding like the outside expert who has arrived with all the answers to their problems, (about which you may actually know very little).

One good approach is to speak well of the child and any qualities which you genuinely admire in him or her. And in discussing basic values, include the parents in your statements as *supporters*. You could say, for example, "I have encouraged Mary to stay in school because I know that you want her to get a good education," or "I've spoken with John about some of the friends he's picked up lately. I know you're concerned about them too."

A parental contact well handled is a good fulfillment of the role of an ambassador for Christ and an agent of reconciliation which Paul describes in 2 Corinthians 5:11-21.

YOUR REVIEW

Contacts with parents, especially in conflict resolution, will happen over an extended period of time. Don't think that one visit or one discussion will be enough. Relationships must be built, and this takes time.

Be sure to follow up on any suggestions or referrals made in the previous meeting, letting parents know how you're doing and finding out whether or not they have kept their end of the bargain.

Strengthen Ties

The follow-up to the initial contact will depend on a variety of factors. In addition to the invitation for the parents to visit church or a special meeting, there are other common interests which can strengthen your ties to a family. These could include repairing a car together, planning a fishing trip, attending PTA or a community social club, going to the football game, and many other activities. Look for ways to be with parents in a natural and open atmosphere.

Obtain Consent

It is always wise to get the consent of the parents for their child to be involved in your programs, and that consent should be formal and in writing if the student is to attend a camp or other outing. The signed form will allow for emergency medical treatment if it is ever needed. While a liability release is not legally binding, it is a responsible gesture, affirming that you are concerned about safety and the parents' permission.

Make Referrals

As the relationship with a family develops, you will have the opportunity to refer them to other resources, individuals, and groups who can provide necessary services. Alcoholics Anonymous, drug rehabilitation centers, professional counselors, discussion groups, churches, special schools, good books, etc., can be helpful in strengthening family members' abilities to meet their own needs.

Write a Contract

Where there is an ongoing conflict between parents and their child, you may be able to make suggestions to both parties which will bring them together. One approach which has been successful many times is to draw up a written agreement with responsibilities, privileges, time frames, and consequences clearly spelled out. Both the parents and the child need to be involved in the preparation of the document and agree to its terms. This has the advantage of clearly defining the areas of difference and the agreed solution which both parties accept. These contracts should be short-term (two to three months) after which there is a time of review where you and both parties sit together and discuss the situation.

SUMMARY

If we are to minister effectively to troubled young people, we must work with their parents. They can be part of the problem and part of the solution. Despite our best efforts, however, we will not always be successful in bringing a family together. Sometimes there are deep-seated problems which are not apparent on the surface, or sometimes a person, either parent or child, is not willing to be honest or make the effort to change. Outside factors may interfere with building harmony—perhaps the attitude or ego of a relative, the demands of an employer, the unrealistic expectations of a parent, or defiance and stubbornness by either the child or parent.

There are times, however, when broken-hearted, consistently disappointed parents have given up hope and don't know which way to turn. When we enter their lives, they rejoice at the fact that someone cares and is willing to help.

Stepping into troubled lives and families and bringing the healing touch of a loving Saviour is a challenging, demanding, and often rewarding experience that takes sensitivity, wisdom, tact, love, and patience. And while it can be frustrating, it will be rewarding to see God at work, changing hurt, broken lives. Thank God He gives us that privilege.

11. Working with Community Services

Richard is one of four boys in the Jackson household. His father, Ron, is a very successful businessman—the owner of Ron's Construction Company. Richard's mother, Sharon, enjoys the freedom that the success of the business provides—living in a series of increasingly expensive homes. But Ron and Sharon argue a lot, usually about money or "working too much," and Richard, as the oldest child, has been in the middle of many of these disputes. In fact, when he thinks about his parents, he usually visualizes them fighting. His earliest recollections include loud shouting matches followed by his father insisting on taking the boys to baseball, basketball, football, or hockey games. At first Richard enjoyed these little excursions, but he soon realized that they were meant to hurt his mother.

Richard's first memorable act of defiance happened during his eighth birthday party. His mom and dad had been arguing again about the trips to sporting events. As their voice volume rose, Richard asked them not to fight, especially in front of his friends, but each one began to pressure him to support his or her point of view. Suddenly Richard exploded. "I hate both of you!" he screamed as he ran from the house. Later he recalled the great feeling of relief that swept over him at that moment. "As if it stopped being my fault that Mom and Dad couldn't get along." This incident began a series of defiant and disobedient acts.

By his eleventh birthday, Richard and his brothers rarely spoke to each other, and his communication with his parents focused only on the things he did wrong. So Richard's relationships were formed away from home, and eventually his friends included boys several years his senior. To gain their respect, Richard provided them with cigarettes and beer from home, and occasionally he would shoplift to impress them.

Just the thought of stealing was exciting to him, and often he would sneak into a store and fill his coat with anything he could find. Though he usually felt guilty about his behavior, Richard kept up a hard, tough exterior like the other guys and became increasingly bold in his stealing.

One day, on a dare from his friends, Richard attempted a daylight theft, and he was caught in the act. After questioning Richard thoroughly for several minutes, Jeff Carpenter, the store manager, sensed that Richard was just a mixed-up young person who needed attention, supervision, and someone to care. And before the "inquisition" had ended, Richard had come to understand that Jeff was fair. When Jeff finally called the police to report the incident, his statement that he was "doing this for your own good" actually seemed to make sense. In fact, Richard thought, maybe now he would be able to tell someone about his struggles and feelings. When the police officers arrived, they told Jeff that Richard would be turned over to the Juvenile Bureau. Jeff asked if there was any way he could help, and the officer gave him a person to call.

That afternoon, the juvenile officer told Jeff that Richard had a history of legal run-ins and would probably be charged with second-degree theft. He further informed Jeff that he had met many times with the parents and that it was their decision whether or not to declare Richard "beyond control for the purpose of seeking juvenile court disposition." This sounded like a foreign language to Jeff, but he finally understood that the juvenile court could declare Richard a court ward and remove him from his home. Having just met Richard, Jeff knew very little about him and nothing about his home situation and how Richard enjoyed "hurting" his parents. Later, Richard's probation officer told Jeff that it would be important for Richard to find someone outside of his family with whom he could confide. Jeff felt a growing conviction that perhaps he could be that person—that friend—and that maybe he could eventually tell Richard about Christ.

A few nights later, Jeff attended a meeting of a voluntary citizen's action group where he heard the Chief Juvenile Probation Officer speak. The message centered on the enormous challenges of crime and juvenile delinquency and how to combat them. "The most effective weapon against crime," he said, "isn't mysterious or expensive. It's public support and voluntary citizen involvement." After supporting his thesis with statistics and examples, the officer concluded his talk by saying, "The widely accepted notion that only 'professional persons' are qualified to treat the offender is a sacred cow that we must eliminate from our thinking because it simply isn't true."

This was the final push that Jeff needed. He was determined to help Richard any way he could. He didn't know anything about "probation" or the juvenile justice system; he just wanted to help.

There are many adults like Jeff Carpenter who know of troubled young people whom they would like to help. Often, however, these adults are intimidated by the prospect of working with the courts, police, schools, or other community agencies. To this point in their lives, they have had no reason to know how these institutions function. They can only guess at what they would be allowed to do and where to begin. These caring adults, therefore, often choose to become involved somewhere else because they are confused and perhaps afraid. Consequently, children like Richard are processed through a system which by its very nature cannot meet one of the greatest needs of the young person—having a friend who cares.

A young person can be brought to the attention of the authorities in many ways. If he has been caught committing a crime, police arrest is likely. If, however, she has been habitually truant or embroiled in conflicts at home, becoming involved is much more informal. Regardless of how troubled youth become involved with the justice system or other agencies, their immediate future is usually determined by those in charge. As a caring adult, therefore, you must know what questions to ask, what the various authorities expect, and when you may be getting in over your head.

The only place to start is with you, analyzing your motives, strengths, gifts, and resources. The following questions will assist in this process.

Your answers will help you better understand yourself and will prepare you to answer the same questions asked by the authorities.

1. Why do you want to minister to this young person? Agencies are not satisfied with answers such as, "It feels good," or "I just like to help people." Your real motive may be found by examining why you waited until now to volunteer. Think through recent events in your life. Often people will volunteer after a personal crisis forces them to reexamine their values.

2. What do you have to offer? An educational degree is not of utmost importance. In fact, personal experience is much more valuable than theory. The crises, struggles, and victories in your life provide a profound resource for helping others. Also, what you know is usually less important than what you are willing to learn. Ask yourself: "What am I good at doing? With which problems can I cope? What are my personality strengths? What do I feel comfortable doing?" You don't need to feel intimidated by the educated and trained professionals in the system.

3. To what extent are you able to become involved? These answers will tell where, when, how much time, and under what conditions you will want to give your time to help a specific young person. List your priorities. Your effectiveness will be limited if the assignment conflicts with what is really important to you. A mother, for example, must decide if she can leave her child with a baby-sitter at a

Testifying in Court

Often, volunteers have a big urge to jump on the witness stand to help their young friend out, and the attorney may not be aware of, or choose to warn, a potential witness of the dangers. Before agreeing to testify, ask yourself several questions and be sure the attorney is aware of the answers:

1. Have I discussed this offense (or previous offense) with the youth?

2. Could questions from the state cause me to break my confidences with the youth?

3. Have I really known the youth long enough to be a credible witness?

4. Have I known the youth long enough to testify of any significant changes, and how can I be sure they are genuine/lasting?

5. Can I follow through on any promises I might make in court (such as promising the youth will attend school every day or go to church with me)?

6. Can I support what I feel, with concrete examples (examples that will hold up and not look foolish in a court of law)?

A desire to help a child is wonderful, but remember that testifying in court will affect your testimony and reputation within the system.

Dottie Cooper, Youth Guidance Staff, Greater Houston Youth for Christ

moment's notice. Some women are uncomfortable with this arrangement, and so they choose volunteer work which doesn't take them out of the home. It is important to be honest when setting your limitations.

4. What do you expect from the agency? Develop a mental list of your needs as a volunteer which should be met by the community agency. These can be objective or subjective. Some people, for example, need regular feedback and affirmation; others desire comfortable surroundings; and others need structure and supervision. Think through your personal expectations—what kind of support, resources, and communication you want from the specific agency.

5. Are you more suited to working directly or indirectly with people? The importance of this question cannot be overstressed. There are many types of worthwhile volunteer work within social service agencies including some tasks which seem far removed from

the person who is ultimately served. An unmarried man who is a computer programmer might enjoy serving as a "big brother," but a mother of four may decide to help as a secretarial assistant. Most community agencies need help with a wide variety of tasks.

UNDERSTANDING YOUR ROLE

To work successfully with a community service, it is important to understand where you fit into the structure and how you should act. The role of a caring adult who wants to help a troubled young person has built-in pressures, expectations, and responsibilities. The key word to remember is *teamwork*. You are not the "lone ranger" who is riding in to rescue the young person in trouble. Instead, you must see yourself as someone who will assist the authori-

someone who will assist the authorities in carrying out their responsibilities. To be an effective team member, you must have these attitudes:

● a willingness to occasionally modify some cherished ideas and concepts;

● the maturity to discuss controversial issues without indulging in personal attacks;

● the ability to see the whole agency at work;

● an awareness that no matter how sure you are that you are "right," the other person probably has sound reasons for his or her ideas also;

● the ability to admit when you are wrong;

● the grace not to "rub it in" when you are right;

● the willingness to serve the paid professional;

● the capacity to put aside your personal preferences, where necessary, to help the young person.

Your role, then, as a caring adult who is working with a community agency and with paid professionals, will not require you to change unless, of course, your attitude needs serious adjustment. To work successfully, you must be a team member, willing to compromise your expectations and to serve within the given structure.

CONTACTING THE RIGHT PERSON

Whether you want to work with the police, schools, courts, or a social welfare agency, the steps to meeting the right person are basically the same. If you have already established a good relationship with the child you want to help, talking to him is the best place to start. Explain that you want

to meet his teacher, probation officer, or social welfare worker. And help the child understand how this "meeting" will benefit him.

If, however, you do not know the young person, or she doesn't know the professional who will be responsible for her (as in the case of Richard and Jeff), you will need to do some investigating. Go to the institution, school, or agency and identify yourself. Explain the situation and your interest in helping.

In both instances, be prepared to answer these basic questions:

1. "Why do you want to work with this specific young person?"

2. "Do you know the parents?" ("Why not?" or "How?")

3. "What do you hope to accomplish?"

4. "What are your qualifications?"

And, if you have given clues in your previous answers:

5. "Where does your religion fit in?"

Be careful in how you answer this last question. As a Christian you expect the unusual and miraculous, but do not promise such results. And avoid typical religious jargon as you talk, without minimizing the importance of the spiritual area of life. Most authorities will be suspicious about being "born again" and "becoming a new creature," but they will acknowledge the value of a religion that works. Allow the professional to probe this area, and answer his or her questions honestly. Do not act like the "all-knowing, all-powerful, wonderful, capable-of-conquering-every-foe Christian social worker." Even an occasional "I don't know" will help them understand that you are a real and sincere human being who is trying to help.

RELATING TO PROFESSIONALS

Your relationship with the paid, professional staff members is crucial to your ministry with troubled young people. The way they view their roles and yours is the key to an effective working relationship. Insecure staff members may feel threatened by volunteers whom they think are intruding into their areas of responsibility. Or you may be highly qualified and capable and thus be seen as a threat to their jobs. And then there are those who have had a bad experience with other "volunteers," and may find it difficult to trust another one.

Concerns

Here are some possible staff concerns and suggested responses which may help you diffuse potential problems. These concerns may be voiced, but many will be unspoken.

CONCERN: *Volunteers may not be effective with clients (young people) and may even cause harm.*

RESPONSE: Develop an attitude which will allow you to serve the professional staff person and to learn from him or her.

CONCERN: *If a volunteer is successful with a young person, this may deprive the staff person of direct client contact.*

RESPONSE: Because you are helping reduce the staff person's client load, be sure to keep him or her updated about the progress of each young person.

CONCERN: *Because volunteers can perform certain staff functions with little or no special training and for little cost, they may be a threat to job security.*

RESPONSE: Support the institutions with which you work and help your staff person by actively lobbying on his or her behalf in the community.

CONCERN: *The volunteer's relationship with a child may upset the status quo.*

RESPONSE: Understand that paid staff are no different than you in this regard. They fear the unknown and believe that you may "rock the boat." Continually build trust with everyone with whom you work.

CONCERN: *Most volunteers do not understand the life-styles of troubled and delinquent youth or the systems which produce antisocial behavior.*

RESPONSE: The truth is that many volunteers come from middle- or upper-class levels of society. They recognize that juvenile delinquency is a problem, but they see the solution exclusively as changing the individual without addressing the system as a whole. If this is the case with you, simply admit your lack of experience and understanding and ask for help and training.

CONCERN: *Volunteers do not understand how the problem of juvenile delinquency is managed within our correctional system and how the young offender is handled by society.*

RESPONSE: You probably have not been exposed to the process of handling delinquents and have not seen juvenile courts, detention homes, jails, or training schools in operation. Again, admit your lack of "hands-on" experience and be willing to learn.

CONCERN: *Most volunteers are successful people and not failure oriented. They may see changing a young person's behavior in very simplistic terms or may have unrealistic expectations about his or her success.*

RESPONSE: Approach the professional with a humble attitude, deferring to his or her education and experience. Also, understand that your progress with a troubled young person may be very slow; avoid the "messiah complex."

Conflicts

You may be thinking that if professional staff members have most or all of these concerns, conflict is unavoidable. In reality, however, staff/volunteer conflicts are unlikely when the roles and expectations for each

Definitions

Juvenile: a person who, by reason of age, falls under the jurisdiction of the Juvenile Court or similar court. Each state has its own definition of the age of majority, but for statistical purposes, a juvenile is usually assumed to be between the ages of ten and eighteen.

Delinquent: a juvenile who has committed an act that would be considered a crime by the state law and local ordinance if the juvenile were an adult.

Status Offender: a juvenile who has committed an act that is only a crime if committed by a juvenile. Such an act is also called "noncriminal misbehavior." An example would be a violation of curfew laws.

person are clearly stated and understood. Often, juvenile courts, police departments, schools, and other social service agencies have written job descriptions and volunteer structures which have been developed over the years. And many have specific staff people who serve as volunteer coordinators who will outline the responsibilities and guidelines for one-on-one contact with young people in trouble.

If, however, the agency with which you want to work has not considered how best to use volunteers, you will have to help them think through their expectations and your job description. As you discuss the situation, be aware of the two major issues which usually arise when volunteers are used in one-on-one contact with troubled youth—supervision and authority. Work out, together, your limits and what you will be expected to do, and agree on the person to whom you will be accountable. This will stop most conflicts before they happen.

THE JUVENILE JUSTICE SYSTEM

What is "the system?"

Despite frequent references in this chapter to *the* juvenile justice system, there is no *one* American system. There are, in reality, innumerable systems variously defined by state and local laws and procedures. Today, there are approximately 2,800 juvenile courts in the United States, most of which were created and authorized by state statute, though they are usually city or county based. These courts have similarities, but they can differ greatly in the way they handle troubled youth. For this reason, this section cannot provide the answers to all the questions that you will have when working with the system in your community.

In the broadest sense, *juvenile justice* refers to a set of processes, laws, and agencies which a community uses to compel juveniles to obey community standards of behavior. These standards differ among communities but are presumed to be vital for general welfare, individual safety, and community stability. More formally, the term refers to the police, prosecution (i.e., District Attorney), courts, and correctional components through which a community enforces its laws.

Our juvenile justice system has changed a great deal over the years. Around the turn of the century, there began a long, gradual movement to

Questions/Answers

Q: Can juveniles have a lawyer represent them in court if they are required to appear?

A: Yes. Juveniles are protected by the 1967 Supreme Court decision involving due process rights. Juveniles and their parents have the right to be advised of right to counsel. If they wish counsel but are unable to retain one, then such counsel will be appointed by the court.

Q: If a child is arrested, does he automatically appear in Juvenile Court?

A: Formal judicial action is not always automatic, either on arrest of a juvenile or at any time during his processing. Many police contacts don't result in arrest, and only about half of those that do, end up in court. Out of this number, 54 percent are handled informally. And it is being urged that certain groups of children, such as truants, runaways, and other status offenders be removed from the court system and helped within the community.

Diversion, the practice of using alternate methods for handling juvenile offenders outside the system, is becoming widespread. Diversion varies in type, purpose, and formality. These programs have been developed at all agency levels, providing such services as counseling, education, training, and psychiatric care. Many agencies are involved that are outside the formal juvenile justice system, but are part of a community's extended juvenile system.

The decision to remand to formal prosecution or refer to an alternative program is usually made by the prosecutor, the police, or the intake officer in the Juvenile Court.

protect youthful offenders from the corrupting influences both of indiscriminate jailing with adult criminals and of hostile, ineffective, or absent parents. Out of this movement developed the present network of juvenile courts, separate codes of justice, and the concept of *parens patriae* (the court acting as substitute parents).

When the English system of courts was transplanted to this country in the seventeenth century, it included the "chancery courts." As courts of equity and fairness, they were charged with the protection of wayward and delinquent children. These courts, however, did not have jurisdiction over children who were convicted of serious criminal acts, and many children "fell through the cracks." Well into the nineteenth century, children who committed criminal acts and who had reached the age of criminal responsibility (as young as seven in some states) were tried as adults. As population and urbanization increased, so did juvenile crime, and with it the frequency and severity of juvenile punishment.

By the end of the nineteenth century, reformers were calling for a separate system of juvenile courts to deal with troubled youth more humanely and effectively. In 1899, the Illinois legislature established the first entirely separate and independent juvenile court system. The statute provided that all juveniles accused of nonadult offenses (e.g., truancy) or adult crimes would be handled by the same court.

These reforms had two immediate effects. First, the juvenile courts would no longer treat minors as "adult criminals" or punish them for criminal conduct because, it was thought, children had neither the understanding nor the motives of adults who commit crimes. Second, treatment and rehabilitation programs for youthful offenders were initiated to correct their "bent" and bring them back into society.

In the mid 1950s to early 1960s, fears began to surface that the same informal, parental nature which gave the juvenile court its special character could be misused to deny a troubled young person his or her legal rights (due process of law). The courts, for example, could impose sentences on minors such as placing them in group homes, assigning them to probation, or locking them up in a juvenile institution without the benefit of a lawyer, trial by jury, or other constitutional rights. In 1969, Howard James won the Pulitzer Prize for his work *Children in Trouble: A National Scandal*, in which he outlined how children and teenagers are often denied their legal rights.

Remember, regardless of how confusing our current system of juvenile justice may appear, it is based on the principle that juveniles are not criminally responsible for their wrong acts and that they can and should be helped. Simply put, the goal of the juvenile justice system is to *reform*, not to punish, young people in trouble. And the system works best when it has the cooperation of concerned parents and caring adults.

Many think that because a young person has been in and out of juvenile court he is a proven criminal. But this is not necessarily true. Remember, these courts also deal with youths who themselves are victims (i.e., abused, neglected, dependent).

Today, many states are making a concerted effort to divert status offenders, nonoffenders, and even some of those who have committed offenses, away from court involvement whenever possible. But these troubled youth need helpful intervention from someone, and so social service agencies and volunteers step into the gap. Caring adults can be the alternative for many of these troubled young people.

How does the system work?

Though there are differences from court to court, the juvenile justice system has a general pattern involving three major steps: *Intake, Adjudication, and Disposition.*

Intake is the process through which a young person comes into the court. During this step, several important decisions are made about his or her case. Someone in the court decides:

● whether to release or to hold the young person in detention while the case is being investigated;

● whether or not to file a petition for a formal court hearing;

● whether or not to dismiss the case entirely;

● whether or not to refer the youth to another agency or court.

Adjudication happens during a court hearing. Here the judge, in consultation with the investigating officer, decides whether the young person is delinquent and responsible for the offense, or dependent and neglected and thus not personally responsible.

Disposition is when the judge decides what should be done. Typically a juvenile court judge will decide whether the young person should be:

● released;

● separated from his or her parents or guardian;

● placed on probation and told to meet certain standards of conduct;

● committed to a detention center, training school, or other correctional facility.

Here's how the system works. If the police determine that a crime has

Entangled in the System

First there was Peter . . . small, blond, freckle-faced Peter was driving the tractor on a rural Maine road when his brother fell off and was killed by a hay baler.

With reason clouded by grief and anger, the parents openly blamed bright, hard-working, 15-year-old Peter for the accident. Peter panicked and ran, staying away three days. When he returned to school some of the students began calling him Killer.

His grades dropped. He gave up sports and started smoking. Then he did strange, defiant things in class, things that upset some of his teachers. Finally he was caught stealing money at school.

It wasn't long before a judge found Peter delinquent and committed him to Maine's reform school for boys.

Peter is just one of the thousands of boys and girls I found locked up. His story, like that of every child, is unique. Some have committed appalling crimes. Many have not. Thousands are sent to reform school by parents under a law that permits them to declare their offspring uncontrollable. Other children simply have no homes.

Howard, James, *Children in Trouble: A National Scandal*, Boston: The Christian Science Publishing Society, 1969, p. 1.

been committed, they send a written report to either the prosecutor's office or a probation officer who is investigating the case. It is this person's responsibility to make sure that there is enough evidence to prove that there was actually a violation of the law. If the prosecutor or investigating probation officer believes that there is proof, he or she charges the young person by issuing a *Written Information* which details the crime committed. Remember, there are many occasions when young people have broken the law but are not arrested or booked into detention. They still will have to go to court if they are charged.

After the young person has been charged, he or she will be served with a *Summons* which contains the date and time of the court hearing. If the person cannot be located or if he or she fails to appear for the hearing, the court will issue a *Warrant* for his or her arrest, which could result in the youth spending time in detention until a hearing is set.

Youth who are arrested and must appear in court have the same rights as adults (except trial by jury), including the right to have an attorney. If the person cannot afford one, the court will appoint a *Public Defender*, at no cost, who will represent the defendant at all hearings and provide legal advice. The young person may also retain a private attorney or waive the right to an attorney altogether.

Usually a young person who has been booked into detention must have a *Detention Hearing* within a certain period of time (3-6 work weeks), or he or she will be released. The purpose of this hearing is to determine if the person should remain in detention or be released pending further hearings. Many courts also hold an *Arraignment Hearing* at the same time. This is when the young person

must plead either guilty or not guilty. If the person is *not* in detention, the arraignment hearing will be the first hearing he or she will attend. With a plea of guilty, the young person gives up the right to change his or her mind or to appeal the outcome of the case.

Next, there will be a fact finding hearing, sometimes called an adjudication hearing or a *Trial*. This is where the prosecutor and/or probation officer assigned to the case presents the evidence for the state to prove the extent of the young person's responsibility. It is the job of the public defender or private attorney to attempt to prove his or her innocence. If guilt beyond a reasonable doubt cannot be determined, the charges against the young person may be dropped. It is likely, however, that the youth could be found in need of supervision and assigned to a probation officer or other agency.

If the young person pleads guilty or is found guilty by the juvenile court judge, he or she will receive a sentence at the *Disposition Hearing*. Here again, the probation officer assigned to the young person's case could give a report to the judge and make a recommendation. At this hearing, the judge can decide whether the young person should be released, separated from his or her parents or guardian, placed on probation, or committed to a correctional facility. If a young person is placed on probation, usually the judge will decide the terms of probation. The judge will also decide whether or not the young person should pay a fine or restitution (compensation to the victim) or do community service (unpaid work for the benefit of the community). The court may also decline jurisdiction by sending the case to an adult court. This can occur if the person is older and has committed a serious offerred to an adult court differs from state to state and from offense to offense.

IN SUMMARY

To work with troubled youth, you will often come in contact with other community services—professional agencies and especially the juvenile justice system. You should, therefore, understand how these organizations and institutions are structured and operate so that you can be most effective.

It is also important, however, to understand your role as a vital helper and *team member* in the process. Professionals need volunteers and vice versa, and they must work together to truly minister to troubled youth.

Ins and Outs—Moving through the System

Arrest: The juvenile justice process often begins with an investigation by a police officer either because he or she observes a law violation or because a violation is reported to the police.

The police officer may decide to release the child to his or her parent(s) with a warning or reprimand, or the officer may release to the parents on condition that the juvenile enroll in a community diversion program.

Or the officer may take the juvenile into custody and refer the matter to the Juvenile Court's intake officer for further processing.

Intake: The intake officer is responsible for determining whether or not a case should move ahead for further court processing.

The intake officer may decide to release the juvenile to the parents with a warning or reprimand or may release the child on condition that the child enroll in a community diversion program or submit to informal probation (supervision) by a Juvenile Court officer.

If not, the intake officer will recommend that a petition be filed, equivalent to filing a charge, and will refer the case to the Juvenile Court prosecutor. The intake officer also makes the initial decision as to whether the child shall be detained pending further court action or released to the parents pending hearing. If the juvenile is detained, the decision is reviewed by a judge or a court administrator at a Juvenile Court detention hearing.

Petition: The Juvenile Court prosecutor reviews the recommendation of the intake officer that a petition be filed. The petition, if filed by the prosecutor, is a formal document that initiates the court adjudication process.

The prosecutor may dismiss the case, or in contrast, may find the allegations so serious that he recommends the juvenile be waived to adult court for trial as an adult.

Adjudication: The Juvenile Court judge must review all the evidence presented at a hearing and determine whether to sustain or reject the allegations made on the petition.

The Juvenile Court judge may reject the allegations made in the petition; then the juvenile is released. In some cases the judge may believe that the allegations are true but withhold adjudication on condition the child agrees to enroll in a community program that the court feels will help resolve the problem.

If the allegations in the petition are sustained, the child is adjudicated delinquent, dependent, or in need of supervision. From there the case moves to disposition.

Disposition: At a hearing, the Juvenile Court judge reviews the recommendations of all concerned parties as to what should happen to the child.

Even now, the judge may decide that a severe form of treatment is not to the advantage of the youth or the community. In this case, the disposition may be probation, a warning or reprimand, some form of community service, a fine, or home detention, in which the juvenile continues to live at home but receives rigorous daily counseling.

Other dispositions are more stringent. They may be such nonsecure custodial treatment as foster care or group home placement—but they may range up to incarceration in a secure juvenile correctional facility. The judge's disposition will depend on the seriousness of the offense and the child's previous court history.

Aftercare: Whatever disposition is made of the case, the court may make the termination of that disposition contingent upon the juvenile's acceptance of aftercare—probation, counseling, enrollment in a community program, or any of a number of other forms of treatment designed to lessen the chance that the youth will get in trouble again.

From *Facts about Youth and Delinquency: A Citizens Guide to Juvenile Justice,* National Institute for Juvenile Justice and Delinquency Prevention.

12. Working with Institutional Youth

To Esther's surprise, her parents showed a great deal of concern following her arrest with three others for robbery. Not only did they see her during the regular visiting hours in detention, but they also arranged for special visits through Esther's probation officer. Their concern almost overwhelmed her.

Esther's dad hired a lawyer for her, and for the first time in years, she began to feel free to discuss her problems with her parents. This remarkable increase in rapport among the three ended abruptly, however, during a conversation involving Esther, her mom, her dad, and the lawyer, as they waited in the courtroom for Esther's hearing:

LAWYER:	If the judge asks you if you're sorry about the robbery, Esther, show real sorrow—a few tears would help.
MOTHER:	She'd better be sorry . . . with all she's putting us through.
ESTHER:	What do you mean by that, Mom?
FATHER:	Your mother means that you have put us through a lot, and now they are threatening to charge us money if you get locked up.
MOTHER:	It's not just the money, Esther. Your father doesn't mean it's just the money.
FATHER:	The hell I didn't! This thing hasn't been cheap.
ESTHER:	But I thought all of this was for me. Instead, you're both worried about the ____ money.
LAWYER:	You better keep your voice down. We're right next to the courtroom.

Unfortunately for Esther, the judge overheard her remarks, and the court baliff drew further attention with his look of dismay as he opened the door.

Sensing the futility of presenting Esther as a contrite, troubled young girl, the attorney skillfully shifted his arguments and stressed the negative, coercive influence of other youth as the critical factor for Esther's participation in the crime. Everyone was impressed by his eloquence . . . except the judge. He acknowledged the lawyer's arguments, but then announced that he would follow the probation officer's report, finding Esther to be delinquent and placing her in a state-operated institution for girls.

On arriving at the institution, called a "training school" by the judge, Esther sized up her status. Here she was not segregated from the "hard-core" delinquents, and she soon adopted the language, demeanor, and attitudes of the rest of the crowd.

When Mitzie, a Christian volunteer, met her some time later, Esther was virtually indistinguishable from the other inmates with her hard exterior and coarse language.

Mitzie worked hard at building their friendship. Every weekend, she would see Esther during visiting hours, and she would go out of her way to stop by after work when she could. During one of their conversations, Esther revealed her feelings about being confined to the institution:

MITZIE: Esther, you confuse me at times. You talk almost as if you liked being here; I hear you say you never want to go home. But you can't mean that.

ESTHER: Well, you'd better believe it because I've had it up to here with home!

MITZIE: But how do you expect to get out of here with that kind of attitude? You *do* want to get out of here, don't you?

ESTHER: Look, they'll let me out of here when my time's up, if I behave right. I won't get out any sooner because I feel something for my parents.

MITZIE: But you're missing the point. We all need a place to turn.

ESTHER: Yeah, but mine ain't home. I wanna get out, but I ain't goin' home.

MITZIE: Well, no one can control the way you feel, Esther.

ESTHER: Right on . . . you got that right!

Mitzie's work had just begun; and unknown to her, five months later, Esther would be paroled to live in a foster home. From there, her expertise at "being delinquent" would bring her back to the training school.

Though not all troubled youth are delinquent, surely most delinquent young people are troubled. Many troubled youth like Esther, therefore, can be found within the walls of institutions: training schools, juvenile halls, reform schools, jails, and other facilities designed to correct and rehabilitate young offenders. Any discussion of ministering to troubled youth, then, must include working with institutional youth.

Historically, churches and other religious groups have had an active ministry in prisons and jails. Most of these efforts have included Sunday services, weekly Bible studies, and personal interaction with the inmates. Unfortunately, however, many of these ministries are "in-one-hour-and-out-the-next" affairs with the Christians coming to the institution, putting on their program and then leaving. If the prisoners fail to respond, these well-meaning adults often become discouraged, and they discontinue the program. Obviously this kind of track record creates skepticism with institutional authorities and official chaplains.

While there are many excellent ministries relating to men and women in prison, there are also many superficial and shallow ones. Nowhere is this more evident than at the juvenile level. Many well-intentioned churches and other Christians seeking to evangelize the youth in these institutions do little more than provide religious services. Others attempt to reach them for Christ by using high-pressure, emotional appeals.

But an effective ministry must be built on meaningful relationships, long-term commitment, and responsible programming.

Correctional institutions can run the gamut from being open—welcoming you and your ministry—to the other extreme of being difficult to work in, with atmospheres charged with tension, fear, hostility, and resistance. Before you design a ministry, therefore, you will need to develop a basic approach, and to understand the institution and its population.

OUR APPROACH

More than once it has been said that we in the Christian ministry are so busy giving people the answers that we never take time to hear their questions. Never is this fault more prevalent than in the typical approach to young people in a correctional institution.

Message

As we attempt to communicate the Gospel with these young people, we must know something more than that Jesus is the answer. Incidentally, we cannot be of ministry service if we know *less* than that. It is an encounter with Christ which changes a life, not simply understanding His teachings or moral principles. We dare not stop at being social "do-gooders" with Bibles under our arms. The young people we meet in institutions need to meet Him and to see Him through our lives in every contact that we have with them.

But we will need more than a simple evangelistic formula or canned speech which we memorize and impose in every situation. During His time on earth, Jesus was a master at addressing large groups and talking to individuals. We could do well to learn from Him.

Consider the different ways Jesus dealt with a wide variety of people: Nicodemus, the religious leader; the Samaritan woman at the well; the rich, young ruler; blind Bartimaeus; the younger boys with the loaves and fishes; and so many more. He dealt with each person effectively and individually at the point of their particular understanding and need.

Don't use heavy theological concepts filled with numerous Scripture references. Follow the example of Jesus who talked to fishermen about fish, to farmers about soil and seed, and to tax-collectors about money. You can relate to young people about their lives if you take time to learn about them: their hobbies, sports, interests, cars, street group structure, etc. It is from life experiences that the best messages come to change hearts.

Our message, therefore, must be Christ-centered and must relate to the specific needs of our audience.

Audience

We must know those to whom we would minister. A missionary would not think of going across the world to a foreign culture, expecting to be effective without taking time to understand the lifestyle and mores of the nationals. This does not mean approving of all their ways, but it might mean having to set aside biases which are often more cultural than scriptural. This is no less true in the institutional world—a culture which is very different from the free community, with its unique pressures, norms, and rules.

Don't approach young people with suspicion. They have a special ability to detect the element of trust or lack

Ministry Foundations

Any ministry to juveniles must be based on lasting, biblical principles. Without a solid biblical base, the ministry will take one of two directions: Biblical directives will be replaced by temporary warm, fuzzy feelings, or the ministry will produce fruit that fails to reach maturity.

In many instances, commitment (on the part of both the youth and the counselor) is directly proportionate to the young person's emotions. When the emotion fades away, so does his commitment.

Fruit that fails to reach maturity is often the result of misdirected commitment—commitment to a certain style of behavior, a certain person (the counselor) or group (a church), but not Christ. Too often Christ is presented only as a Saviour who helps someone out of a tight spot instead of the Lord who desires to direct a person's life.

God requires that His servants be competent and mature in their ministries. He provides the adequacy to be responsible before the institutional staff, the courts, the parents, peers, and Him. A worker must not handle God's Word as if it were just another product on the shelves of psychological therapy. Ministers of God's living and powerful Word are to be responsible, compassionate, and mature.

of it, and this is especially true of an institutionalized youth. He knows a con artist when he sees one. (He may be a good one himself!) But remember that young people will usually live up to what is expected of them, good or bad. This is not to say that you should be naive or gullible. That will earn no respect. But you should always look for the potential in young inmates, not just what you see on the surface. And encourage them to see what they can be with Jesus in control of their lives.

Whenever possible, learn who the natural leaders are in a group and make friends with them. They may respond positively to your message or at least pave the way for you to influence the peer groups they lead.

Learn the different attitudes inherent in a group. Latino young people, for example, will tend not to look you in the eye when talking (this is a rather strong Anglo trait). When the Latino young person looks down, he is showing respect, not rejection. An Asian young person usually will not respond well to the "get to the point" conversation approach used by most middle-class Americans, and she will not like to question or disagree with

Answers for Troubled Teens

If you pursue an active ministry to troubled teens you will be looked to for support, encouragement and answers to many questions, pressures, and needs. Your reflex may be to provide a ready answer or a Scripture verse that applies, and many times that will meet immediate needs. There will be times, however, you will be faced with questions which have no easy answers: Why did God put marijuana on earth if we are not supposed to smoke it? Why was I raped by my father and uncle? Why did my sister have to die? What's wrong with selling my body? At least it helps me to survive.

There will be difficult questions which have no easy cures or answers. I counsel with a family where the pieces no longer fit together: mother, father and four children. They look to me for answers to their particular pain and sometimes I just do not have them.

Could God somehow have wanted it to be that way? Could it be that there are times when I am to be at a loss for words, counsel, advice . . . and answers? I think so, for then I must focus on Him and seek Him alone. God never intended for us to have all the answers; He intended that we should have Him.

God intends that we have such a relationship with Him that we are at one with His perfect sovereign will even as Jesus was; that we be so intimate with Him that we become one with Him; that the abiding consciousness of life is God, not merely thinking about Him.

Count it a blessing when you are at a loss for words, counsel, advice, and answers; for there the abiding consciousness of God has opportunity to push itself to the front.

In the quiet moments after those difficult questions, thank God that you are being drawn closer to Him. Then reach out and touch that special person and say, I don't know . . . but I do care, and that's why I'm here. And sometimes that's the greatest answer in the entire world.

Harvey Hook, Executive Director, Greater Columbus Youth for Christ.

anything that is said by someone she respects. You may presume agreement and understanding when it is not there. For example, to an Asian youth, it is far more important to build respect and trust than it is to accept an idea. Taking time to build the friendship with him or her, will be better than any other approach.

Expectations

Don't expect changes overnight. Accepting the Lord takes only the moment necessary to open the door of a life to Him, but conversion is a lifetime process of learning, maturing, and growing in the faith. Young people who accept Christ will not necessarily live up to your expectations or standards. But that's all right. Allow the Holy Spirit to do His work in each life. God is not in a hurry; too often we are. Physical growth can't be forced and neither can spiritual maturity.

Don't spend too much time worrying about the sincerity of those to whom you minister in custody. Remember, the issue is between them and God, not between you and them. Also, understand that one of the most difficult places to take a stand for the Lord is in a cell block or a juvenile hall. The pressure from other inmates and even staff is nearly all the other way. The new believer is mocked and ridiculed and sometimes physically abused—problems about which you will have very little knowledge as you go home after your ministry time. Most young people who have trouble getting on their feet in the Christian life are not insincere—they are immature in some area of their lives and need support. Keep encouraging, keep praying, and keep believing.

Be prepared to help youth being released readjust to the community. Certainly you can't do everything for them, nor should you. Nor is it helpful to allow them to take advantage of you. The soundest rule is, "I'll help you as you help yourself to . . . find a job . . . enroll in school . . . meet new friends . . . get into a caring church group." Walk with them at their rate and only as they are ready. Don't push or demand (and then get disappointed). At this point these young people need insight, honesty, and patience. The result can be a young person genuinely turned around to be a trophy of God's grace—knowing, walking, and growing with Him.

INSTITUTIONS

There are federal, state, and county institutions, each of which has maximum, medium, and minimum security facilities. Closely associated with these are detention centers which offer rehabilitation programs. Each institution has its own clientele, philosophies, and procedures which will give you certain advantages and disadvantages. Identifying the institution and understanding its limitations will save you time and trouble.

Most correctional institutions are open to almost any person or group who wants to help. But as you begin your work as a "minister," you may have to work hard to overcome the negative stereotypes in the minds of the staff members, developed by years of associating with well-meaning but misguided religious volunteers. You will need to demonstrate by the quality of your life and the competence of your work that you are a caring and qualified person who deserves the respect and cooperation of those in charge.

Realize that the main goal of these facilities is *control* and that the tight security and rigid policies were designed to protect the inmate population and the staff. Any outsider,

The Many Faces of God

The juvenile institution is a marketplace of need. To venture in is to open your life to becoming a vessel of hope and change in young broken lives. To be effective you must be aware of how best to relate to incarcerated teens.

God has many faces, as He has many children—black, white, brown, red. Let me explain. Statistical evidence has shown that the majority of incarcerated kids are of minority races and low socioeconomic backgrounds. With this information in hand we are faced with a demanding question: How can we best minister to a multiracial and multiethnic population?

God calls us to a holistic ministry, one that emphasizes the needs of the total person: mental, social, physical, and spiritual. This is best accomplished by reaching out to others for assistance. It is a great advantage to your work if you develop a team of volunteers who directly reflect the incarcerated teenage population you are ministering to.

It is, therefore, imperative to network with other groups, churches, and Christian minorities to develop the most effective team. The resulting ministry will be greatly enhanced because it fosters identification, positive community contact, follow-through care, and ministry growth.

We are God's messengers of peace to young lives. We bear in our lives the marks of Christ, and carry in our hearts the gift of His love. When you touch a kid's life, he will see the face of God expressed through your life. When others of different backgrounds and races join you, he and others will see the many faces of God.

Harvey Hook, Executive Director, Greater Columbus Youth for Christ.

therefore, must fit into the existing structure. Remember that you are a guest and not a VIP, and be ready to submit to the staff and not expect them to rearrange their programs to fit your needs. Courtesy and politeness will go a long way toward building a smooth working relationship, but don't expect *all* the problems to be solved. You may have to live with certain inconveniences or institutional idiosyncrasies.

Try to establish a regular schedule for your visits to the institution. This will help establish you as a responsible and committed resource person and an integral part of the program, providing a variety of nonthreatening, theraputic, and normalizing experiences for their young people.

Credibility, however, is not built overnight. Only the program demonstrating a long-term commitment will win the respect and admiration of the professional staff members. Institutional ministry to incarcerated youth can be difficult, frustrating, and heartbreaking. Only those who are willing to be involved over an extended period of time should accept this challenge.

Working well within an institution depends primarily on the following factors:

● *Building credibility and solid relationships with the professional staff members*—It is important to be sensitive to their needs, roles, pressures, and desire for recognition and attention. Spend time getting to know them.

● *Maintaining proper roles*—Don't criticize the institution and the staff in order to be accepted and liked by the young people. Also, don't act like an authority by relating to the youth in the same way as the staff. Respect the roles of staff, inmate, and volunteer.

● *Cooperating with other ministries and volunteers*—Remember, you are not competing with others who also want to help. Work with these other helpers.

● *Developing a reputation for dependability and consistency*—Be the kind of person on whom the staff and young people can depend. Keep appointments and be on time.

Understanding the institution and following these simple guidelines will help open the door to the lives of young people inside.

INCARCERATED YOUTH

Characteristics

The typical young person in a juvenile detention or treatment facility is a complex mixture of rebellion, confusion, hurt, loneliness, despair, hostility, and other needs and personality characteristics. His or her actions often speak louder than words, revealing a desperate search for understanding, love, and acceptance. But he or she is also a bundle of potential—a wonderful creation of God and a person for whom Christ died—with special talents, abilities, and gifts.

Being placed in an institution means losing freedom; it is a time of personal crisis for the young person. And adults may be seen as threats, authority figures, "means" to various ends, or representatives of the system that put him or her there.

Young men and women are placed in correctional institutions when they are judged to be threats to themselves or others. They have proven by their actions that they cannot function appropriately in society, and so they are to be "rehabilitated."

Don't assume, therefore, that these young people are simply wayward children who will blossom and change with a little love and understanding. Instead, you may be manipulated, lied to, rejected, and verbally abused at times. And perhaps the greatest obstacle to overcome is their unrealistic expectations for you and your program. Many of these young people want desperately to change or to be released, and they want it right away. The truth is, however, that much of their progress will be "three steps forward and two steps back." These experiences can hurt deeply; but if you are aware of such possibilities, you will avoid becoming bitter and disillusioned. In reality, anyone working with institutionalized young people walks a very fine line between suspicion and naiveté. You must demonstrate trust and respect for each individual while at the same time being realistic. Call them to a "higher" level of life and help them realize their potential, but don't give up when there are setbacks.

Guidelines

Though it will take time to develop the ability to relate naturally to institutionalized youth, the following guidelines should be kept in mind:

1. Have a nonjudgmental attitude. As the young person describes his or her attitudes and past behaviors, refrain from judging or sermonizing. Accept what is said and move on.

2. Be "shockproof." By listening attentively but without gasps, "oh, no's!" or amazement, you will encourage the young person to be real and not sensational in his or her

One-to-one Volunteer Staff

A good way to meet the maximum number of residents' needs is to provide caring one-to-one relationships for youth via volunteers. After consulting with the institutional staff to determine which youth have the greatest needs, pair committed volunteers with individual youth. The volunteer can be seen as a big brother or big sister who will provide many hours of friendship and community contact.

Volunteers should understand that they are to befriend their assigned youth and, in that process, provide informal counseling. His or her approach should be to love and unconditionally accept the young people and to cooperate with the staff's proposed treatment plan. The volunteer should provide off-campus opportunities (if permitted) as well as many solid hours of relationship-building time on campus.

Volunteer partnerships work best in long-term institutions. But they can also be used to follow a juvenile from the institution into the community to continue to service him effectively in the referral or neighborhood setting.

Volunteers can also be used to disciple two or three youths who have become Christians. And they can run on-campus Bible studies for youths who are not permitted off the grounds. This on-campus study can take place at the same time as the Bible study for those with off-campus privileges.

Volunteers should receive training to acquaint them with the needs and characteristics of delinquent youth as well as the special dynamics involved in the lock-up situation. They should be closely supervised, supported and encouraged as they provide pertinent feedback on their youth to their counselor.

Working with Girls

Many well-intentioned men have found themselves out of the ministry due to accusations by girls with whom the men felt they were having a significant ministry.

Society has dealt some children a cruel blow by robbing them of a significant relationship with their fathers, but research reveals that daughters suffer much more than sons. Consequently, the girls don't understand how to relate to men and father-type figures.

Our society is also very sexually oriented, with pornography downgrading the position of women, and child/teen sexual abuse reaching alarming figures. Many institutionalized girls (some estimate 98 percent) have been sexually abused in some way—through incest, prostitution, or pornography. Therefore, simple gestures (a hug, a pat on the back, even a handshake), simple courtesies (opening a door, getting a chair), simple words (I care about what happens to you; you're a nice person; or you sure look pretty this morning) are often misinterpreted to be sexual advances and invitations.

Any man who chooses to work with girls must guard himself about ever being misinterpreted and should be warned he would probably be much safer in a mine field.

Dottie Cooper, Youth Guidance Staff, Greater Houston Youth for Christ.

openness

3. Listen with intense, active concern. Focus on what the person says and watch for nonverbal messages.

4. Don't talk constantly about yourself, your problems, and your needs. The idea is to get the young person to open up and talk; two-way sharing can develop later.

5. Ask questions to help the young person tell you about him/herself. Questions about family, pets, school, sports, and interests can lead to deeper levels of communication. Or you could ask, "Where is your home?" "How are you being treated?" Make sure that your questions cannot be answered by a simple yes or no.

6. Follow factual statements with questions about feelings. It is important to get beneath the surface facts and opinions. You could ask, "How did you feel about getting caught?" "Was the court fair?"

7. Provide feedback, support, affirmation, and acceptance. Whenever possible, let the individual know that you think he is special and that you care about him. And be sure to give all sorts of positive feedback when he does the right thing. This will help build the relationship and encourage constructive behavior.

8. Be honest and "real" when you talk about yourself. Though you should not "stretch" your own experiences to establish common ground with the young person, you should share what has really happened to you and how you felt (i.e., "My brothers never raped me, but I was scared and hurt when they beat me up.").

9. Look for symptoms of unheard and unseen attitudes and feelings. This does not necessarily mean asking questions–rather it involves listening carefully as the young person talks about her past, her family, and other topics.

10. Understand the young person's need for confidentiality. Make it clear that your purpose is to minister, not to be the eyes and ears of the administration. Explain that you will not discuss his or her problems unless you can help by working with a staff person. Remember, you are obligated to report anything that you may learn about something which may endanger a person's safety. If the counselee understands these simple rules, he can feel free to talk with you, and you can maintain your integrity with him and the institution.

11. Determine the educational level of the youth with whom you are working. You want to communicate with the young person and not talk down to her or over her head.

12. Attend employee training sessions whenever possible. This will provide valuable information and build rapport with the staff.

13. Be aware of the young person's need for nonsexual physical affection. You can demonstrate your affection by handshakes, pats on the back, and hugs.

14. Know that your ability to bring love and compassion will be directly related to the vitality of your relationship with God. Pray for these young people and for your ministry among them, and study the Bible regularly.

After you think through your basic approach and you understand the institution and its young people, you are ready to design the ministry.

THE MINISTRY

Detention Centers

The juvenile detention center is often the entry point of youth into the "secure" environment of the juvenile justice system. It may also be their first experience with incarceration. Most young offenders remain in detention facilities only until they can be released to the custody of their parents or until the court makes another disposition in their cases. (In many smaller communities and in some counties, the youth detention facilities may consist of a unit or several cells in the adult jail.)

Because of the extremely high turnover rate in such institutions, relationships cannot be built over an extended period of time. Many of the contacts made with youths in such facilities, therefore, will be limited in intensity, depth, and duration. But detention centers can provide excellent ministry opportunities. Because this may be the young person's first time in confinement, the personal trauma and shock can push him into thinking seriously about himself and God. And many of these youths who are detained for the first time are released back into the community and can be seen again and integrated into your ongoing program.

Of course some young people may see God as a way to escape their present predicament, or they may grasp for the supernatural, hoping to ease their trauma. This type of religious motivation is not very deep and lasting, but it can serve as a starting point.

To develop a ministry with more than one young person in a short-term facility, remember the following points:

The Plan

● *Type of program*—A very serious or heavy religious program will probably be ineffective, so don't try to duplicate your church youth program in the institution. Because of the high turnover rate, many of the young people may only be seen once, others a number of times. Your programs, therefore, could include films, music,

games, or a combination. Be sure to vary the program to avoid boredom. A short talk can be used to communicate a biblical verse or principle. Most of these meetings will not produce a large crowd, but they can open up discussions with individuals.

● *Length of program*—try to keep the programs moving quickly and limited to about an hour. This will be long enough—especially for the first program. Eat a meal or spend time with young people individually on the day of your program.

● *Frequency of program*—You should visit the institution at least once a week. Young people will soon realize that your visit is not just a "one-time thing" and that you will return.

Institutional Analysis

These questions and others should be asked before designing a program:

● Is it a locked-down setting that never provides opportunities for youth to go off campus?

● Are youth permitted off grounds on a wide or a limited basis? If so, with what restrictions?

● Are outside youth allowed in the institution? How many staff must accompany an outing?

● Is there an all-purpose room that can be used for programs, Bible studies and related activities?

● What kind of recreational activities are provided for the youth?

● Are there chances for social interaction?

● Do any of the youth have serious hygiene or physical needs?

The Preparation

● Determine the needs of the juvenile center.

● Know how the juvenile center relates to the court system (e.g., average length of stay, etc.).

● Make appointments with court personnel you know. Ask them if your plan is realistic and if they know of people at the center who can help.

● Meet and communicate with the superintendent or person in charge.

● Enlist volunteers. Church members and Christian college students make excellent volunteers. It is best not to have more than five volunteers involved in one program.

● Get to know the floor supervisor and staff. The more the staff at the juvenile center get to know you, the easier will be your task.

The Follow-through

Always do whatever you promise. This includes keeping appointments with staff and young people. Don't take on more than you can handle.

Spend time with individuals. The group programs are helpful tools, but most of the ministry will occur one-to-one. Follow through, therefore, with individuals who are in the center, who are placed outside the center, or who are on parole. The juvenile center staff may limit your time with young people at first—until they realize that your program involves personal follow-through. Follow-through is especially important for new Christians.

The Program

● *Bible study/"insight"*—Though it may take several weeks to build relationships before you can start, Bible studies are a vital part of ministering in institutions. Your topics can be general or specific, and material can be borrowed or adapted. As we have mentioned previously, your vocabulary and communication must be on a concrete level to be understood.

If possible, try to have your Bible studies "off campus." Maybe the youth could be transported to a private home or a casual, church lounge. Being locked up makes young people forget what being normal is like. Meeting in a "warm" home will help them remember that there is a world waiting for them to succeed. It will also help break down barriers and give them something fun and exciting to anticipate.

As you prepare for a Bible study, remember these factors:

● *Natural groupings*—Detention centers usually are separated into units or divisions based on sex, age, and physical characteristics. It is important to design your Bible studies to build on each group's strengths. Mixing different groups may foster feelings of competition for recognition and squelch any natural spontaneity.

● *Size*—For informal interaction, the ideal size is five to twelve in a group. Anything larger can diminish the level of intimacy which should characterize the small-group process. As the group's size increases, active participation and involvement decreases.

● *Time*—Schedule the study at a time which will coincide with the institution's needs and which will not conflict with attractive alternatives (i.e., gym or recreation times).

● *Location*—Where the study is held will be a major influence on the group process. A chapel, a room apart from the living unit, or a room off campus will remove the youths from as many distractions as possible. Institutionalized youth relish any opportunity to be away from the area

WORKING WITH INSTITUTIONAL YOUTH 199

in which they spend most of their time. If possible, select a room which they can decorate and one which will provide comfort and warmth. Make the Bible study an attractive alternative to the monotonous hours spent in the unit.

● *Sunday services*—Many youth in detention have church backgrounds, and when placed in a crisis situation, most of them will feel the emotional, psychological, and spiritual need to worship. Your ministry can play a significant part in helping to meet that need.

● *Team approach*—Youth in detention need to be exposed to the healthy and diverse body of Christ with its various spiritual gifts. In your services, therefore, use a variety of volunteers and local church personnel. Church choirs, seminary students, and others can help you provide meaningful worship experiences.

● *Worship*—Young people need the opportunity to worship. There is no need for gimmicks or games in the worship experience. A certain amount of informality will enable young people to open up, but the atmosphere must be reverent.

● *Music*—Use music as much as possible. Music will attract the uninterested young person. It will also set the tone and atmosphere of the worship experience and add life and vitality.

● *Response*—An "altar call" isn't necessary and is often misunderstood. Mass response is common among institutionalized youth because many want to change but do not understand the commitment which is necessary. If you give the invitation to receive Christ, make sure you have immediate follow-up and discipleship sessions for the new believers.

● *Alternative programs*—Choirs,

Asking Questions of Troubled Youth

Coming from a typical middle-class background was not my best asset in learning to talk to troubled youth. I would often try to use questions my Sunday School teachers had asked me in the past, such as, "What does your father do?" Asking this of a young person who does not know his father can be somewhat stressful for the youth (and embarrassing for the asker). Stating, "My goodness, you sure don't look like your brother," only to find out all the children in the family had different fathers, made me very aware of the importance of asking good questions, questions that would both make the young person feel safe in revealing himself to me, and help me to learn about this person. I have found these family-type questions to be most helpful:

1. Who do you stay with?

2. Do you have brothers and sisters? What are their names and how old are they?

3. Who in your family do you get along with the best?

4. Who in your family do you not get along with?

Dottie Cooper, Youth Guidance Staff, Greater Houston Youth for Christ

---

puppets, drama, concerts, films, recreation, small groups, and holiday celebrations will attract and help many young people.

● *Literature*—Many organizations provide literature for use in institutions (free or at a nominal cost). Literature can be a tremendous help in reaching and discipling young people

One-to-One

One-to-one relating is the bottom line of all institutional ministry, particularly in detention centers. It is within this relational framework that the youth begins to share himself. This is the beginning of the process of responsible evangelism and healing to which you are called. Spending quality time with individual young people develops credibility with both the youth and the detention center staff that can't be built any other way.

for Christ. To obtain books, pamphlets, magazines, and other needed literature pieces:

— Use institutional stationery and addresses in all your correspondence;

— the particular institution (e.g., (chaplain);

— Make a duplicate copy for institution records;

— Be sure you have the financial resources to underwrite any expenses incurred by this program.

● *Correspondence*—Virtually all young people in detention and other forms of incarceration are very interested in any caring contact with the outside world. Because of this interest, an ongoing correspondence ministry can be developed.

Begin by clearing your plan with the institution's administration. Then, identify those individuals and church groups who are willing to write to selected youth. Next, select the interested youth and match them with the appropriate "writers." (Note: It is a good idea to match males with males and females with females so that no romantic motives will be as-

sumed. Also, be aware that some youths may attempt to visit their pen-pals on release and seek special favors. Consider using a church address to protect the volunteer's privacy if desired.)

To be most effective, a correspondence program should concentrate on those young people who will be incarcerated for an extended period of time. Correspondence can be a very effective tool to reach young people and to follow through with those who cannot be discipled and loved in person.

Long-term Juvenile Correctional Institutions

Long-term institutions, which house offenders for more than six months, afford a significant ministry opportunity. In such settings, young people are often detained a year or longer, depending on the nature of the institution. Because there is less turnover in the resident population, you will have a much greater opportunity to build solid relationships.

The caring adult must establish a sensitive and reliable ministry program in order to develop credibility with both the young people and the staff. This will happen over time as you get to know the staff and work faithfully within their guidelines.

After you have made the initial contact and are given the opportunity to spend time at the institution, you must determine your focus. Select a specific cottage, unit, cellblock, or section in which to work, and make sure that those young people need your services. Then spend time in the unit talking with both staff and youth, discovering areas of need and learning the system of discipline and privilege.

Juvenile institutions are filled with troubled youth, and they can provide

troubled youth, and they can provide a significant opportunity to minister to those very needy young people. The challenge will be great, but the rewards even greater as you begin to see young men and women turned around in their relationship with God and society.

13. Handling Special Problems

t first glance, Patty looked to be about fifteen. She was well developed physically, but a closer look revealed her soft, childish, twelve-year-old face, despite the overdone makeup. As she spoke, Patty displayed very little emotion, offering bits of information in a casual, off-hand or matter-of-fact style to Sandy, a volunteer youth worker, during their first visit over a Coke.

"My mom left my younger brothers and sisters at my grandma's one day. She ran off to Oregon with her boyfriend. He sent for her after he got out of jail. It's weird the way she did it too 'cause she had just gotten married to my second stepdad, and they'd only been married two days when she ran off."

"So where is your mom now?"

"I dunno—somewhere in Oregon, I guess—with that jerky boyfriend. She called my grandma and said she might come back in a few months. It makes me so mad . . . but it doesn't matter what I think anyway. I'm glad I don't live with her anymore. She blames me for lots of her problems."

"What do you mean 'blames you?' For what?"

"Oh . . . just stuff that happened when her boyfriend lived with us."

At this point in their conversation, Sandy sensed a barrier because further attempts to talk about Patty's mother were met with shrugs and nervous glances around the room. Patty pulled some snapshots out of her wallet, spread them on the table, and explained who was who. Sandy's head spun as she tried to follow the confusion of two stepfathers, stepbrothers and sisters, and stepaunts, uncles, and cousins, all of whom had been a part of Patty's life.

"Do you have a picture of your father?"

"No. He left when I was a baby. See this picture? This is my new sister at my foster home. We're roommates."

When Sandy drove Patty to her house and walked her to the door she asked, "Are you and your roommate the only foster children living here?"

Patty laughed. "I wish! There are five girls besides the two kids my foster parents have. Come on in if you want to meet them."

The living room was cramped and stuffy, and a stale odor met Sandy as they walked through the door. Noise from the TV, a radio, and shrill voices fought for attention. A heavy girl with bad acne sat at the dining room table as two other teens chased each other into the kitchen yelling, "Food fight!" Someone lay asleep on the couch, covered with a well-worn blanket. The foster mother appeared with a toddler on her hip as Patty disappeared down a hallway. She held out her free hand to Sandy in greeting.

"Hope you can get through to Patty," she whispered. "No one else seems to be able to. We try hard to show her love; even the other girls try. But Patty's hard to open up. She tries to act tough, you know, like she's hurting." After a few more minutes of conversation and meeting various "family" members, Sandy left with mixed emotions about Patty's home environment.

Later, the social worker confirmed for Sandy that everything Patty had said about her real mom was true. In addition, Sandy learned that Patty had been sexually abused by her mom's boyfriend and by her first stepfather.

Over the next few months, Sandy's weekly visits with Patty produced only a small measure of rapport. Patty was talkative, but she was unwilling to be honest about her feelings, speaking mostly about boys she was dating or fights with girls at school who called her names. From her comments, Sandy picked up clues about Patty's sexual attitudes. But because of Patty's young age, she was not prepared for the phone call she received from the foster mother late one evening. "Thought you'd want to know that Patty ran away three days ago. We caught her with a boy in her bed. Seems like she snuck him in late at night. Anyway, she ran away after we grounded her, but we think we know where to find her."

This incident began a cycle for Patty of running away and being brought back, again and again. She was found at various apartments and houses with boys in their late teens. Each time she was stoned on drugs or drunk or both, and there was evidence of sexual "bondage" acts.

Then Patty disappeared for three weeks until, according to the foster mother, she was returned by the police after they found her in an apartment, the "home" of some other street kids. "A well-known pimp was paying the bills. They busted the place for drug dealing and illegal weapons. Patty's in the hospital with a bad urinary and female tract infection, and they're checking her for two kinds of V.D."

When Sandy visited Patty in the hospital, she tried to reason with her about her lifestyle. With I.V.'s taped to her arm, and with no makeup, Patty looked like the frail twelve-year-old she really was. Yet she defiantly stated, "I'm gonna go back to the streets when I get out of here. I like being on my own." Patty ran away from the hospital that night. She was found the next day in the same apartment building. Then, at the foster mother's request, Patty was sent to a facility for incorrigible girls.

Sandy was hurt and discouraged. How could she help Patty now? Running away, drugs, and prostitution were problems about which she knew absolutely nothing!

Troubled youth come in all shapes and sizes, and their problems range from the relatively minor and simple to the very serious and complex. We have said that loving, caring relationships are foundational for ministry with troubled young people and that your friendship, support, and counsel can work wonders. God can and will work through you to reach these hurting children. But no one person should expect to do *everything* in ministry, to solve all the problems, answer all the questions, and meet all the needs. It is important, therefore, to see yourself as a member of a team of people, a network of resources, working together to reach troubled youth. And at times you may encounter young people like Patty, struggling with a combination of severe and seemingly insurmountable problems. Consider how you would respond if you were Sandy.

The goal of this chapter is to sug-

gest ways to handle these special and very troublesome situations.

Space limits us from providing exhaustive answers to every potential struggle faced by young people, so we will highlight a few of the major areas and provide practical responses as well as suggestions for follow-through and key Bible verses which may be helpful for counseling or teaching.

ALCOHOL ABUSE

Identifying the Problem

Alcohol dependency affects people physically, socially, and mentally. Once viewed solely as a moral or spiritual problem, it is recognized today by the American Medical Association as a "disease" or "illness." One of the main reasons for this decision is that, like other diseases, alcoholism can be "cured" through properly prescribed treatment. This designation also implies that:

● the illness can be described;

● the course of the illness is progressive and predictable;

● the illness is primary; that is, it is not a symptom of another disease;

● the illness is permanent and terminal if left untreated.

Alcohol abuse in young people has grown dramatically. Because nearly everyone in their world drinks—parents, older brothers and sisters, neighbors, television personalities, and former athletic heroes—drinking seems natural and appropriate in certain circumstances. It also makes them feel good, helps them fit in with a certain crowd, or cope with problems and pressures. Over time, the amount of alcohol and time spent consuming it increase because they need greater amounts to feel "high" or because drinking becomes a habit.

As this dependency grows (physi-cally, socially, and mentally), the alcohol becomes a necessary part of the alcoholic's body chemistry and begins to take control of their actions and reasoning. At this point, they begin to withdraw from activities and people, drink almost continually, and become extremely unreliable.

Alcohol affects the brain, dulling thinking, perception, coordination, and motor control. Left untreated, alcohol will destroy the brain, heart, liver, and pancreas as it poisons and kills those cells.

Those who are dependent on alcohol seldom realize their dependency until there is a crisis or confrontation. Instead, they tend to rationalize their drinking with statements like, "I wasn't getting drunk, only feeling good with my friends," or "I don't drink as much as _____ ; she really has a problem!"

Confusion follows rationalization, but the final step toward alcoholism

What Have We Done to Our Kids?

There is a conditioning process which helps explain the irrationality of youth. Why else would healthy boys and girls inject wretched drugs into their veins, or give sexual favors to virtual strangers, or dye their hair orange and green, or even commit suicide? Their behavior has been warped by enormous social pressures in an environment of unmet needs. Now obviously, teenagers possess a free will and I would not excuse those who engage in irresponsible behavior. But they are also victims—victims of a peer-dominated society that can only leave them lost and confused. And my heart goes out to them.

How passionately I feel about the plight of today's children. How sorry I am for the pressures we have allowed to engulf them. How regretful I am for the sexual enticements that reach their ears during elementary school—teaching them that virginity is a curse and sex is an adolescent toy. How I grieve for the boys and girls who have been told, and now they believe, that they are utter fools and will fail in each of life's endeavors. How tender I feel toward the wounded children, the blind or deaf or retarded or cerebral palsied, who believe themselves to be cursed by God and man. Somehow, we must make a new effort to reach this generation with a message of confidence and hope and love and respect. And ultimately, we must secure the Gospel of Jesus Christ in their hearts and protect it from the assault of hell.

(from the May 1986, "Focus on the Family" letter, by James Dobson)

is denial, when the person blames his or her problem on someone or something else. For example, "If my parents weren't arguing so much I wouldn't drink so much." "My friends expect me to drink." "I have to drink to be one of the guys." Denial is the major obstacle to recovery.

Besides these physical and mental symptoms, there are social effects involving family and friends. The alcoholic's family members become resentful, fearful, embarrassed, suspicious, disappointed, and isolated, and they often blame themselves for the person's drinking problem.

Handling the Situation

Most attempts to help alcoholics are ineffective because they spring from a poor understanding of the dynamics of alcoholism. Instead of being confronted with their condition as a progressive and deadly illness affecting their entire lives, alcoholics are often told that they ought to quit drinking or that drinking is wrong. As long as the communication with the young alcoholic is on this level or the problem is related only to judgments connected with drinking, he will not seriously consider stopping or changing. Instead, he will see himself as no different than most normal people who occasionally make mistakes.

Effective intervention can only come through a crisis which is significant enough to break through this defense system. Even then, however, the confrontation must not be condescending or demeaning or focused on symptoms. It must be factual, nonjudgmental, firm, and loving. When you confront the alcoholic with his problem, be sure that you have the facts straight. Slowly, firmly, and quietly relate your observations of his behavior and explain the effects and ultimate results of his lifestyle. Let

---

Stages of Alcohol Abuse

Teenage alcohol abuse is on the rise, and it usually runs through five stages:

1. *Curiosity* in a world where alcohol is readily available;

2. *Learning the mood swing.* Children and adolescents learn how easy it is to feel good with few if any consequences, except perhaps mild guilt;

3. *Seeking the mood swing.* Rather than using alcohol as an accompaniment to social events, the youngster decides to get drunk as a goal and arranges to have his or her own supply;

4. *Preoccupation with the mood swing.* Being drunk is the main goal of life. Students who drink daily may plan their days around trips to euphoria;

5. *Drinking to feel OK (addiction).* The euphoria becomes harder to achieve; larger amounts are needed.

Alcoholism in teenagers is also accompanied by drops in school performance, deterioration in family relationships, negative personality changes and depression, physical changes such as red eyes or a dull attitude, legal problems such as vandalism or traffic accidents, and shifts in friendships.

(from *Campus Life Leaders Guide*, May/June 1986.)

---

him know that his drinking has caused this crisis and that he must bear full responsibility. Refuse to cover for him or to bail him out anymore. It is important to use facts, not suppositions or opinions.

It will also be helpful to involve two or more other caring people-his friends. The alcoholic's defense systems are too developed to be breached alone. This loving confrontation should take place when he is sober. He will be more receptive to your message when he is remorseful and introspective.

If he begins, then, to admit his problem, the next step is to refer him to one of the many very helpful resources, including Alcoholics Anonymous and its related agency, Alateen. You will find many others listed in the telephone directory under "Alcoholism, Information and Treatment." In addition, the National Council on Alcoholism provides information, referrals, and counseling for problem drinkers and their families. Other resources are also in the phone book.

Following Through

Remember that lasting change is seldom easy or quick. Alcoholism is a persistent and recurring disease, and the alcoholic will need continual support and prayer. Because you already have a good relationship with this person, you should be able to talk freely with him about the problem. Let him know that you are available to help in any way you can.

Because you are a valuable member of the recovery team, continue to learn about alcoholism, and keep in touch with those who are trying to help your young friend. Also, begin to surround him with others who will support him in the decision to stop drinking. This is when positive peer pressure is needed.

Key Bible Verses

Matthew 10:1; 16:19; 28:18; John 8:36; 1 Corinthians 3:16-17; 6:9-11, 19-20; 15:33; Ephesians 4:22-24; 5:18.

DRUG ABUSE

Identifying the Problem

Alcohol abuse and drug abuse are very similar. There is no single type of young person using drugs, and no one has been able to accurately predict those individuals who are predisposed to drug usage. There are, however, certain motivational factors for drug use and abuse.

● People take drugs because they want to.

● People use drugs to "feel better" or to "get high." Young people experiment with drugs because of curiosity, anxiety, hope of acceptance, or low self-esteem.

● People have been taught by cultural example that drugs are an effective way to make them feel better or to solve problems (TV advertisements, peers, adult drinkers, and so on).

● People don't stop using drugs until they find something "better."

Though the specific symptoms will vary with the drug, here are the common ones of which you should be aware. A combination of many of these symptoms will be evident in the life of someone who is using drugs.

● extremely dilated or contracted pupils

● increased restlessness

● lack of interest

● excessive talkativeness

● increased rebelliousness

● excessive sleeping (like being knocked out)

● trancelike staring (as in a drunken stupor)

● quickly shifting eye movements

● rapid breathing

- unusual withdrawal

- violent behavior

- theft

- sudden change of friends

- secretive conversations

- giddiness or laughing at common events

- deterioration of personal hygiene

- increased lying (covering for friends and hiding activities)

Handling the Situation

When you suspect that a young person is using drugs, don't panic and rush into the situation with accusations and judgments flying. Because you have a good relationship with this person, you should be able to take him aside and discuss your observations lovingly and quietly. During this conversation, be frank, honest, and to the point. Explain what you know to be true and your inferences drawn from the facts. Encourage him to be open with you and explain that you will keep what he says in strictest confidence unless the information will be harmful to him or others.

If this is an occasional or first-time use of drugs and perhaps you caught the person in this act, your discovery and confrontation may be enough to shock him into wanting to change. If it is a more serious situation, however, more drastic measures may be necessary. This may involve intervention with others, as outlined in the section on alcohol abuse. Be careful of being manipulated or lied to; listen to what the person says about how he is going to change, but remind him that "actions speak louder than words."

Because drug usage comes from the desire to feel good, it is important to help the individual develop al-

ternatives. If he wants adventure or challenge, suggest a survival training experience or bike racing. If he wants physical satisfaction, try to get him involved in athletics, dance, or hiking. If he wants sensory excitement, suggest that he try sky-diving. The idea is to help these young people become "high on life"—to have fun and thrills without destroying themselves.

Following Through

As is true with the alcoholic, the drug abuser has tremendous physical

---

Fighting Addiction

What is addiction? Addiction is the loss of choice. It occurs when the object of our affection becomes the object of our obsession. Youth tend to become addicted because they are seekers of immediate gratification. Alcohol or drugs work—right now. Always. They never let the young person down. Life lets him down. School lets him down. Friends let him down. But alcohol or drugs never do.

Kids also like to live without ambiguity. They tend to think and feel in black and white. They think, "Either I feel good, or I feel bad." They have a very hard time tolerating the middle-of-the-road, average feeling-level.

Addiction can consume the teen and distract him or her from all other involvements; it is not a pleasurable experience. The object of obsession becomes the answer to and then the root of fear, anxiety, and guilt. Addiction is signaled by an inability to choose not to do something.

(from *Campus Life Leaders Guide*, May/June 1986).

Characteristics of Pot Smokers

1. Avoid teachers, parents, other family members, and church members.
2. Hang around a new group of peers.
3. Seem to be with others all the time—never alone. Being alone is not comfortable at all.
4. Fighting behavior is increased.
5. Exhibit loud, raucous behavior, belligerent and hostile.
6. Move from group to group, changing friends often.
7. Abuse others' rights.
8. Family seems miles away. Afraid to get close to loved ones.
9. Paranoid when authority figures are around.
10. Overreact to ordinary situations.
11. Mood changes often.
12. No goals or direction.
13. Frustrated easily.
14. Increased number of fears.
15. Feeling of inferiority.
16. Becoming passive.
17. Ignore responsibilities.
18. Active, defensive, and angry.
19. Need others to make decisions for them.

Most people who abuse drugs:

1. Don't see the importance of personal hygiene. They don't dress neatly, and hair and grooming go downhill.
2. Skip meals often.
3. Change eating habits often. Lots of junk food to keep up with the munchies.
4. Wear clothes that show rebellion.
5. Change their sleeping habits.
6. Catch some illnesses easily.
7. Have a change in complexion.
8. Often have bloodshot eyes.
9. Find it harder to concentrate.
10. Take a who cares attitude toward life in general.
11. Become easily depressed.
12. Often think of suicide as a way out.
13. Have very little spiritual emphasis on life.
14. Become very private—locked drawers.
15. Leave joints in shirts, car, or room; become very careless.
16. Look at lying as justified.
17. Often have new acquaintances appear around home.
18. Deny drug usage or possibility of being hooked.
19. Sometimes carry weapons of defense to protect themselves.

(from *Tough Turf*, Bill Sanders, Fleming H. Revell, 1986, pp. 138-139)

needs. With serious abusers, stopping "cold turkey" will be virtually impossible without professional help. The young person, therefore, will need a program designed specifically for dealing with chemical dependency. Many fine programs and agencies are available in most areas, and you can refer young people to them. If a young person is in a residential treatment program, be sure to check to see if you can visit. Usually the staff will welcome and encourage the development of positive and healthy relationships. Also, discuss the individual's situation with his doctors to see what you can do to help after he is released.

Follow-through is important. Maintain contact with these needy young people and check on their progress. Be aware, however, that they may slip back into their old patterns of drug usage and then either avoid you or try to fool you. Remind them that you genuinely care about them, and encourage them to be open and honest with you.

Key Bible Verses

Proverbs 13:13; Jeremiah 23:24; 1 Corinthians 3:16-17; 6:19-20; 10:13; 2 Corinthians 5:17; Ephesians 4:22-24; Hebrews 4:13.

CHILD ABUSE

Identifying the Problem

Child abuse is a problem which is becoming increasingly prevalent at all levels of our society. Abuse can take many forms and doesn't always leave visible marks.

There are four categories of child abuse: physical, emotional, sexual, and neglect.

Physical abuse involves physical injury of a child or a series of destructive incidents which are not caused accidentally, including multiple fractures in the long bones, fractures of the skull, bruises and injuries in the soft tissues, and subdural hematomas.

To recognize physical abuse, look for these symptoms: cuts, welts or swelling; burns (e.g., from cigarettes or "doughnut-shaped" from immersion in scalding liquids); or burns with a pattern (e.g., from a heating element); fractures; scars with peculiar patterns (e.g., looped or rounded); bruises; bite marks. In most instances of abuse, the child will seem to display the symptoms successively; that is, he or she will always have one or more injuries.

The short-term effects of physical abuse reflect the constant tension and anxiety which the child has been experiencing: sleep difficulties, thumbsucking and nail-biting (in younger children); fearfulness, listlessness or apparent apathy. Other effects of abuse do not surface until the child is older and exposed to additional outlets such as drug or alcohol abuse, sexual promiscuity, and criminal activity. Victims of abuse tend to react with either aggression or withdrawal. Children who have been severely abused and exposed to continual violence are apt to develop violent patterns in their own lives. Aggression is perceived as the way to

---

A Survey

From *USA Today* research: a 1985 random survey of 100 callers, ages 12 to 19, to a national cocaine hot line, revealed that 64 percent were dependent on more than one drug. Most common: cocaine and alcohol; 68 percent said grades dropped because of drug use; 57 percent said they bought most of their drugs right at school; and 18 percent had attempted suicide.

Crisis Intervention

A person in a state of crisis normally experiences three stages of reaction to the situation:

1. *Impact.* The person is shocked, confused, bewildered, and may try to deny what has happened. All that can be done is to keep the person safe and warm because they are unable to cope.

2. *Recoil.* The person feels anxiety, shame, anger, depression, and may be agitated and unable to act efficiently. Emotions are uncontrolled. The counselor needs to help the person sort out the feelings and identify them. Once emotions are aired and defined, the person is ready to move on to the next stage.

3. *Adjustment.* The person seeks to return to normal and begins to look for resources and defenses against the emotional turmoil. At this stage the solving of practical problems can begin, and the counselor can work with the person and help him or her find constructive solutions.

Here are five pointers on how to help someone deal with a crisis:

1. *Give emotional support.* Let the person express his or her feeings, and make sure the person knows you care and are optimistic about his or her future.

2. *Be alert for information* that will help you to understand the problem and assist in arriving at a good solution.

3. *Offer realistic hope.* Let the person know that other people encounter this problem too, and that he or she can reasonably expect to handle it, as those others have.

4. *Give future-oriented guidance.* Help the person understand the problem and see it realistically. He or she will feel better knowing what to expect in advance so that emotions can be prepared and ways to deal with things can be planned.

5. Turning to problem solving, *discuss possible solutions with him or her.*

confront problems, personal relationships, and responsibilities. They have learned that hostility, evidenced in rebellion toward authority figures and personal aggression toward others, is the only available outlet for their anxiety. Some children resort to other forms of destructiveness, such as setting fires or vandalism, to vent their aggressive and hostile tendencies.

A psychological condition caused by the parent or guardian, *emotional abuse* is much more difficult to define than physical abuse, simply because there is often no tangible evidence of parental aggression or neglect. Emotional abuse may be the refusal of parents to offer consistent love, attention, and protection, depriving the child of those things which meet his or her emotional and psychological needs. It can be as simple as subjecting the child to unusual ridicule or humiliation, or as complex as isolating him or her from peers or adults who want to help. Whatever the forms, this abuse can be just as emotionally crippling as physical abuse.

The results are similar to the long-term effects of physical abuse. These young people become fearful, and they act aggressively to gain attention. Usually they have very low self-esteem and feel insecure and rejected, and they are unable to express their emotions in a healthy manner. They also have a difficult time developing positive relationships, and this may lead to alcohol and drug abuse, sexual promiscuity, learning difficulties, and habitual truancy. Other signs may include eating disorders (anorexia, bulimia, etc.), sleepiness, fatigue, and running away.

The definition of *sexual abuse* ranges from indecent exposure to full sexual intercourse and rape. In 75 percent of reported cases of sexual abuse, the offender was known to the child or family, usually a family member or relative.

To determine sexual abuse, look for these symptoms: physical complaints with no physiological basis, including sleep disturbances, fatigue, weakness, headaches, bed-wetting or excessive urination, and anxiety. Physical symptoms include bruises of or bleeding from external genitalia, vagina, or anal regions; presence of semen; pregnancy; positive tests for sexually-transmitted diseases; torn or bloody underclothes; pain or itching in the genital area.

The emotional results of sexual abuse are even more devastating than the shorter-lived physical effects. Children who have been sexual victims generally tend to place the blame heavily on themselves. They react as other abuse victims do, by withdrawal, delinquent activities, or involvement with drugs and alcohol.

But victims of sexual abuse also react differently. As many as 90 percent of young prostitutes have been found to be abuse victims. Early in life these individuals see themselves as sexual objects, and so they begin to dress and act accordingly.

Neglect, simply put, is when the parents or guardians pretend that the child doesn't exist, failing to provide basic and necessary care. Often these young victims are called "throwaway kids" because they are unwanted and ignored.

This kind of abuse may surface through injuries and other needs which have not been adequately met. The symptoms could include lack of cleanliness, inappropriate dress, frequently-expressed hunger, frequent sickness, lack of parental supervision, lack of bandages, and so on.

How to Handle the Situation

When confronted with an abusive situation, the usual response of a caring adult is anger directed against the abuser. While a crime may in fact have been committed and while the appropriate action should be taken, remember that the offender is not just a violent person. He or she is a person in need. Your anger is easy to understand, but it will not be helpful if expressed in a verbal diatribe against the guilty party. Here is what you can do.

As soon as you suspect abuse or neglect, you should report it to the proper authorities. Most states require a report to the state's child protective agency which may also be supplemented by a written report to the police. (You must, by law, inform the child protective agency of that action.) The police can be contacted if an incident is in progress. In many states, the child protective agency operates 24-hour "hot lines," where the police are notified simultaneously of the suspected incident. In severe cases, the police may investigate immediately in tandem with the child protective agency.

It is not legally required, but many child protective agency personnel ask that the reporter inform the parents of the decision to report. Though the parents may respond with a variety of emotions from anger to fear, you should approach them with a caring attitude, letting them know that your decision to report abusive or neglectful behavior stems from your concern for the child and for the preservation of the family.

Most states require an investigation into the alleged abuse incident 24 to 72 hours after the report has been filed. After this initial investigation, the child protective agency decides within 60 days whether the report is valid, unfounded, or undetermined. (Extensions of up to 30 days are possible.)

In an unfounded report, all information identifying the subjects is removed from the records. Reports with an "undetermined" finding are closed after a specified period of time.

Those reports with a valid (or "indicated") finding may follow a procedure through the judicial system including criminal court and juvenile court.

It is important to try to understand the abuser. Usually, particularly in cases of abuse which have been substantiated, the abuser will be ordered by the court to undergo treatment and counseling. When this happens, you should refrain from counseling involvement with the abuser. Whatever the disposition of the case, try to establish a relationship of trust and friendship by being open and caring, listening and encouraging. Because you are not a professional, however, you should avoid crisis intervention, giving advice, and trying to counsel or change behavior.

The initial response to the abused child should be love, acceptance, and assurance of help. But you should also inform him or her of your responsibility to report the situation to the authorities.

Following Through

Some parents who are aware of their problems may be referred to self-help groups such as Parents Anonymous. These organizations stress a group approach to helping parents with similar tendencies find understanding, support, encouragement, and assistance in breaking out of their abusive tendencies.

Other types of supportive resources are:

● *home support programs*-qualified lay counselors or "parent aides" who can give advice and support within the home environment. These are trained and supervised volunteers.

● *hotline telephone services*—crisis counseling and intervention designed to help parents cope with their tendencies to abuse or with actual abuse incidents.

● *crisis nurseries and emergency drop-off centers*—residential support and care for children who can be dropped off for short periods in order to give the parents time to "cool off."

● *child care and parenting instruction*—classes to teach parents practical ways to discipline and care for their children, including how to cope with children during times of stress.

The abused young person needs:

● a caring relationship with a mature adult (you);

● positive peer group experience;

● reinforcement of positive self-worth and enhancement of healthy self-image;

● communication and demonstration of the love, hope, and peace of the Gospel.

As you continue to relate to the

abused young person, therefore, it is vitally important that you demonstrate consistency and long-term care, nonjudgmental acceptance of the individual, unconditional positive regard, patience, and allowance for the purposeful expression of feelings. Also, you should help the victim learn to make decisions and take responsibility for him or herself.

The needs of victimized children cannot be easily addressed or met; however, many abused children grow up to lead happy and productive lives, seemingly unscarred by the horrors of their childhood. The healing may come to the entire family through the attention of people like you and professional counselors.

Key Bible Verses

Leviticus 18:6; Mark 9:36-37; 10:13-16; Acts 16:31; 1 Corinthians 5:1-13; 1 John 1:9.

DEPRESSION

Identifying the Problem

According to the American Psychiatric Association in their *Diagnostic and Statistical Manual of Mental Disorders* (3rd ed., Washington, D.C., 1980), the major symptom of depression is the fairly prominent and persistent loss of pleasure and interest in normal activities and pursuits. Even for troubled young people this includes feelings of sadness, lost hope, and discouragement. Other symptoms which usually accompany depression are:

● low self-esteem

● fatigue—loss of energy

● inability to think and to concentrate

Depression

Depression (or melancholia, as it was once known) has been recognized as a common problem for more than 2,000 years. Recently, however, it has come so much into public attention that some are calling our era the age of melancholy, in contrast to the age of anxiety which followed World War II. Depression is something which everyone experiences in some degree and at different times in life. Depression has been considered as by far the commonest psychiatric symptom, and one which is found both as a temporary condition in a normal person who has suffered a great personal disappointment and as the deep suicidal depression of a psychotic.

The signs of depression include sadness, apathy, and inertia which make it difficult to get going or to make decisions; loss of energy and fatigue which often are accompanied by insomnia; pessimism and hopelessness; fear; a negative self-concept often accompanied by self-criticism and feelings of guilt, shame, worthlessness and helplessness; a loss of interest in work, sex, and usual activities; a loss of spontaneity; difficulties in concentration; an inability to enjoy pleasurable events or activities; and often a loss of appetite. In some cases, known as masked depression, the person denies that he or she feels sad, but sad events in one's life accompanied by some of the above listed symptoms lead the counselor to suspect that depression is present behind a smiling countenance. In many cases the symptoms of depression hide anger which has not been expressed, sometimes isn't recognized and, according to traditional psychiatric theory, is turned inward against oneself.

(from *Christian Counseling*, Gary R. Collins, Word Books, 1980, pp. 84-85)

● feelings of worthlessness and guilt

● preoccupation with death or suicide

● excessive sleepiness or the inability to sleep at all

● decreased or increased appetite resulting in a significant weight change

● inability to sit still; pacing; hand-wringing; outbursts of complaining or shouting (the reverse may also occur with slow body movements and low, slow speech)

● other reactions, including crying, feelings of anxiety, irritability, fear, hallucinations, and delusions.

Look for these symptoms or a combination of them. Adolescent boys who become depressed, for example, often become negative, antisocial, restless, grouchy, aggressive, and uncooperative. They may talk about leaving home, have problems at school, practice poor personal health habits, become sensitive to rejection, and begin to use alcohol and drugs.

Though the reasons are not fully understood, most experts agree that depression has multiple causes which will differ for individuals or groups depending on life history, psychological makeup, environment, and biological factors. For example, depression may be "frozen anger" or it may be the result of a deep disappointment or hurt. Whatever the causes, depression runs rampant in our society.

Handling the Situation

Because depression can often be traced to a time of emotional stress, the depressed young person needs to be loved and cared for. It is important, however, not to overreact to the youth's emotional needs. Here is what you can do.

● Develop a caring, trusting relationship so that the young person will experience love, acceptance, and a positive adult model.

● Try to identify the source of the young person's depression and antipathy.

● Help the person ventilate and release feelings of anger, guilt, and self-doubt.

● Provide opportunities for him or her to experience success—identify strong points, build on them, and help others notice them.

● Help the young person meet and build relationships with others.

● Help the individual understand that God loves him or her—he or she is not a failure in God's eyes.

Following Through

If, after taking these steps, depression persists, refer him or her to a physician or counselor for professional help. Be sure to continue to check up to see how he or she is doing and to express your love and concern.

Key Bible Verses

Matthew 5:2-12; Romans 5:3-5; 8:28, 31-39; 14:22; 2 Corinthians 4:8-9; Philippians 4:4-7; James 1:2-4.

HOMOSEXUALITY

Identifying the Problem

Behavior that might be branded as homosexual occurs more frequently than is generally believed. In early adolescence, this is often experimental in the sexual awakening process and should be separated from confirmed, adult homosexual preference. The behavior may be extended if the young person has inadequate heterosexual interaction, and frequently is found in correctional institutions where contact with members of the opposite sex is limited.

In *Counseling Teenagers* (Group Books, 1984), Dr. Keith Olson points out that homosexuality is usually caused by a combination of the following factors:

● genetic tendencies;

● sex-drive intensity from glandular functioning and hormones;

● early orientation through experiences with homosexual adults;

● emotional and psychological development (i.e., sexual abuse);

● family dynamics;

● heterosexual segregation (i.e., being segregated in juvenile centers, group homes, jails).

Dr. Olson states, "It is important to recognize behavioral aspects that indicate the direction of the adolescent's psychosexual development. These are:

1. The emergence and continuation of homosexual behavior, especially guilt.

2. The absence or delayed onset of masturbation, especially without fantasies (suggesting internal conflict or excessive sexual inhibition).

3. The presence of fantasies where the fantasizer is beaten, tortured, or injured, and where someone is forced to be cruel to another.

4. Boys who maintain strong feminine identifications through adolescence, especially when the mother is domineering and the father is either weak or absent.

5. Fears about heterosexual involvement during adolescence that cause such repression that little or no desire for sexual experience is felt at the conscious level.

6. A deep and persistent attachment to an older person of the same sex that takes on the characteristic of exclusiveness that is typically found in love relationships.

7. A sincere, conscious, and firm conviction from the adolescent that he or she is a homosexual" (p. 426).

Handling the Situation

First, you should understand that homosexual, sexual involvements are sin, but so are heterosexual, sexual relationships outside of marriage. It is important, therefore, to see the homosexual person as a creation of God and someone for whom Christ died. He or she should not be isolated or singled out for special condemnation.

Many young people with homosexual tendencies want help. They are confused by their feelings and by the mixed messages of society. Here's how you can respond.

● Avoid strong rejection or heavily focused disapproval with young people in the developmental stages. It will only exacerbate their problem with self-image.

● Encourage healthy interaction with members of the opposite sex in appropriate circumstances.

● Be a model of heterosexual attitudes, emotional responses, and acceptance. If you are married, let your young people see how you relate to your spouse.

● Match young people with a male and female team (i.e., husband and wife) for friendship and counseling.

● Help the young person discuss the problem and let him or her know that change is possible through Christ.

● Be ready to refer the person to a professional counselor.

Following Through

Changing a young person's sexual orientation does not come quickly, and quite possibly, he or she should be under the care of a Christian psychiatrist, psychologist, or counselor. As these young people begin to desire to change, they will be afraid of leaving their old lifestyle, knowing that the break with the past will be difficult and painful. This is where your time and relationship backed up by prayer is essential. Let them know God's requirements and forgiveness and that you will be with them to help.

Key Bible Verses

Proverbs 13:20; Mark 10:27; John 8:36; Romans 1:18-32; 12:1-2; Philippians 4:8; Hebrews 10:23-25.

PREGNANCY

Identifying the Problem

Young, unmarried girls who are pregnant usually will exhibit the following symptoms:

- tenderness in breasts
- frequent urination
- constipation
- morning sickness
- change in clothing and appearance
- hygiene problems
- insomnia
- mood swings
- apprehension
- feelings of guilt, fear, depression
- less interest in sex

Handling the Situation

If you suspect that a girl is pregnant, you should talk to her about it with extreme sensitivity and care. Explain the symptoms that you have observed and assure her of your acceptance and support. Then move on to the appropriate steps listed below.

If the girls *tells you* that she is pregnant, follow these procedures.

- Counsel her. Most likely, she came to you because she trusts you. Do not let her down.

- Help her verify the fact medically. Use the family doctor or one of many clinics.

- If her parents (stepparents, guardian) have not been told, help her to be able to face them. (There is not a time when a good understanding of the home situation is more important.)

Abortion Destroys Life

"Children are a gift from God" (Psalm 127:3). "Suffer the little children to come unto Me; forbid them not; for to such belongs the kingdom of God. . . .And He took them up in His arms and blessed them" (Mark 10:14-16).

Children have always been special to our Lord. In the Scriptures, they are called gifts and blessings. He not only gives them life; He also gives them strength, talents, and abilities. He gives them parents who have the responsibility of teaching them to develop these gifts to their fullest potential. Their lives are *His*.

But not all of His precious children are allowed to be born. Over 1,500,000 children (4,100 per day; 3 per minute) lose their lives to abortion each year.

(from Bethany Christian Services, Grand Rapids, Michigan. Bethany has a pregnancy hotline: 1-800-BETHANY.)

Tips for Counseling Pregnant Teens

1. Accept the person as an individual.
2. Help the person clarify the problem, the feelings involved, and alternative ways of coping with it.
3. Support the person in making a decision.
4. Be sure to give full and accurate information on all of the alternative ways of coping with the problem.
5. The womans right to decide must be respected and enhanced by courteous listening.
6. Provide privacy and an atmosphere of comfort and confidentiality.
7. Allow the woman to tell her own story.
8. You may want to consider:
   - Whom she has told about the pregnancy and their reactions.
   - Feelings experienced by the woman.
   - Significant others close to the woman who have been involved in this crisis, the attitudes, expectations, and pressures they may bring to bear on the decision-making process.
   - How strongly the client feels about the decision she has formulated.
9. Relate to her specific situation and deal with the reality issues.
10. Endeavor to reduce the anxiety level by encouraging her to make a decision by exploring the total situation.
11. Indicate your confidence in her ability to make a good decision.

- Make sure the school is aware of the situation.

- Continue to love her. This is not doomsday, and she did not get pregnant to hurt you. Continue to counsel her during the pregnancy. She is going to have big problems and she needs your love.

- Do not be afraid to bring the family in on the counseling.

- Help her (with the family) to determine the infant's future—keeping the baby, giving the baby up for adoption, etc. She may want to consider abortion; let her know that this would not be the right option.

Following Through

Much of what we have just discussed continues well after the pregnancy has been determined and the news broken to the parents or guardians. It is important to stay close to this girl throughout the pregnancy, letting her know that you are available to help in any way you can.

If you know the father-to-be, try to put him in touch with an adult male who can offer friendship and counsel.

Advise the young woman about adequate prenatal care, medically, nutritionally, and socially—putting her in touch with a good doctor, helping her choose the right kind of foods, and introducing her to young people who will accept her.

Also, some girls have had abortions either before or after telling anyone they were pregnant. With these cases the parents usually do not know. Suicide may also be considered by a young woman struggling with guilt feelings after an abortion. Be alert to these possibilities.

Key Bible Verses

Exodus 20:14; Psalm 32:5; Proverbs 28:13; Jeremiah 31:34; Hosea 3:1-3;

John 8:1-11; Romans 8:1; 1 Corinthians 6:9-11; Galatians 5:19-26; 1 John 1:9.

RUNNING AWAY

Identifying the Problem

Running away from home has become a frequent phenomenon among adolescents and even preadolescents. In fact, in 1986 over 1 million young people will run away.

Running away may be an attempt to escape parent-child conflicts, unreasonable family expectations (as viewed by the child), guilt over some act, abusive home situation, or futility of school. Running away may be motivated by running to something or someone such as a boyfriend or girlfriend, another parent who may be viewed as less demanding, a friend who would be a shield from reality or problems, a warmer climate, or more permissive community.

Young people who have run before have predictable patterns or places to which they run. These may give clues as to where they might be found.

Running away is a message to the rest of the family and an act of self-assertion. Even if they first deny it, parents eventually have to admit that their child is missing.

Handling the Situation

If a young person tells you about his plans to run away, encourage him to stay and work out the problem with your help, or suggest positive alternatives. Help him develop a more mature perspective on family conflict, emphasizing his role and responsibility. And encourage him to contact Mom and Dad even if he chooses not to return home.

Help the family resolve the immediate crisis first, and then use the problem as a lever to move the family toward confrontation, communication, and change.

Remember that there are risks with young people on the run, including their turning to robbery or prostitution or other inappropriate actions in order to survive. Therefore, they need to be found as soon as possible and encouraged to return.

Following Through

Responsible follow-through requires you to continue to be involved with both the young person and the parents, helping them communicate and resolve their conflicts. In cases of abuse, refer to the guidelines presented earlier in this chapter. Consider offering your home as a temporary home for the child until the immediate crisis passes. This can help facilitate problem-solving while keeping the young person safe.

For further information about runaway and exploited youth, consult these resources (the addresses are in the Appendix).

- National Network of Runaway and Youth Services, Inc.

- National Runaway Switchboard
  1-800-621-4000 (outside Illinois)
  1-800-927-6004 (Illinois)

- Runaway Hotline
  1-800-231-6946 (outside Texas)
  1-800-392-3352 (Texas)

Key Bible Verses

Luke 15:11-32 (the Story of the Lost Son); Acts 18:10; Ephesians 6:1-4; Colossians 3:20-21; Philippians 4:11-13; Hebrews 13:5-6.

SUICIDE

Identifying the Problem

Suicide and suicide attempts have skyrocketed in the past few years among young people. In fact, suicide is now the second cause of death for the 15–24 age-group (after accidents and before homicides), according to the U.S. Department of Health, Education, and Welfare's National Center for Health Statistics, Public Health Service. Here are a few other important facts from "Project SHARE" (see Appendix for address).

● Suicide is very rare before the onset of puberty, but becomes more common with each advancing year, reaching a peak around age 23.

● Suicide occurs three to four times more often among boys than girls.

● Suicide is more common among white teenagers than blacks.

● Most suicides are carried out with a gun. Hanging is the second most common method of death in this age-group.

● There is no consistent relationship to the type of community where the child lives. In some parts of the nation, rates are highest in rural areas; in others, they are higher in urban or suburban areas.

● An unknown proportion of teenage suicides occur in "clusters." That is, a community which normally experiences very few cases, will suddenly face an epidemic of teenage suicides.

Causes

The causes for suicide vary widely, depending on the individual and his or her personality, emotional makeup, and circumstances. Here are some of the more common ones:

● low self-esteem

● drastic change in personal appearance

● depression

> ## Suicide Statistics
>
> From the *Chicago-Tribune* wire service: a study published by Metropolitan Life Insurance Company said there has been an increase of almost 800 percent among youngsters under age 15 committing suicide in the last 35 years. It is estimated that 300 youngsters committed suicide last year (1985), up from fewer than 40 in 1950. It added that the overall national suicide rate has remained stable. Last year, about 28,500 people killed themselves in the U.S., making suicide the nation's eighth leading cause of death.

● overwhelming sense of guilt/shame; feelings of worthlessness

● life crises including death of a loved one, separation/divorce of family members, injury or illness of self or loved one, pregnancy, romantic breakup, etc.

● severe disappointment

● psychiatric illness

According to a study of 108 adolescent suicide attempts from 1977 to 1979 by C.L. Tishler, P.C. McHenry, and K.C. Morgan ("Adolescent Suicide Attempts: Some Significant Factors," *Suicide and Life Threatening Behavior* vol. 11 [2]: pp. 86–92, Summer 1981), the adolescent's attempt to take his or her life is grounded in a combination of longstanding problems coupled with the impact of a recent event.

Fifty-two percent of these precipitating events involved problems with parents; 30 percent involved problems with the opposite sex; 30 percent with school; 16 percent with siblings; and 15 percent with peers.

Family disruption plays an important part in adolescent depression and suicide behavior. A history of suicide attempts by family members and relatives is also often prevalent.

Symptoms

The symptoms of emotional pain are not as obvious as those of physical pain, and often we miss them. But most suicide victims do give signals for which we should be especially sensitive. According to psychologist John Q. Baucom in *Fatal Choice, The Teenage Suicide Crisis,* the self-destructive cries for help include:

● Withdrawal—from people as well as from habits or objects

● Inappropriate sexual behavior—attempting to find a measure of unconditional acceptance

● Accident-proneness—a subtle, subconscious cry for help or attention

● Unsafe driving habits—self-destructive behavior which says "I don't care what happens to me."

● Alcohol and drug abuse—self-destroying and a way to "dull the pain"

● Eating disorders—often these are systematic and methodical versions of suicide

● Depression

● Aggression—uncontrolled fighting or destructive behavior

● Melodrama—through music, writing, and story telling, the individual "acts out" his or her feelings. This can also include talking about suicide.

● Plans and preparations to die—including suicide notes

Handling the Situation

The most important resource that you bring to a potential suicide situation is relationship. Your love, concern, and friendship with a young person can literally be life-saving. If you suspect that someone is suicide prone, don't be afraid to talk to him or her about it, assuring the person of your love and willingness to help. Many young people turn to suicide because they think nobody cares; let the person know that you care and that you want to see him or her again.

If a young person tells you that he is thinking about killing himself, your best response is to give him something to look forward to, even if it just means talking to you again. At the end of your time together, schedule a specific time when you will see him, and give him an assignment, a plan of action. This assignment should consider what you have learned about his situation, feelings, and the precipitating factors, and should be designed to reduce the risk of a suicide attempt. It should also include realistic goals—something concrete to do. For example, you could have him write down the experiences at various stages in his life where he achieved success and felt good about himself. Agree to review this with him the next day at a specific time and place.

Be sure to take any suicide talk or threats seriously, even if they are said in a casual or joking manner. It is vitally important that you seek professional help for this person as soon as possible. Remember, your promise of confidentiality does not cover matters of life and death.

Following Through

Your follow-through with a person who has attempted suicide is very similar to that of the other crises discussed above. Continue to demonstrate your acceptance and affirmation of the individual, letting him know that you really care and that you enjoy his company.

If the young person is receiving professional counseling, keep an open communication line with the counselor, letting him or her know that you are willing to be a part of the healing team.

Key Bible Verses

Psalm 31:9-10; 34:18; 42:5-8; 43:5; Proverbs 23:7; Matthew 18:10, 14; 25:35-40; John 3:11, 18; 1 Corinthians 13:4-7; Ephesians 6:4; James 1:9, 2:14-17.

AIDS

Identifying the Problem

AIDS, or Acquired Immune Deficiency Syndrome, is a disease caused by a virus that reduces the body's natural ability to defend itself against disease or infection. Like it or not, AIDS is real, and troubled young people are at risk because of their sexual and substance abuse practices.

Some of the symptoms of the AIDS virus include:

● fatigue

● swollen glands

● persistent cough

● fever

● night sweating

● chronic diarrhea

● gradual unexplained weight loss

● oral thrush—white spots in the mouth

● persistent blue and brown skin lesions.

Handling the Situation

Not everyone who has the HIV virus develops AIDS. Some may have very few or no symptoms at all, but they do have continual infections and are likely to infect others. AIDS is thought to be transferred by blood and other body fluids.

Helping and Prevention

Certain behaviors may reinforce suicidal gestures. These responses are often intended as helping. Occasionally, however, they can actually strengthen the possibility of subsequent suicide attempts.

Parents need to insure that attention is paid to adolescents when they are not acting out or behaving in self-destructive fashion. Attention strengthens behavior. Therefore, one way to increase healthy responses is to reward them with attention. If the only time a teenager has a lengthy discussion with a parent is in crisis periods, there are likely to be more crises. If a teenage girl can only get attention from men by flirting, she is more likely to flirt. Basically, an adolescent will do whatever is necessary to get attention from others. If the teenager is given sufficient positive attention for proper and appropriate behavior, usually positive behavior will continue.

(from *Fatal Choice*, John Q. Baucom, Moody Press, 1986, pp. 120-121)

If you suspect your young person has AIDS, you need to:

● decide up front whether you're willing to go the distance

● avoid being judgmental

● encourage him or her to seek early treatment

● protect yourself

● support, support, support your young friend.

Dealing with AIDS is a frightening proposition. There is currently no successful treatment or cure. A person infected with AIDS is infected for life.

The following has been adapted from Gerald Egan's book, *Skilled Helper,* and Barbara O'Keen's book, *Effective Helping: Interviewing and Counseling Techniques.*

Helping Behaviors

Verbal

1. Uses understandable words.
2. Reflects and clarifies client's statements.
3. Interprets appropriately.
4. Summarizes for client.
5. Responds to privacy message.
6. Uses verbal reinforcers.
7. Calls client by first name or you.
8. Gives information appropriately.
9. Answers questions about self.
10. Uses humor occasionally to reduce tension.
11. Is nonjudgmental.
12. Adds greater understanding to clients statement.
13. Phrases interpretations tentatively so as to elicit feedback from client.

Nonverbal

1. Tone of voice similar to client's.
2. Good eye contact.
3. Occasional head-nodding.
4. Facial animation.
5. Occasional smiling.
6. Occasional hand-gesturing.
7. Close physical proximity.
8. Moderate rate of speech.
9. Body leaning toward client.
10. Occasional touching.

Hindering Behaviors

Verbal

1. Advice giving.
2. Preaching.
3. Placating.
4. Blaming.
5. Cajoling.
6. Exhorting.
7. Excessive probing and questioning—especially why questions.
8. Demanding.
9. Patronizing.
10. Overinterpreting.
11. Using words client doesn't understand.
12. Straying from topic.
13. Intellectualizing.
14. Overanalyzing.
15. Talking about self too much.

Nonverbal

1. Looking away from client.
2. Sitting far apart or turned away from client.
3. Frowning.
4. Scowling.
5. Having a tight mouth.
6. Using gestures which distract.
7. Yawning.
8. Closing eyes.
9. Speaking in an unpleasant tone of voice.
10. Speaking too slowly or too rapidly.

Anyone dealing with people in high-risk categories, and that includes troubled young people, needs to decide ahead of time what level of involvement he or she can handle. You are going to have to deal with your own fears, most notably the fear of exposure to the disease itself and of the loss of your young person.

If you suspect that your teen has AIDS, you need to get him or her medical attention. Good medical care is essential. While there is no cure for AIDS, there are dozens of drugs that are being clinically tested and that may be useful against AIDS. Good medical support often helps to slow the progress of the disease.

What your teen does not need at this point is panic, accusations, or a judgmental attitude from you. God still loves him or her. On the other side, this vulnerable young person is now facing his mortality and may have a lot of spiritual questions. Gather some good resources and be prepared. You may have the opportunity to share the salvation message with this hurting person.

Following Through

Once your young person has been di-agnosed with AIDS, he or she will travel through the whole grieving process—denial, anger, withdrawal . . . the whole gambit. And you'll probably go through it with him or her. Your support is critical. AIDS patients say that one of the worst aspects of the disease is the isolation from, and rejection by, other people.

Don't be afraid to touch the infected person. The virus cannot be transmitted by a hug or a touch. AIDS is spread mainly through sexual contact or through shared hypodermic needles and other equipment used to inject drugs. It's also not recommended that razors, toothbrushes, and other items that could possibly have blood on them be shared. But you get the picture: brushing elbows while watching the Super Bowl won't put you at risk.

Check your resources. Find out what volunteer groups have been organized in your community. Many areas have hot lines, financial and legal help, as well as therapy for AIDS patients and their survivors. Some cities also have funding to shelter AIDS patients who have been evicted because of their disease. The local public health department is a good place to start.

EPILOGUE

Troubled young people are often invisible; they are unwanted and ignored in our neighborhoods, at school, and even at home. Often the only way they can be noticed is to become young people in trouble; then they receive the headlines and the attention. The news is filled with reports of adolescent crime, gangs, abortions, drug abuse, runaways, rebellion, sex, and suicide.

Unwanted by society, these children are loved by God. They are His very special creations, and He sent Christ to die for them.

We are told that "Everyone who calls on the name of the Lord will be saved. How, then, can they call on the One they have not believed in? And how can they believe in the One of whom they have not heard? And how can they hear without someone preaching to them? And how can they preach unless they are sent? (Romans 10:13-15) Perhaps God is sending you to minister to these very needy, very valuable children of His— troubled youth. Go . . . in His strength and with His blessing.

RESOURCES

ABORTION COUNSELING LIFELINE 1-800-238-4269 (1-800-BE-THANY). Provides counseling for the pregnant woman and family. Bethany also provides adoption placement services.

ALCOHOLIC HELPLINE 1-800-252-6465. Run by Doctor's Hospital. Provides referrals for the alcoholic and family nationwide.

ASSOCIATION FOR CHILDREN WITH LEARNING DISABILITIES 4156 Library Road, Pittsburgh, PA 15234, (412)341-1515.

EVANGELICAL CHILD AND FAMILY AGENCY 1530 North Main Street, Wheaton, IL 60187, (708)653-6400 (24-hour hotline). Also has a Wisconsin District office: 2401 N. Mayfair Road, Suite 302, Milwaukee, WI 53226, (414)476-9550. Provides family counseling, abortion counseling, residential care for unwed mothers, and adoption services in Illinois and Wisconsin.

NATIONAL NETWORK OF RUNAWAY AND YOUTH SERVICES, INC. 1319 F St. NW, Suite 401, Washington, DC 20004 (202) 783-7949.

NATIONAL RUNAWAY SWITCHBOARD 3080 N. Lincoln, Chicago, IL 60657, 1-800-621-4000 (outside Illinois); 1-800-621-3230 (inside Illinois).

PRISON FELLOWSHIP P.O. Box 17500, Washington, DC 20041, (703)478-0100. An organization set up to minister to inmates within the state and federal prison system. Ministry is done by local chapters throughout the United States and abroad.

YOUTH FOR CHRIST/USA For local ministry information, contact the national headquarters at (303)843-9000.

STATE LIST

The following listings indicate that agency within each state whose responsibility it is to oversee and coordinate juvenile justice, child care services, or both. While some states have other agencies sharing in different aspects of youth services, the agencies we indicate should be able to refer you to another office when necessary.

ALABAMA
Department of Youth Services
Box 66
Mount Meigs, AL 36057
(205) 215-8100

ALASKA
Department of Health and Social
　Services
P.O. Box 11601
Juneau, AK 99811-0601
(907) 465-3030

ARIZONA
Department of Economic Security
Administration for Children, Youth,
　and Families
1789 W. Jefferson St
Box 6123
Site Coe 940A
Phoenix, AZ 85007
(602) 542-3981

ARKANSAS
Department of Human Services
Division of Youth Services
1320 C Brookwood Drive
Little Rock, AR 72201
(501) 682-1001

CALIFORNIA
Department of the Youth Authority
4241 Williamsbourgh Dr.
Sacramento, CA 95823
(916) 262-1480

COLORADO
Division of Youth Services
4255 S. Knox Ct.
Denver, CO 80236
(303) 762-4695

CONNECTICUT
Department of Children & Families
170 Sigourney St.
Hartford, CT 06105
(203) 566-3661

DELAWARE
Department of Correction
80 Monrovia Ave.
Smyrna, DE 19977
(302) 739-5601

DISTRICT OF COLUMBIA
Youth Service Administration
25 M SW
Washington, DC 20024
(202)727-5804

FLORIDA
Children, Youth, and Family Services
Department of Health and
 Rehabilitative Services
2811 Industrial Plaza
Tallahassee, FL 32301
(904)488-8762

GEORGIA
Dept. of Children and Youth Services
2 Peachtree St. NE—5th Floor
Atlanta, GA 30303-3139
(404)657-2400

HAWAII
Office of Children and Youth
P.O. Box 3044
Honolulu, HI 96802
(808)586-0110

IDAHO
Division of Family and Community
 Services
450 W. State St.
Boise, ID 83720
(208)334-5700

ILLINOIS
Department of Children and Family
 Services
406 E. Monroe St.
Springfield, IL 62701
(217)785-2509

INDIANA
Juvenile Services
302 W. Washington—Room E334
Indianapolis, IN 46204
(317)565-5711

IOWA
Adult, Children & Family Services
Department of Social Services
Hoover State Office Building
Des Moines, IA 50319
(515)281-5521

KANSAS
Department of Social and
 Rehabilitation Services
Docking State Office Building
915 SW Harrison—6th Floor
Topeka, KS 66612
(913)296-3271

KENTUCKY
Department for Social Resources
Children's Residential Services
275 E. Main St.
Frankfort, KY 40621
(502)564-7220

LOUISIANA
Office of Youth Development
Department of Health and Human
Resources
P.O. Box 94304—Capital Station
Baton Rouge, LA 70804-9304
(504)342-2644

MAINE
Department of Mental Health and
 Retardation
State House Station 40
Augusta, ME 04333
(207)287-4220

MARYLAND
Juvenile Services Administration
321 Fallsway
Baltimore, MD 21201
(410)333-4418

MASSACHUSETTS
Department of Youth Services
2743 Wormwood St.
Boston, MA 02210
(617)727-7575

MICHIGAN
Department of Social Services
235 S. Grand Ave.
Lansing, MI 48909
(517)373-2046

MINNESOTA
300 Bigelow Bldg.
450 N. Syndicate
St. Paul, MN 55104
(612)642-0200

MISSISSIPPI
Department of Youth Services
939 N. President
Jackson, MS 39205
(601)354-6649

MISSOURI
Division of Children and Youth
    Services
Box 447
Jefferson City, MO 65102
(314)751-3324

MONTANA
Family Services
316 N. Park
PO Box 817
Helena, MT 59624
(406)444-2030

NEBRASKA
Probation Administration
State Capitol
Box 98910
Lincoln, NE 68509
(402)471-2141

NEVADA
Family Services
711 E. 5th St.
Carson City, NV 89710
(702)687-5982

NEW HAMPSHIRE
Division of Children and Families
Concord District Office
40 Terril Park Dr.
Concord, NH 03301
(603)271-6200

NEW JERSEY
Department of Corrections
Whittlesey Road, Box CN863
Trenton, NJ 08625
(609)984-0203

NEW MEXICO
Children, Youths, & Families
P.O. Drawer 5160
Santa Fe, NM 87502-5160
(505)827-7613

NEW YORK
Division for Youth
52 Washington St.
Rensselaer, NY 12144
(518)473-8438

NORTH CAROLINA
Division of Youth Services
Department of Human Resources
705 Palmer Dr.
P.O. Box 29527
Raleigh, NC 27626-0527
(919)733-3011

NORTH DAKOTA
Department of Human Services
Children and Family Services
600 E. Boulevard Ave.
Bismarck, ND 58505
(701)224-2316

OHIO
Department of Youth Services
51 N. High
Columbus, OH 43266-0582
(614)466-8783

OKLAHOMA
Office of Juvenile Justice
Juvenile Services Unit
Box 25352—Rm 300
Oklahoma City, OK 73125
(405)521-2197

OREGON
Children Services Division—
    Administration
2nd Floor
500 Summer St. NE
Salem, OR 97310-1017
(503)378-4121

PENNSYLVANIA
Department of Social Welfare
Office of Children, Youth, and
    Families
P.O. Box 2675
Harrisburg, PA 17105
(717)787-3422

RHODE ISLAND
Children, Youth and Families
610 Mt. Pleasant
Providence, RI 02908
(401)457-4708

SOUTH CAROLINA
Vocational Rehabilitation
Juvenile Justice
5000 Broad River Rd.
Columbia, SC 29210
(803)896-7655

SOUTH DAKOTA
Board of Charities and Corrections
115 E. Dakota Ave.
Pierre, SD 57501-3216
(605)773-3478

TENNESSEE
Department of Correction
Rachel Jackson Bldg.
320 6th Ave. N
Nashville, TN 37243-0465
(615)741-2071

TEXAS
Texas Youth Commission
4900 N. Lamar
Austin, TX 78751
(512)483-5000

UTAH
Division of Youth Corrections
Department of Human Services
120 North 200 West—4th Floor
Salt Lake City, UT 84103
(801)538-4330

VERMONT
Social Services Division
Department of Social and
        Rehabilitative Services
103 South Main St.
Waterbury, VT 05671-2401
(802)241-2131

VIRGINIA
Department of Corrections
Box 26963
Richmond, VA 23261
(804)674-3000

WASHINGTON
Department of Social and Health
    Services
Division of Juvenile Rehabilitation
P.O. Box 45720
Olympia, WA 98504-0095
(206)753-7402

WEST VIRGINIA
Division of Corrections
Youth Services
112 California Ave.–Room 300
Charleston, WV 25305
(304)558-2037

WISCONSIN
Division of Corrections
State Office Building
One West Wilson St.
Madison, WI 53702
(608)266-2471

WYOMING
Department of Corrections
Herschler Building 1 East
Cheyenne, WY 82002
(307)777-7405

STATE CHILD PROTECTIVE AGENCIES

The following listings indicate the agency within each state responsible for the protection of children and youth in matters of neglect and abuse.

ALABAMA
Alabama Department of Human Resources
Division of Family and Children's Services
Office of Protective Services
64 North Union Street
Montgomery, AL 36130-1801

During business hours, make reports to the county's Department of Human Resources, Child Protective Services Unit. After business hours, make reports to the local police.

ALASKA
Department of Health and Social Services
Division of Family and Youth Services
Box H–05
Juneau AK 99811

Ask the operator for Zenith 4444 to make reports in state. Out of state, add area code 907. This telephone number is toll free.

ARIZONA
Department of Economic Security
Administration for Children, Youth and Families
P.O. Box 6123
Site COE 940A
Phoenix, AZ 85005

Make reports to local offices of the Department of Economic Security.

ARKANSAS
Arkansas Department of Human Services
Division of Children and Family Services
P.O. Box 1437
Little Rock, AR 72203

CALIFORNIA
Office for Child Abuse Prevention
Department of Social Services
714-744 P Street, Room 950
Sacramento, CA 95814

Make reports to the county's Department of Welfare and the Central Registry of Child Abuse (916) 445-7546, maintained by the California Department of Justice.

COLORADO
Department of Social Services
   Central Registry
P.O. Box 181000
Denver, CO 80218-0899

Make reports to the county's Department of Social Services

CONNECTICUT
Connecticut Department of Children
   and Youth Services
Division of Children and Protective
   Services
170 Sigourney St.
Hartford, CT 06105

Make reports in state to 1-800-842-2288 or out of state to (203) 344-2599.

DELAWARE
Delaware Dept. of Services for
   Children, Youth & Their Families
Division of Child Protective Services
330 East 30th Street
Wilmington, DE 19802

Make reports in state to 1-800-292-9582

DISTRICT OF COLUMBIA
District of Columbia Department of
   Human Services
Commission on Social Services
Family Services Administration
Child and Family Services Division
500 First St. N.W.
Washington, DC 20001

Make reports to (202) 727-0995

FLORIDA
Florida Child Abuse Registry
1317 Winewood Boulevard
Tallahassee, FL 32301

Make reports in state to 1-800-342-9152 or out of state to (904) 487-2625.

GEORGIA
Georgia Department of Human
   Resources
Division of Family and Children
   Services
878 Peachtree St. N.W.
Atlanta, GA 30309

Make reports to the county's Department of Family and Children Services.

HAWAII
Department of Social Services and
   Housing
Public Welfare Division
Family and Children's Services
P.O. Box 339
Honolulu, HI 96809

Make reports to each island's Department of Social Services and Housing Child Protective Services reporting hotline.

IDAHO
Department of Health and Welfare
Field Operations Bureau of Social
   Services & Child Protection
450 West State, Tenth Floor
Boise, ID 83720

Make reports to regional offices of the Department of Health and Welfare.

ILLINOIS
Illinois Department of Children and
   Family Services
Station 75
State Administrative Offices
406 East Monroe St
   Springfield, IL 62701

Make reports in state to 1-800-25-ABUSE or out of state to (217) 785-4010.

INDIANA

Indiana Department of Public
  Welfare—Child Abuse and Neglect
Division of Child Welfare—Social
  Services
141 South Meridian St.—Sixth Floor
Indianapolis, IN 46225

Make reports to the county's Department of Public Welfare.

IOWA

Iowa Department of Human Services
Division of Social Services
Central Child Abuse Registry
Hoover State Office Building—
  5th Floor
Des Moines, IA 50319

Make reports in state to 1-800-362-2178 or out of state (during business hours) to (515) 281-5581.

KANSAS

Kansas department of Social and
  Rehabilitation Services
Division of Social Services
Child Protection and Family Services
  Section
Smith—Wilson Building
2700 West Sixth St.
Topeka, KS 66606

Make reports to area offices of the Department of Social and Rehabilitation Services.

KENTUCKY

Kentucky Cabinet of Human
  Resources
Division of Family Services
Children and Youth Services Branch
275 E. Main St.
Frankfort, KY 40621

Make reports to the county offices in fourteen state districts.

LOUISIANA

Louisiana Department of Health and
  Human Resources
Office of Human Development
Division of Children, Youth, and
  Family Services
P.O. Box 3318
Baton Rouge, LA 70821

Make reports to the parish's Protective Service Unit.

MAINE

Maine Department of Human
  Services
Child Protective Services
State House, Station 11
Augusta, ME 04333

Make reports to the regional Office of Human Services, in state to 1-800-452-1999 or out of State to (207) 289-2983. Both operate 24 hours a day.

MARYLAND

Maryland Department of Human
  Resources
Social Services Administration
Saratoga State Center
311 West Saratoga St.
Baltimore, MD 21201

Make reports to the county's Department of Social Services or to local law enforcement agencies.

MASSACHUSETTS

Massachusetts Department of Social
  Services
Protective Services
150 Causeway St.—11th floor
Boston, MA 02114

Make reports to the department's area office of the Protective Screening Unit or in state to 1-800-792-5200.

MICHIGAN
Michigan Department of Social
    Services
Office of Children and Youth Services
Protective Services Division
300 South Capitol Avenue—9th floor
Lansing, MI 48926

Make reports to the county's Department of Social Services.

MINNESOTA
Minnesota Department of Human
    Services
Protective Services Division
Centennial Office Building
St. Paul, MN 55155

Make reports to the county's Department of Human Services.

MISSISSIPPI
Mississippi Department of Public
    Welfare
Bureau of Family and Children's
    Services
Protection Department
P.O. Box 353
Jackson, MS 39205

Make reports in state to 1-800-222-8000 or out of state (during business hours) to (601) 354-0341.

MISSOURI
Missouri Child Abuse and Neglect
    Hotline
Department of Social Service
Division of Family Services
P.O. Box 88
Broadway Building
Jefferson Building
Jefferson City, MO 65103

Make reports in state to 1-800-392-3738 or out of state to (314) 751-3448. Both operate 24 hours a day.

MONTANA
Department of Family Services
Child Protective Services
P.O. Box 8005
Helena, MT 59604

Make reports to the county's Department of Family Services.

NEBRASKA
Nebraska Department of Social
    Services
Human Services Division
301 Centennial Mall South
P.O. Box 95026
Lincoln, NE 68509

Make reports to local law enforcement agencies or to local social services offices or in state to 1-800-652-1999.

NEVADA
Department of Human Resources
Division of Welfare
2527 North Carson Street
Carson City, NV 89710

Make reports to the local offices of the Division of Welfare.

NEW HAMPSHIRE
New Hampshire Department of
Health and Welfare
Division for Children and Youth
    Services
6 Hazen Dr.
Concord, NH 03301-6522

Make reports to the district office of the Division for Children and Youth Services or in state to 1-800-852-3345 (ext. 4455).

NEW JERSEY

New Jersey Division of Youth and
   Family Services
P.O. Box CN717
One South Montgomery Street
Trenton, NJ 08625

Make reports in state to 1-800-792-
8610. District offices also provide 24-
hour telephone services.

NEW MEXICO

New Mexico Department of Human
   Services
Social Services Division
P.O. Box 2348
Santa Fe, NM 87504

Make reports to the county's social
services offices or in state to 1-800-
432-6217.

NEW YORK

New York State Department of Social
   Services
Division of Family and Children
   Services
State Central Register of Child Abuse
   and Maltreatment
40 North Pearl Street
Albany, NY 12243

Make reports in state to 1-800-342-
3720 or out of state to (518) 474-9448.

NORTH CAROLINA

North Carolina Department of
   Human Resources
Division of Social Services
Child Protective Services
325 North Salisbury Street
Raleigh, NC 27611

Make reports in state to 1-800-662-
7030.

NORTH DAKOTA

North Dakota Department of Human
   Services
Division of Children and Family
   Services
Child Abuse and Neglect Program
State Capitol
Bismarck, ND 58505

Make reports to the county's Social
Services Office.

OHIO

Ohio Department of Human Services
Bureau of Children's Protective
   Services
30 East Broad Street
Columbus, OH 43266-0423

Make reports to the county's Department of Human Services.

OKLAHOMA

Oklahoma Department of Human
   Services
Division of Children and Youth
   Services
Child Abuse/Neglect Section
P.O. Box 25352
Oklahoma City, OK 73125

Make reports in state to 1-800-522-
3511.

OREGON

Department of Human Resources
Children's Services Division
Child Protective Services
198 Commercial Street, SE
Salem, OR 97310

Make reports to the local offices of
the Children's Services Division and
to (503) 378-4722.

PENNSYLVANIA
Pennsylvania Department of Public
  Welfare
Office of Children, Youth and
  Families
Child Line and Abuse Registry
Lanco Lodge, P.O. Box 2675
Harrisburg, PA 17105

Make reports to CHILDLINE 1-800-
932-0313 or out of state to (713) 783-
8744.

RHODE ISLAND
Rhode Island Department of
  Children and their Families
Division of Child Protective Services
610 Mt. Pleasant Ave.
Bldg. 9
Providence, RI 02908

Make reports in state to 1-800-RI-
CHILD or 742-4453 or out of state to
(401) 457-4996.

SOUTH CAROLINA
South Carolina Department of Social
  Services
1535 Confederate Ave.
P.O. Box 1520
Columbia, SC 29202-1520

Make reports to the county's Department of Social Services.

SOUTH DAKOTA
Department of Social Services
Child Protection Services
Richard F. Kneip Building
700 Governors Dr.
Pierre, SD 57501

Make reports to the local social services office.

TENNESSEE
Tennessee Department of Human
  Services
Child Protective Services
Citizen Bank Plaza
400 Deadrick St.
Nashville, TN 37219

Make reports to the county's Department of Human Services.

TEXAS
Texas Department of Human Services
Protective Services for Families and
  Children Branch
P.O. Box 2960, MC 537—W
Austin, TX 78769

Make reports in state to 1-800-252-
5400 or out of state to (512) 450-3360.

UTAH
Department of Social Services
Division of Family Services
P.O. Box 45500
Salt Lake City, UT 84110

Make reports to the district offices of
the Division of Family Services.

VERMONT
Vermont Department of Social and
  Rehabilitative Services
Division of Social Services
103 South Main Street
Waterbury, VT 05676

Make reports to the division's district
offices or to (802) 241-2131.

VIRGINIA
Commonwealth of Virginia
Department of Social Services
Bureau of Child Protective Services
Blair Building
8007 Discovery Dr.
Richmond, VA 23229-8699

Make reports in state to 1-800-552-
7096 or out of state to (804) 281-9081.

WASHINGTON

Department of Social and Health
  Services
Division of Children and Family
Child Protective Services
Mail Stop OB 41–D
Olympia, WA 98504

Make reports in state to 1-800-562-
5624 or to local offices of the Department of Social and Health Services
Offices.

WEST VIRGINIA

West Virginia Department of Human
  Services
Division of Social Services
Child Protective Services
State Office Building
1900 Washington Street East
Charleston, WV 25305

Make reports in state to 1-800-352-
6513.

WISCONSIN

Wisconsin Department of Health and
  Social Services
Division of Community Services
Bureau for Children, Youth, and
Families
1 West Wilson Street
Madison, WI 53707

Make reports to the county's Social
Services Office.

WYOMING

Department of Health and Social
  Services
Division of Public Assistance and
  Social Services
Hathaway Building
Cheyenne, WY 82002

Make reports to the county's Department of Public Assistance and Social
Services.

SOURCE: U.S. National Center on
Child Abuse and Neglect, *Child Abuse
and Neglect: A Shared Community Response* (Washington, DC: U.S. Department of Health and Human Service,
March 1989), pp. 16-23.

AGE CHARACTERISTICS

	9-12 years	12-15 years
Physical	Loves activity, exuberant Strong and healthy Noisy, enjoys fighting Loves the out-of-doors Likes competition and difficult tasks	Self-conscious and awkward due to rapid growth Alternating periods of energy and fatigue Coordination improved, loves sports
Mental	Development of reasoning powers Interested in nature and collecting Inquistive Good memory	Capable of real thinking Makes snap judgments Imagination active Frequently critical Wants to make own decisions
Emotional	Enjoys humor Has few fears May be quick-tempered	Emotions fluctuate—moody Emotional life unstable— cannot control emotions Emotions intense Feels misunderstood
Social	Enjoys group activity— loyal to gang Hero worships adults Growing social consciousness Demands justice, fair play Decreasing shyness Can accept responsibility Does not like authority over him/her	Wants to be grown up Wants to be independent of adults Wants to belong Has a strong sense of loyalty Follow-the-crowd spirit, gang loyalty Craves status, self- importance Wants reality, pretends indifference
Spiritual	Recognizes sin as sin Emotions not involved in his/her religion Has questions about Christianity	Wants a practical answer to spiritual problems Doubts and lack of belief Beginning to think on intellectual level Needs step-by-step explanation of Christian basics

GLOSSARY

ADJUDICATION: A Juvenile Court decision, after a hearing, to uphold a petition by finding a child delinquent, a status offender, or dependent, or else to dismiss the petition and release the child from the court's custody.

AFTERCARE: Supervision or treatment given children for a limited time after they are released from a correctional program, but still under the control of the Juvenile Court, to enable them to adjust to society.

CHILD ABUSE: Willful causing of physical hard to a child. Frequently brings the child under the protection of the Juvenile Court. Foster care is usually indicated.

CHILD NEGLECT: Willful failure to provide for one's child or ward adequate food, clothing, shelter, education, or supervision. Frequently brings the child under the protection of the Juvenile Court.

DEINSTITUTIONALIZATION: Moving juveniles out of secure care facilities, detention centers, or jails and into community-based programs or back into the community.

DELINQUENT: A juvenile whom a judicial officer of a Juvenile Court has adjudged to have committed a delinquent act.

DEPENDENCY: Legal status of juveniles over whom the court has assumed jurisdiction on a finding that their care by parents or guardians has fallen short of proper legal standards.

DETENTION: Holding a child in physically restrictive, secure facilities until court disposition or another court order is given.

DETENTION CENTER: A secure facility in which juveniles are detained until court orders are written or adjudication proceedings are held.

DETENTION HEARING: A proceeding before a judge or other judicial officer to determine if a child is to be detained, if detention is to continue, or if the child is to be released.

DISPOSITION: The Juvenile Court's decision after a hearing regarding the future treatment of the child with regard to the delinquent act or status offense.

DIVERSION: Handling the juvenile petition through resources other than the Juvenile Court. This may include outside agencies and counselors. This step may be taken at any point in the formal processing.

FAMILY COURT: A court whose jurisdiction includes neglect, delinquency, paternity, support, and other noncriminal misbehavior.

GAULT DECISION: A decision handed down by the US Supreme Court in 1967 which recognizes the rights of a juvenile as being similar to an adult's constitutional rights. The decision forbids the denial of basic rights to a juvenile, and ensures the rights of legal counsel, specific charge, confrontation of witnesses in cross-examination, and presumption of innocence. It also includes the privilege against self-incrimination.

GROUP HOME: A nonsecure residential facility established for the purpose of providing access to community activities (school, for example) and an approximation of family life for adjudicated juveniles.

GUARDIAN AD LITEM: A person appointed by the judge to look after the legal rights of a court client who, for one reason or another, cannot speak for himself. Such clientele might include a juvenile, handicapped individual, or a young child involved in an abuse or neglect situation.

INTAKE: The process of receiving a juvenile into the juvenile justice system. Decisions are made at this time regarding the future course of the case—such as, the filing of a petition, releasing the juvenile, or referral.

JUVENILE COURT: A court whose jurisdiction includes persons who by law are defined as juveniles, and alleged to be delinquents, status offenders, or dependents.

PAROLE: A conditional release from a secure detention or correctional facility, with supervision continuing until the term of disposition has expired.

PETITION: A document filed in Juvenile Court, usually by a prosecutor, requesting the court to take jurisdiction over a juvenile adjudged to be delinquent, or a status offender, or dependent.

PROBATION: A conditional release of an adjudicated offender into the community, for a set period of time, and under specified conditions and supervision.

RESIDENTIAL CARE FACILITY: A facility other than a detention or shelter care facility that is licensed by a government to provide living facilities, care, and treatment for children and youths. Examples include foster homes, group homes, and halfway houses.

RESTITUTION: Restoring by the offender of what a victim has lost through a crime or delinquency. Juveniles, ordered to make restitution, may be required to pay back or repair damages to the property or victims, or perform community service.

RUNAWAY: A juvenile whom a Juvenile Court has found to have committed the status offense of leaving the custody of a parent or guardian and has not obtained permission to do so, and has not returned within a reasonable amount of time.

STATUS OFFENSE: An act prohibited by statute, but only for juveniles. The same act, if committed by an adult, would not be an offense. Examples include running away from home or truancy.

SUBPOENA: A court issued document compelling an individual to appear at a court hearing, either as a witness, or to supply records necessary for the disposition of a case.

SUMMONS: A court issued document stating the specific charge, the legal rights of an individual, and time and date of the hearing. The summons must be served within a specified amount of time to each person required to appear at the hearing. If this involved a juvenile, the summons would have to be served on the juvenile and his or her parents or guardians.

TAKEN INTO CUSTODY: Securing the physical custody of a juvenile alleged to be delinquent by a law officer. Arrest would be the comparable adult term.

TRANSFER OR WAIVER TO ADULT COURT: A decision made by the Juvenile Court, after a hearing, that relinquishes its jurisdiction over a juvenile and permits the case to be heard in criminal court. This action would be taken when the juvenile is accused of committing a particularly serious crime. The juvenile is then tried and treated as an adult.

TREATMENT: The Juvenile Justice and Delinquency Prevention Act of 1974 states that this ". . . includes but is not limited to medical, educational, special education, corrective an preventive guidance, and training, and other rehabilitative services designed to protect the public, including services designed to benefit addicts and other users by eliminating their dependence on alcohol or other addictive or nonaddictive drugs or by controlling their dependence and susceptibility to addiction or use." This would include rehabilitative programs designed to change the behavior of an individual.

BIBLIOGRAPHY

Baucom, John Q. *Fatal Choice: the Teenage Suicide Crisis.* Chicago: Moody Press, 1986.

Blum, R.H. *Society and Drugs.* San Francisco: Jossey-Bass, 1972.

Carkhuff, Robert R. *Art of Helping.* Amhurst, Mass.: Human Resource Development Press, 1980.

Carter, Velma Thorne, and J. Lynn Leavenworth. *Caught in the Middle: Children of Divorce.* Valley Forge, Pa.: Judson Press, 1985.

Davis, Samuel M. *The Rights of Juveniles.* New York: Clark Boardman, 1974.

Empey, Lamar T. *American Delinquency: Its Meaning and Construction.* Homewood, Ill.: The Dorsey Press, 1978.

Erikson, Erik. *Identity: Youth and Crisis.* New York: Norton, 1968.

Giallombardo, Rose. *Juvenile Delinquency.* New York: John Wiley, 1966.

Gifford, Carla, Felisa Kaplan, and Salus Marsh. *Parent Aids in Child Abuse and Neglect Programs.* Washington, D.C.: U.S. Department of Health, Education, and Welfare, 1979.

Glasser, William. *Reality Therapy.* New York: Harper and Row, 1965.

Goldstein, Joseph, Anna Freud, and Albert J. Solnit. *Beyond the Best Interests of the Child.* New York: The Prepress, 1973.

James, Howard. *The Little Victims: How America Treats Its Children.* New York: David McKay Co., 1975.

Jenkins, Richard L., Preben H. Heidemann, and James A. Caputo. *No Single Cause: Juvenile Delinquency and the Search for Effective Treatment.* College Park, Md.: American Correctional Association, 1985.

Kesler, Jay, and Ron Beers, eds. *Parents and Teenagers.* Wheaton, Ill.: Victor Books, 1984.

Kesler, Jay, Ron Beers, and Lavonne Neff, eds. *Parents and Children.* Wheaton, Ill.: Victor Books, 1986.

Magee, Bill. *Runaways, Throwaways.* Scottsdale, Ariz.: Good Life Productions, 1980.

Malmquist, Carl P. *Handbook of Adolescence.* New York: Jason Arenson, 1978.

Martin, Harold P. *Treatment for Abused and Neglected Children.* Washington, D.C.: US Department of Health, Education, and Welfare, 1979.

McLean, Gordon. *What's a Parent to Do?* Wheaton, Ill.: Victor Books, 1983.

Narramore, Clyde. *Counseling Youth.* Grand Rapids, Mich.: Zondervan, 1966.

Olson, G. Keith. *Counseling Teenagers.* Loveland, Colo.: Group Books, 1984.

Powell, John. *Why Am I Afraid to Tell You Who I Am?* Niles, Ill.: Argus, 1969.

Romig, Dennis A. *Justice for Our Children.* Lexington, Mass.: D.E. Heath, 1978.

Sanders, Bill. *Tough Turf: A Teen Survival Manual.* Old Tappan, N.J.: Revell, 1986.

Schlossman, Steven L. *Love and the American Delinquent.* Chicago: The University of Chicago Press, 1977.

Scott, Sharon. *Peer Pressure Reversal.* Amherst, Mass.: Human Resource Development Press, 1985.

Stacey, William A. and Anson Shupe. *The Family Secret: Domestic Violence in America.* Boston: Beacon Press, 1983.

Steinmetz, Susan K. *The Cycle of Violence: Assertive, Aggressive, and Abusive Family Interaction.* New York: Praeger Publishers, 1977.

Swihart, Judson, and Steven Brigham. *Helping Children of Divorce.* Madison, Wis.: InterVarsity Press, 1982.

Talbot, Nathan B. *Raising Children in Modern America.* Boston: Little, Brown and Co., 1976.

U.S. Department of Health, Education, and Welfare. *A Curriculum on Child Abuse and Neglect, Leader's Manual.* Washington, D.C., 1979.

U.S. Department of Justice. *The Shadows of Distress; Reports of the Juvenile Justice Assessment Centers.* Washington, D.C., 1980.

Welter, Paul. *How to Help a Friend.* Wheaton, Ill.: Tyndale, 1978.

Worldwide Publications, *The Christian Worker's Handbook.* Minneapolis, 1981.

Yablonsky, Louis, and Martin Haskell. *Juvenile Delinquency.* Chicago: Rand McNally College Publishing, 1974.

Youth for Christ/USA, Youth Guidance Division. *Child Abuse and Neglect Handbook.* Wheaton, Ill.: YFC, 1983.